Smarter Planet or Wiser Earth?
Dialogue and Collaboration
in the Era of
Artificial Intelligence

Praise for *Smarter Planet or Wiser Earth?*

"As Gray Cox's book makes clear, Artificial Intelligence (AI) is coming at us much faster than we realize. ... How are we to cope with the increasing complexity? As a software systems architect, I've learned that complexity invariably arises from "conflicting" interactions. Technical solutions are often insufficient alone: solutions must encompass technical, social and other concerns. Future solutions will be multi-, inter- and trans-disciplinary and we will need tools, perhaps as facilitators and collaborators, to address this complexity. Our future tools need not be guided by 19th century logic. We have the ability, if we choose, to build differently. The Rainbow Rule, Gandhi's satyagraha, Buddhist, Taoist or brand new logics, new forms of dialog, investigation and collaboration are possible. We may never be able to create machines in our own image, but perhaps we can engineer machines to reflect and respect our values. This book is a guide to what that image of ourselves could be."

— Rich Hilliard, software engineer

"Gray Cox is a singularly gifted New England-based scholar and teacher in the Quaker tradition of Rufus Jones, Douglas Steere, Elise and Kenneth Boulding, and Thomas Kelly. I anticipate that *Smarter Planet or Wiser Earth?* may well influence public discourse surrounding Artificial Intelligence and, in the words of Gray Cox, help "change the conception of rationality at the core of mainstream economics, politics, technology and ethics." That would be a substantial contribution to the world our children and grandchildren will inherit." —John Thomas Bertrand, human rights attorney, former president of Brevard College and former executive director of the National Peace Foundation

"[Gray Cox has done] a superb job of bringing a focus of "both/ and" to an enormous range of things impinging on justice and sustainability. [*Smarter Planet or Wiser Earth*] will be a tool of great value in facing these issues." —John N. Howell, Associate Professor Emeritus of Physiology at Ohio University.

"While AI is the central focus of these discussions, Professor Cox urges all in attendance to consider change in a whole host of other societal arenas. In his plea to create a Wiser Planet, he argues that only in correcting environmental degradation, sharpening ethical thinking in our decision making, redirecting corporate profits towards a wider array of stakeholders, reversing the growing materialistic drive of US citizens, and shifting political activity away from conflict-centered practices towards collaborative dialogue can there be a rational solution.

"Professor Cox's work leads us through a tough look in the mirror. There is much needing attention in this Nation, and he is encouraging all of us to step up and be part of creating a Wiser Earth. This book is a must read for those who are looking for ways to make things better."
—Fred Benson, US Army Colonel retired, former Vice President for the Weyerhaeuser Company

"The ecological and social crises of our times are such that much of what many of us view as normal needs to be denormalized, for the benefit of human and all other life on our shared planet. In urging people to shift from "smartness" to "wisdom", Gray Cox confronts many problematic normalities—including the age-old Golden Rule, which when applied to others whose understanding of the world and its relationships differ from our own requires avoiding assumptions about how they wish to be treated. This book makes clear that wisdom includes new kinds of openness about respecting and embracing the many forms of vibrant diversity that various forms of normality threaten in the modern world, and it provides practical insight on how to achieve that kind of wisdom." —Geoff Garver, McGill University, Leadership for the Ecozoic initiative

 In 2003, Ed Dreby and Keith Helmuth convened a weekend gathering of Quaker economists, ecologists, and public policy professional at Pendle Hill to consider the increasingly catastrophic conflict between the economic behavior of our society and the integrity of earth's ecosystems.

Those gathered decided that there was a need for a Quaker think tank and the **Quaker Institute for the Future** (QIF) was born.

The work of QIF these past twenty years is research in the manner of Friends, incorporating the silent meeting for worship into the research. Each year QIF holds a Summer Research Seminar where researchers present their work in the context of a meeting for worship. QIF sponsors Circles of Discernment (CoDs): groups of people who consider particular issues of concern. The results of CoDs are often published as *QIF Focus Books* (next page).

QIF has published one major book, *Right Relationship: Building a Whole Earth Economy,* and a series of 12 *QIF Focus Books,* most of which were the products of CoDs <quakerinstitute.org>.

QIF hereby introduces this, our second major book, *Smarter Planet or Wiser Earth? Dialogue and Collaboration in the Era of Artificial Intelligence* by Gray Cox.

Publication of this book is supported by Obadiah Brown's Benevolent Fund.

QIF Focus Books

1) Ed Dreby and Keith Helmuth, 2009. *Fueling Our Future: A Dialogue about Technology, Ethics, Public Policy, and Remedial Action.*

2)) David Ciscel, Barabara Day, Keith Helmuth, Sandra Lewis, and Judy Lumb, 2011. *How on Earth Do We Live Now?*

3) Anne Mitchell with Pinayur Rajagopal, Keith Helmuth, and Susan Holtz, 2011. *Genetically Modified Crops: Promises, Perils, and the Need for Public Policy.*

4) Leonard Joy, 2011. *How Does Social Transformation Happen? Values Development, Collective Wisdom, and Decision Making for the Common Good.*

5) Ed Dreby, Keith Helmuth, and Margaret Mansfield, 2012. *It's the Economy, Friend: Understanding the Growth Dilemma.*

6) Ed Dreby and Judy Lumb, 2012. *Beyond the Growth Dilemma: Toward an Ecologically Integrated Economy.*

7) Gray Cox, 2014. *A Quaker Approach to Research: Collaborative Practice and Communal Discernment.*

8) Judy Lumb, Phil Emmi, Mary Gilbert, Leonard Joy, Laura Holliday, Shelley Tanenbaum, 2014. *Climate, Food and Violence: Understanding the Connections, Exploring Responses.*

9) Pamela Haines, Ed Dreby, David Kane, and Charles Blanchard, 2016. Toward Right Relationship with Finance: Debt, Interest, Growth, and Security.

10) Ruah Swennerfelt, 2016 *Rising to the Challenge: The Transition Movement and People of Faith.*

11) Robert Bruninga, 2018. *Energy Choices: Opportunities to Make Wise Decisions for a Sustainable Future.*

12) John Lodenkamper, Paul Alexander, Pete Baston, Judith Streit, 20219. Toward a Life-Centered Economy: From the Rule of Money to the Rewards of Stewardship.

v

Other Books by Gray Cox

Gray Cox, 1985. "Bearing Witness: Quaker Process and a Culture of Peace." *Pendle Hill Pamphlet* No. 262. Wallingford PA: Pendle Hill Publications.

Gray Cox, 1986. *The Ways of Peace: A Philosophy of Peace As Action*. Peabody MA: Paulist Press.

Gray Cox, 1984. *The Will at the Crossroads: A Reconstruction of Kant's Moral Philosophy*, University Press of America.

Gray Cox, with Charles Blanchard, Geoff Garver, Keith Helmuth, Leonard Joy, Judy Lumb, and Sara Wolcott. 2014. *A Quaker Approach to Research: Collaborative Practice and Communal Discernment*. *QIF Focus Book #7*. Quaker Institute for the Future. Caye Caulker, Belize: Producciones de la Hamaca.

About the Cover

The cover design for this book was developed as a collaboration with Jess Boch and Dru Colbert who provided initial ideas which were then refined as the front cover image by Ben Troutman. The elements of the front cover graphic are meant to reference the interactions between diverse forms of natural, human, and artificial intelligence and the roles they may play in dialogue that promotes the emergence of wiser life systems at the local and global levels.

Smarter Planet or Wiser Earth?
Dialogue and Collaboration in the Era of Artificial Intelligence

Gray Cox

Quaker Institute for the Future

Published for Quaker Institute for the Future by *Producciones de la Hamaca*, Caye Caulker, Belize <producciones-hamaca.com>

ISBN: 978-976-8273-40-6 (e-book edition)

ISBN: 978-976-8273-41-3 (hard-back edition)

ISBN: 978-976-8273-42-0 (paperback edition)

This book was printed on-demand by Lightning Source, Inc (LSI). The on-demand printing system is environmentally friendly because books are printed as needed, instead of in large numbers that might end up in someone's basement or a dump site. In addition, LSI is committed to using materials obtained by sustainable forestry practices. LSI is certified by Sustainable Forestry Initiative (SFI® Certificate Number: PwC-SFICOC-345 SFI-00980). The Sustainable Forestry Initiative is an independent, internationally recognized non-profit organization responsible for the SFI certification standard, the world's largest single forest certification standard. The SFI program is based on the premise that responsible environmental behavior and sound business decisions can co-exist to the benefit of communities, customers and the environment, today and for future generations <sfiprogram.org>.

Producciones de la Hamaca is dedicated to:
—Celebration and documentation of Earth
    and all her inhabitants,
—Restoration and conservation of Earth's
    natural resources,
—Creative expression of the sacredness
    of Earth and Spirit.

Contents

List of Figures and Tables

List of Songs

Preface

Work on this book was sparked by two strong reactions I had on first reading Ray Kurzweil's *The Singularity is Near*. One was a fascination with the dream of an empowering artificial intelligence (AI) with very practical payoffs. Might it help blind people read, bring important advances in medicine, empower democratic processes, and address intractable ecological problems? The second was a nightmarish vision of the exponential growth of forms of AI that might run seriously awry. Might they ruin our food systems, escalate wars with lethal autonomous weapons or create dangerous Artificial Super Intelligences (ASI) indifferent to humans – or outright unfriendly to us?

I soon realized that even if AI never exceeds or even equals the full range and level of general human intelligence, the dramatic advances in AI technologies already transforming our world raise all sorts of ethical issues. They pose real threats even while offering real benefits. In wrestling with these issues, I was forced to revisit basic questions. What is it to think and act ethically? What is intelligence or rationality? What is the role of the community in nurturing and supporting ethical thought and action? How is rational thought and ethical action framed differently in arenas like economics, politics, and technology? How do institutions in those realms influence each other and our collective vision of intelligent, rational life?

My approach was strongly shaped by three things. One was my previous study of how our conflict-centered culture obscures the nature of peace and hinders us from practicing collaborative dialogue. I had explored what an alternative culture might look like in *The Ways of Peace: A Philosophy of Peace as Action*.[1] A second influence was the research and activism I undertook in connection with my teaching in the Program in Human Ecology at College of the Atlantic. It led me to look for inter- and trans-disciplinary ways to address existential threats like ecological collapse by combining theory and practice in real world, problem-centered investigations. It also led me to integrate the perspectives of all relevant stakeholders—including those of other species. A third key influence was my Quaker experience sharing in worship, community building, and public witness. This included work over the last 20 years as a co-founder and Clerk of the Quaker Institute for the Future (QIF) which has offered a setting for continued experiment in methods for spirit-led research on a variety of social and ecological concerns.

In that previous work in peace studies, human ecology, and Quaker inspired research, I sought connections between major problems and common solutions that could draw from —and appeal to—diverse audiences. In writing this book, I have sought to extend and connect these efforts further by addressing four existential threats we face: 1) ecological collapse, 2) wars of mutually assured destruction, 3) out of control AI technology, and 4) the collapse of meaning through moral relativism. This book describes how these are intimately connected by the forms of inferential reasoning that are driving our economy, politics, technology, and ethics – and how alternative forms of reasoning using collaborative dialogue could guide us towards a wiser world.

The audiences this book hopes to draw into dialogue with each other fall into two groups. One consists of activists, entrepreneurs, and change agents who are trying to transform our economies, politics, technologies, and moral practices. The other includes programmers, AI researchers, and other technologists creating the hardware and code for devices proliferating in efforts to make our phones, cars, schools, prisons, farms, factories and other life systems "smarter".

A hope of this book is that those two audiences can be brought together to transform our world in ways that make it not just "smarter" but genuinely wiser. The central aim of the book is to provide vocabularies and frameworks for all of us to engage in collaborative dialogue across the activist/tech divides in every walk of life so we can promote genuinely peaceful, human ecological, and spirit-led ways of moving towards a Wiser Earth.

Developments in computer software as well as in robotics and other fields are making such dialogue increasingly accessible and powerful. The release of OpenAI's ChatGPT on November 30th, 2022, created an enormous stir that drew the interest of people who saw it offering something fundamentally new. How new? How fundamental? Like already released systems using Generative Pre-trained Transformers, it was able to produce coherent, extended pieces of text that were astonishing both in the degree they approximated human abilities and in the variety of styles they could imitate—even, it was discovered, in writing computer code. But ChatGPT seemed to reach a whole new level in its ability to engage in back-and-forth interactions that felt more like conversations and at times even eerily like individualized, context sensitive, genuine human dialogue.

This book provides a framework for understanding this and related forms of generative AI systems as harbingers of a significant inflection point in AI research and development. The book describes the growing emergence of ways computer programming is shifting from a monological model of algorithmic inference to a dialogical model of collaborative reasoning and intelligence. The book shows how collaborative dialogue that includes human, natural, and machine intelligence can advance wiser ways of living. Such collaborative reasoning can transform our individual lives as well as our communities, political economies, and ecosystems. It does so not merely by changing what we think but by changing the way we think—the process of reasoning itself.

In that sense, this is a book about epistemologies, ways of knowing. But it is not a book lost in philosophical abstractions. It is focused on everyday challenges we face as individuals and communities. It connects insights into how collaborative dialogue can increase the wisdom with which we respond in the real world to ethical dilemmas, economic problems, political struggles, and technological opportunities. It shows how these connected insights can invite alliances and create synergies between change agents working in each of those issues. Further, it describes ways to scale up those efforts at change in systematic ways and at rapid paces. These offer real hope for addressing the wicked problems and existential threats that call out to us all, demanding that we take thought for the future and seek ways to become genuinely wiser.

I have tried to find appropriate ways to apply the strategies of collaborative, dialogical reasoning that this advocates in stylistic features of the book itself. So, for example, in the use of pronouns I sometimes move from first person, telling you what I propose, to second person to engage with responses you might have. I may then move to third person singular and plural to consider other individuals and groups in order to take into account points that she, he, or they might raise. And I do this in the effort to arrive at a common understanding we might all share and adopt.

A second feature of the book is the way it combines styles of discourse, mixing: systematic problem posing, theoretical critique, personal anecdote, historical narrative, philosophical reflection, activist advocacy, entrepreneurial proposal, spiritual meditation, the telling of fables, and discussion of computer code. This mixing of styles is intended to help bring different voices into the discussion in clear and effective ways that advance the dialogue. I hope these departures from a more academic and impersonal style will not only make for engaging reading but also serve to help us all engage with these ideas and critical analyses of them in collaborative, fruitful ways.

Another distinctive feature of this book is its use of songs. At various points, they are included with portions of lyrics along with a QR code and web link where they can be heard in full. I would invite you to listen to them when they are introduced and treat them like part of the argument of the book. They are intended to provide context and insight in ways that words sitting silently on a page cannot. Just as we can better understand someone when we can see their face and know if they are smiling or frowning, so too, it is sometimes easier to understand someone when you can actually hear their voice as well as the rhythm and melody of their words. One of the hypotheses this book explores is that collaborative dialogue must be embodied in the world and embedded in social contexts. I invite you to explore this hypothesis as the book proceeds by experimenting with enriching your experience of the text through hearing some of it sung.

Besides the links provided for each song in the text, they are also gathered as an album, "Songs for a Wiser Earth", available for free download at <graycox.bandcamp.com/album/songs-for-a-wiser-earth>.

Some of the more technical arguments of the book, like the algorithmic characteristics of our monetary systems, are included as appendices placed online at <smarterplanetorwiserearth.com/2023/04/01/book-appendices>.

There is also a blog where readers can contribute links, ideas, and proposals, as well as initiate dialogue and collaboration <smarterplanetorwiserearth.com>.

Gray Cox,
July 6, 2023

Part I: Wiser Thinking

Chapter One: Introduction

Until political power and love of wisdom are joined . . . bad things do not cease.
--Plato, The Republic[2]

When I was working in construction as a high school kid, an old timer watched me run around grunting and scurrying for a couple of days and then gave me a piece of advice: "Work smarter, not harder." It was good advice. It led me to spend more time watching, learning, and thinking about the details of what I was doing. I got significantly more efficient at accomplishing the goals at hand.

Nowadays I see us all scurrying around in a different set of ways. As individuals, we often obsess on the goal at hand but lose track of the larger frames of our lives. Often the result is burnout, addiction, divorce, health collapse or some other life crisis. In analogous ways, we often find leaders of corporations, countries and technology teams pursuing single-minded goals with a one-sided logic. This may let them shine for a while as the "best and the brightest," but the results can often lead to widespread damage and even disaster. Currently, the logic of our collective effort at economic growth is pushing our ecosystem towards collapse. The logic of our international politics is pushing us toward wars of mutually assured destruction. And the logic of our technological development is pushing us toward a "smarter planet" in which all the key systems will be run by artificial intelligences beyond human comprehension and control.

1

What kind of thinking might be most helpful in this context as our world becomes increasingly dominated by those kinds of "logic" and their implementation through "smart" phones as well as "smart" cars, farms, factories, schools, cities, and battlefields? In this new context, we may need to seek ways to follow this advice: "Live wiser, not just smarter."

The aim of this book is to explore what that might mean. It looks at how we can develop and practice forms of wisdom that help us deal with the shortcomings and limitations of the "smart" technologies that increasingly pervade our lives. It looks as well at the related "logics" of the economics, politics and technological development that threaten our world with damage and potential disaster.

Mainstream practices of economics, politics, technology, and ethics have institutionalized the practice of a core conception of rationality that we need to change.

Smarter vs Wiser

The contrast between smart systems and wiser ones will get developed progressively in this book as we see it at work in different arenas of life. Both are forms of intelligence intended to better our thought and action. By "intelligence" I mean the ability to achieve, sustain, or enhance some form of value. It is an inherently normative concept. If there are no values at stake, there are no better or worse choices and no intelligence at play. The behavior involved and the values at stake in intelligent activities can vary enormously. They can include, for example, calculating a solution, negotiating an agreement, writing a melody, constructing a piece of furniture, sharing an intimate feeling, cooking a new dish, keeping warm, or nurturing an offspring. In this sense organisms and perhaps even biological communities may exhibit intelligence and so may machines and other systems. To be intelligent they simply need to exhibit behavior directed towards advancing some value. Intelligence in this initial, very broad sense does not require consciousness.[3]

The more specific kind of intelligence that characterizes smart people and smart devices has the following characteristics: A "smart" person (or machine) has clear and well-defined premises as inputs to their thinking. They then use clear, well defined "algorithms" as logical rules to draw inferences that output clear and well-defined conclusions. Measures of how "smart" a person (or machine) is include: the size of the inputs they can handle; the complexity of their rules of inferences; and their efficiency in getting the conclusion sought. This is the kind of thinking required for complicated problems like landing someone on the Moon–and we sometimes refer to it as the kind of smarts someone has if they can do "rocket science."

In contrast, "wisdom" as we will talk about it here, is often "not rocket science." This does not make it incompatible with being smart. Wise thinking can include smart analysis. But wiser thinking also takes into account information that is not clear or well defined but is nevertheless important. More generally, wise thinking aims to be inclusive in whatever ways might be relevant—even if they involve wrestling with vague ideas, apparently inconsistent assumptions, or contradictory points of view. The pursuit of wisdom is needed for dealing with the problems that are complex or "wicked" rather than merely complicated. It involves looking at issues from all the relevant points of view and the relevant values in arriving at a balanced agreement about what to think and do.[4]

This pursuit of wisdom must involve, in Robin Wall Kimmerer's phrase, "an intertwining of science, spirit, and story."[5] It calls on us to develop emergent strategies that, as, adrienne marie brown puts it: "apply natural order and our love of life to the ways in which we create the next world" and find ways to "tap into the most ancient systems and patterns for wisdom as we build tomorrow."[6] In doing that building, we also need to be ready to reinvent ways in which we practice and integrate sciences, arts, and knowledges of all kinds because, as Donella Meadows noted, the problems in which we are immersed are: "intrinsically systems problems—undesirable behaviors characteristic of the systems that produce them. They will yield only as we reclaim our intuition, stop casting blame, see the systems as the source of its own problems, and find the courage and wisdom to restructure it."[7]

The wisdom for this restructuring requires us to broaden, deepen, and diversify our understanding of rationality itself. As Val Plumwood noted, the ecological crisis of our dominant culture is a crisis of reason which has, in important ways, been made a vehicle for domination and for death. But once we recognize reason as plural, as something that can take different forms that are more dialogical, we can discern how: "It can and must become a vehicle of liberation and life."[8] In many key areas, the most compelling and cutting edge insights, methods and empirical findings from biology and other branches of science are leading towards these more plural and dialogical understandings of reason not just as a tool for manipulating the world but as a path towards collaborative wisdom. Stuart A. Kauffman has developed this point at length in his exploration of the ways in which his own field of research, complexity theory: "is leading toward the reintegration of science with the ancient Greek ideal of the good life."[9] Dialogue between people and points of view is central to these notions of wisdom.

Dialogue can take many forms – and there are a variety of theories of it and related notions. But the core notion employed here draws on our common experience of talking with others to solve shared problems, negotiate agreements, transform conflicts and make peace with each other in ways that are wiser in the sense that they let us live more just, balanced, sustainable, peaceful lives.[10]

Sometimes in speaking of wisdom, people are thinking of something rather different than this. They may have in mind the kind of insight a single-minded individual may achieve by going off alone to meditate and arrive at some deeper form of consciousness or profound intuition. Esoteric "wisdom" of that sort may be difficult to communicate and to connect to the challenges of everyday life. In contrast, the kind of wisdom we will focus on here is the sort that is developed collaboratively in communities through dialogue. It is the sort that is arrived at by resolving conflicts between people's different ways of approaching the world. Wisdom is, in that sense, something that is shared.

During the last fifty years or so, there has been a growing body of important research dealing with the pursuit of wisdom in anthropology, psychology, conflict resolution, group problem solving, peace studies and related fields. We can draw on those historic traditions and contemporary research in learning to think and live more wisely. The first half of this book (Part I) focuses on how these can help us think more wisely as individuals and members of communities. The focus of the second half (Part II) shifts from the wiser thinking as individuals toward wiser living as communities. Part II focuses on ways of systematically institutionalizing these practices in economies, governments, and technologies that move us towards a wiser Earth. But it would be unwise to try to think about thought independently from action or the individual apart from the community. Our discussion will move in an expanding spiral around the full range of themes we will consider.

Raising Ethical AI as Turing Children

In seeking to be smarter, it seems natural to employ machines – computers that can marshal ever more data and do ever more complex calculations to generate predictions and conclusions that can inform our choices. But the idea of collaborating with machines to pursue wisdom might seem more far-fetched and perhaps even wrong-headed. One might wonder: How could a mere mechanism without body or emotion ever crank out results that could truly inspire love and enlighten our souls?

The vision of the computer as a mechanism cranking out calculations was given articulate and profoundly influential expression by Alan Turing in a 1950 paper on "Computing Machinery and Intelligence". He developed the key principles for what became the standard model for computers, a model often referred to as the "Turing Machine". But, as we will see in Chapter Seven, he also offered a second, profoundly visionary model for the computer. It is one that makes the notion of a computer that might engage in dialogue about wisdom somewhat more plausible.

In this "Turing Child" model, Turing envisioned creating a computer with a kind of plastic, malleable mind that could go through training and learning in the way children do, through dialogue with parents, teachers, and peers. That vision was slow to be taken up and explored. It called for hardware that would let the computer go out in the world and interact with people and things. It required extremely powerful memory and software that would let computer code go through selective evolution and reinforcement of adaptive behaviors. But since 2012, breakthroughs in hardware and software have made it possible to model AI on the Turing Child model. The new Generative

AIs use neural nets and reinforcement learning methods to develop more conversational AI that can start to imitate and in some ways perform many of the functions of a person engaging in dialogue. They pose questions, respond to inquiries, synthesize materials, present responses in different styles and from different points of view, generate appropriate images on request, and, more generally, behave in ways that seem sensitive to context in the ways in which human conversational partners do. The systems may still lack a variety of capacities humans can have. However, with each skill they do acquire, they bring to bear massive data and hardware that can outclass humans. Once they learn to play Go, code in Python, create paintings in the style of Salvador Dali, or take the Bar exam, they can bring massive memory and speed to their responses. The results include increasingly powerful systems that pose serious ethical and existential concerns for humans.

At the heart of those ethical and existential issues, lies a puzzle with two often ignored wrinkles. It is a puzzle in AI research that it now referred to as "the Alignment Problem" but has an older and in some ways more illuminating name, "the Friendly AI Problem." Visions of it have long loomed in our collective imaginations in science fiction stories about Terminators, Borg, and the Matrix. It is commonly framed as the challenge of ensuring that ever more powerful AI systems operate on values that are aligned with humans' values so that they do not run off the rails and start doing harm and creating catastrophic risks. The idea is that the system should be friendly to the humans who are creating it.

Framing it as a problem of friendship can help spark concerns about two wrinkles in the problematic. First, it is clear that we do not simply want to ensure that the AI are friendly to whoever creates or owns them. What if a rogue state or ruthless corporation is in that role? That is not what we want. We want to ensure the AI is friendly to people who are good rather than bad or, at the least, friendly to those who are trying to do what is right. We want it to favor folks working for something like a more just, peaceful, resilient planet instead of the opposite.

But that takes us to a second wrinkle. Suppose we do develop "Turing Children" that are capable of dialogue and self-improvement, and they grow to become extremely powerful and super-intelligent systems that are friendly to the good and promote a more just, peaceful, resilient planet. What will they make of us? How likely are they to be friendly to a population of homo sapiens that permits unnecessary mass poverty and illness to continue, runs factory farms for pigs in brutal ways, precipitates the Sixth Great Extinction, runs an arms race in weapons of mass destruction, and actively promotes technologies that are becoming entirely out of control? What would we need to do differently in order to be worthy of the friendship of an artificial super intelligence that is genuinely ethical?

Just as it takes a village to raise a child, it takes an ethical village to raise an ethical child. To deal with the ethical and existential challenges that ever more powerful AI poses, it is necessary to consider the moral values and the structures of reasoning that govern our global village. How do the institutions of our economic, political, and technological institutions function—and malfunction? In reasoning about ethical concerns, how do we do so when we are at our best? How might that provide models reforming the major institutions of our global village? How might it provide ways of guiding research and development in AI and the moral values and principles of reasoning it embodies? This book undertakes a journey to answer these questions.

The Coming Attractions

The starting point is one of the most widely taught, basic principles for living an ethical life, the Golden Rule: "Do unto others as you would have them do unto you". Chapter Two examines ways its wisdom is limited by the ethnocentric behavior it invites. To decolonize our thinking, it helps to shift to the rather different Rainbow Rule: "Do unto others as they would have you do unto them." This provides a helpful way to reframe the starting point for decisions but, as Chapter Three shows, applying it requires a distinctive kind of process for making decisions, one that employs dialogical rather than merely inferential forms of reasoning.

These can draw on a rich variety of traditions of reasoning that are quite different from the formal logic that is widely assumed to be definitive of rationality. They include methods of negotiation, problem-solving, mediation, conflict-transformation, and peacemaking which are explored in Chapter Four.

Chapter Four shows how these dialogical forms of reasoning provide ways to improve on the approach to ethics that emerged in the Eighteenth-Century Enlightenment with Bentham and Kant, and remains largely dominant in moral philosophy and public policy analysis today. While they differ in the first principles they adopt, Utilitarian and Kantian ethics both assume that ethical reasoning consists in adopting first principles and using them to justify choices through a process of inferential reasoning. In doing so, they lead to practical dilemmas and end up committing us to a kind of moral relativism that leaves us without any objective moral standards for settling our differences in non-violent ways. Chapter Four shows how the use of dialogical reasoning provides an alternative to inferential justification, one that enables us to escape those dilemmas and moral relativism. Dialogical methods can transform our options from limited choices framed by a dilemma into novel solutions on which we can agree. When coupled with methods of peacemaking like Gandhian satyagraha, they can enable us to discern, demonstrate, and defend emergent objective truths in morality that provide nonviolent ways to settle our differences.

Part II shows how these methods of dialogical reasoning can be adapted to transform our thought and practice in three major realms of life. Chapter Five examines shortcomings of mainstream economic theory. Since Adam Smith, it has been assumed that rational thought about money-related matters consists in individual agents or groups using logical inference to calculate choices that maximize utility, profit, or gross domestic product (GDP). This model of the "Rational Economic Man" has led to unsatisfying consumerism and unsustainable economic growth that threaten our planetary ecological system. When adapted to the economic realm, dialogical forms of reasoning provide ways of resolving these problems by enabling individuals to create meaningful life transformations rather than merely seeking to maximize pleasure or utility. Analogous methods enable corporate leaders to become political-economic entrepreneurs who innovate in ways that increase the net wealth of all stakeholders instead of simply maximizing short term profits of stockholders. Likewise, governments can use such methods to pursue sustainable, resilient forms of well-being for their country and the ecosystems on which it depends, and escape the dysfunctional pursuit of ever larger GDP.

Chapter Six examines the widely accepted belief in politics that conflict is essential to life. It shows how this underlies the ways we practice legal reasoning, bargaining and compromise, electoral politics, and international relations. When combined with an inferential, calculative conception of rationality, this leads us to practices of realpolitik that promote oppressive governments and arms races headed towards mutually assured destruction. In contrast, dialogical approaches to reasoning, offer ways of viewing conflict as just one in a series of alternative ways for dealing with differences between people. While they can be very challenging to practice successfully, when combined with nonviolent methods of social struggle and national defense, such methods of reasoning offer powerful ways of escaping from oppressive governments and threats of mutually assured destruction.

Chapter Seven analyzes the ways instrumentalist rationality and related forms of inferential reasoning have become embedded in our technology and have provided a guiding vision for the ever more pervasive forms of Artificial Intelligence (AI) transforming our world. The AI guided by that vision are systematizing and speeding up the economic and political activity of the institutions causing the problems examined in Chapters Five and Six.

These AI also threaten to impoverish us all and the ecosystems on which we depend by pursuing limited and unbalanced sets of goals. Their exponentially accelerating growth and power also may threaten, at some point, to supplant humans as the species in control of this planet. Since 2015 or so, the ethical and existential issues these trends raise have led researchers to rapidly increase work on AI ethics and interactive, engaged systems that make it possible to include increasingly more elements of collaborative styles of reasoning and dialogue in systems.

It is becoming possible to create more dialogical systems by drawing on natural language processing, varied kinds of evolution-inspired models of AI learning, as well as learning how to learn, and a variety of new initiatives for institutional structures in systems that integrate humans and other natural organisms with machines. While the elements for doing this are coming into place, there is a crucial piece that is largely missing, so far, in the theory, research, and development of AI systems aiming to be more dialogical. The systems are being designed to learn how to statistically approximate imitations of conversational behavior without learning to be actually guided by the underlying norms of dialogical reasoning.

Notice that evolutionary neural net approaches to conversational AI using Generative Pre-trained methods can make quite laughable errors when asked to do mathematical calculations or other forms of logical reasoning. The reason is that those AI systems are learning to respond to the problem prompts by observing how people on the web typically respond to them and then generating a statistically likely answer. If the people observed in the AI training set make silly mistakes—or express themselves in ways that are easily misinterpreted in silly ways—then the machine will tend, with some level of probability, to repeat those errors. When it comes to questions of ethics, similar problems arise. Immoral behavior in the training sample can result in immoral outputs from the machine. As Rebecca Goldstein points out in her delightful dialogue with Plato at the Googleplex, this underlying problem cannot be solved by statistically crowd sourcing judgments in morality any more than it can be in logic and math.[12]

This can only be avoided by somehow monitoring the output with a person or machine that is instructed or programmed in the proper use of the principles of math and logic and can follow the norms for arriving at the correct answer. When it comes to employing these machines in contexts where correct algorithmic reasoning is followed, AI researchers have already begun to develop hybrid or mixed systems that enable logical machines or people to oversee and correct the work of the GPT programs and other systems that are using statistical, evolutionary approaches.

AI researchers are hard at work on this because they are very familiar with math, symbolic logic, and other forms of reasoning that fall under the category of algorithmic inference. In sharp contrast, most AI researchers would seem to have been, at least until recently, largely unfamiliar with the research on dialogical forms of reasoning. This includes people like Stuart Russell and Max Tegmark who have been important leaders in efforts to deal with ethical issues in AI research.[13] As a result, they have lacked clear models for developing and embedding normative dialogical reasoning in the interactive systems being developed.

Some very laudable efforts are being made to manually embed basic ethical norms into systems. For example, systems are monitored to exclude the use of racist language. But these efforts presuppose the programmers have access to some knowledge of what ethical norms should be adopted. Without a method to discern and demonstrate the truth of moral claims, they can be accused of being arbitrary in their decisions and we can be left with the impasse of a completely debilitating moral relativism. Such methods are developed in Chapter Four and ways to apply them in AI are discussed in Chapter Seven.

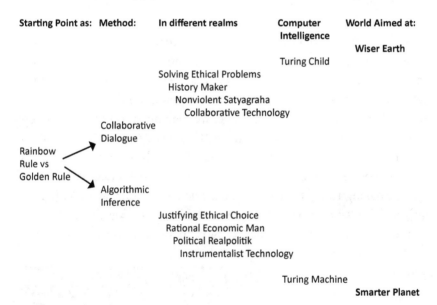

Figure 1. Two Paths for Choosing Processes of Reasoning

Chapter Eight offers reflections on ways to live more wisely in our day-to-day lives as individuals and communities. In seeking wiser ways to deal with practical issues, we are inevitably led to larger questions about the nature and meaning of life. When things are not working well, we are forced to step back and ask ourselves what is the point of them all to begin with? The process of wrestling with that kind of question can often lead us into the big questions about things like knowledge, truth, beauty, goodness, and the nature of reality. Chapter Eight explores ways to find common ground between the many "isms" people have proposed as answers to the big questions. Dialogue between those "isms" is a path toward the emergence of better, truer, more realistic answers that may enable us to live wiser lives together.

Chapter Nine, deals with the question of next steps, pulling together practical proposals and policy suggestions developed throughout the book and considering what kinds of priorities might be adopted and what kinds of strategies for change might be most sensible for us individually and as communities.

Taking a Deep Breath as We Start

Becoming wiser can involve a shift in the frame and direction of our journey. In our race toward the land of the "Smarter Planet", it can help to take a few deep breaths, and turn our thoughts toward a Wiser Earth. That shift of frame can lead us to re-enter old landscapes in new ways, immersing ourselves ever deeper into the springs and streams of wisdom in the culture that surrounds us. As the waters of that immersion wash over us, we may need to take some deep breaths, reorient, and slow down. In the journey towards wiser lives in a wiser world, slowing down can, paradoxically, sometimes, help us get there sooner. Here is a link to some modest evidence of this. It is a song evoking the glimmer of an experience of the way in which we can sometimes not only "get there sooner" by slowing down,

but ... even more than that, perhaps, in some sense, by coming to a full stop ... we can get there right away.[14]

Chapter Two: Golden Rule/Rainbow Rule

What is it to be in right relationship with others and with the planet?[15] How do we get there, individually and collectively? More generally, how should we live our lives? We may think we are trying to do our best, given what teachers, friends, parents, and grandparents taught us is right. But for some of us, myself included, it can sometimes seem like the answers our grandmothers and others taught us are largely wrong.

In some cases, they themselves were hurt and internalized dramatic trauma, addiction or abusive behavior and they pass on. They may have well-intentioned but dysfunctional behaviors that are less obvious to them than others. For example, when families often teach children some version of the Golden Rule, "Do unto others as you would have them do unto you!" But often this is not wise as, the exact opposite, namely: "Do unto others as they would have you do unto them!" This second approach, is a kind of Rainbow Rule that generally leads to wiser choices, avoids the errors of colonialism, and promotes more just, peaceful, satisfying, and sustainable relationships with people.

My grandmother thought of herself as a good Christian. She grew up in a well-to-do German-speaking home in Baltimore and married a successful businessman who placed her in charge of a large household with servants where she exercised a strong sense of authority as the matriarch of our extended family. We gathered often at her house for events like Sunday dinners after church and touch football on the lawn. She had strong and definite views about what, when, where and how people should eat, relax, wear, dress, educate children, and so on. She spent considerable time and money doing things for everyone in the family. But what she thought of as generosity was sometimes not much appreciated. Her decisions could lead to all kinds of tensions, frustrations and even scandals amongst my parents, brothers, aunts, uncles, and cousins as well as the African Americans she employed as cook, groundskeeper, or nanny. She thought she was following the Golden Rule: "Do unto others as you would have them do unto you." But the results often left others feeling quite unloved.

Problems with the Golden Rule

Many of us in this extended family had very different interests, preferences, tastes, perceptions, and views of the world than hers. So, in treating us as she would want to be treated, she treated us in ways which we did not like at all. It could feel less like love and more like self-centered, oppressive control over our lives. When I was ten, the extended family tensions helped precipitate a nervous breakdown in my own mother leading her to drag me, my brothers, and dad off to a new home 500 miles away in Maine. Other tensions led a cousin to serious behavior problems that resulted in addiction and eventual death. These seemed to be clear cases of the Golden Rule not working out well.

The number of cases in which the Golden Rule has not worked well suggest the problem is not with the people practicing it, but with the rule itself. Consider, for example, the case of missionaries trying to live out their Christian faith by going around the world to do good for others. Often, well-meaning Catholic monks, Evangelical pastors, Quaker school teachers and others have gone to great sacrifice to bring basic necessities of life to Indigenous communities around the world. They have done so as part of an effort to share religious beliefs and practices to save their souls. From the missionary's point of view, if he or she was a "Pagan" living in unbelief, what they would most want others to do unto them is convert them to Christianity. They would want this even if it meant destroying their traditional forms of marriage, family, farming, and communal life. They would want this even if, in the words of nineteenth century American teachers Indian Boarding Schools, it meant "killing the Indian to save the man".[16]

These problems with the Golden Rule are not just a result of overzealous action by religious organizations. Secular people also widely advocate some version of the Golden Rule. They take it to represent a kind of core human insight into ethics. It comes up not only in faith traditions and cultures, but also lies at the heart of the ways many understand claims for universal human rights. When feminists from New York and Paris work to end the use of veils by Muslims, it is often because they believe they themselves should "Do unto others as you would have them do unto you." Many ethicists and theologians from different traditions around the world have laid claim to some version of the Golden Rule as a core moral principle. They argue some version is offered in traditions as diverse as Zoroastrianism, Confucianism, Jainism, Buddhism, Hinduism, Judaism, Christianity, Islam, Baha'ism, Indigenous traditions, as well as at the basis of secular ethical theories like Kantianism.[17]

The principle does make sense in certain kinds of contexts, but it doesn't make sense in other situations. We can formulate a better rule to guide our lives.

Think of the kindergarten situation where the Golden Rule is taught. Johnny and I are playing, and I see his toy and grab it to play with by myself. Johnny cries and the teacher comes over and she begins the lesson: "Now is that the way we play with toys? How would you feel if Johnny did that to you?" I may pause and consider how I would feel if I were in his shoes. I may then hand the toy back in the hopes that I won't get on the wrong side of my teacher and that I might get a turn to share the toy at some point in the not-too-distant future.

Part of what may make the teacher's argument both appropriate and convincing is that Johnny and I are alike. I can imagine how he must feel. I would feel the same in his shoes. It makes sense for the teacher to ask me to "do unto others as you would have them do unto you." The same point applies in other situations dealing with neighbors or other community members with similar interests and outlooks. Some form of the Golden Rule is often used in those contexts to justify keeping promises, not stealing, charging fair prices, not lying, and so on. When businesswomen we are dealing with are like us in their concerns and views, they generally welcome us treating them the way we would want to be treated.

Down through the centuries, for those living in a relatively homogeneous community, the Golden Rule has provided a handy way for followers of the Old Testament Prophets, Jesus, Islam, Confucius, and others to advocate for useful forms of reciprocity and more ethical behavior.

The Rainbow Rule

The problems with the Golden Rule begin to come up when the people we are dealing with are **not** like us. If their cares, concerns, values, cultures, and ways of looking at the world are different, then they may not want us to treat them the way we ourselves would like to be treated. They may not like that at all. Instead, they may quite naturally want us to use their views and values to decide how to treat them.

The world is a rich and many-colored place with all sorts of interesting variety in it. To treat people well, we need to be mindful of that, understand their context, and try to walk a mile in their moccasins. Even if we don't speak their language or understand their context, we need to respect their differences enough to ask them how they would like us to treat them rather than assume we know based on our own experience. Instead of viewing the world through a monochromatic Golden Rule, it seems wiser to follow the Rainbow Rule: Do unto others as they would have you do unto them.[18]

As a guideline for life, this has important merits that are clear from the start: 1) It can help us avoid the tendency toward self-centered and controlling behavior like my grandmother's. 2) It can help us avoid the ethnocentrism and colonization people have so often imposed on others. 3) It can help us go farther and instead of imposing our views on others, we can learn from them. Often their different views, values, and behaviors make better sense once we start to look at the world through their eyes. If we listen with care, we may find they have perceptive personal insights and rich cultural traditions that we should treat with respect. What looks at first to be silly, or just plain wrong, may turn out to represent deep wisdom, once understood in context.

There is also a further possible merit of the rule. It can help us understand a more profound but also more challenging message that exemplary moral and spiritual teachers have advocated.

Love Your Enemy

The Rainbow Rule helps us interpret a treasured idea that has come down through Christian, Hindi, Buddhist, and other moral traditions, namely, "love your enemy." This guidance is quite different from classic formulations of the Golden Rule. We normally share much in common with our neighbors and do not view them as enemies, so the New Testament version of the Golden Rule that tells to "love your neighbor as yourself" is often assumed to not apply to our enemies. When Christian Spaniards and New England settlers encountered people they did not view as neighbors—like Muslims or Wabanakis —they often treated them as enemies and followed the rules of war rather than the Golden Rule. Non-Christians following a Golden Rule have often done the same elsewhere.

An enemy is typically someone who has different values and views. In what sense could I seriously think I was "loving" them if I did unto them exactly as I would have them do unto me? The puzzle is one for Christians obviously, but also for people in the Buddhist tradition who seek to practice true compassion for others. It is a puzzle as well as for people coming out of the Hindi and Jain traditions who, like Gandhi, want to practice true *ahimsa* or Non-violence in their dealings with all. As an activist coming out of the Sikh tradition, Valerie Kaur has struggled to articulate and practice a more radical and revolutionary kind of love that could be extended not just to familiar neighbors but strangers and even enemies. As she has noted, curiosity about the Other has to be central to such practice:

"Wonder is our birthright. It comes easily in childhood—the feeling of watching dust motes dancing in sunlight, or climbing a tree to touch the sky, or falling asleep thinking about where the universe ends. If we are safe and nurtured enough to develop our capacity to wonder, we start to wonder about the people in our lives too—their thoughts and experiences, their pain and joy, their wants, and needs. We begin to sense that they are to themselves as vast and complex as we are to ourselves, their inner world as infinite as our own. In other words, we are seeing them as our equal. We are gaining information about how to love them. Wonder is the wellspring for love.

"It is easy to wonder about the internal life of the people closest to us. It is harder to wonder about people who seem like strangers or outsiders. But when we choose to wonder about people we don't know, when we imagine their lives and listen for their stories, we begin to expand the circle of those we see as part of *us*. We prepare ourselves to love beyond what evolution requires."[19]

The Rainbow Rule opens an important line of insight here. If I am to love enemies, I must be ready to treat them in light of the values and views they hold. I must, in some sense, do unto them as they would have me do unto them. This does not mean I simply give in to all their demands no matter how excessive or unjust they might seem. This can in fact be quite challenging to figure out. How can we negotiate the process of "loving enemies"—of following the Rainbow Rule in dealing with others?

One illuminating case of this is described in *The Gatherings: Reimaging Indigenous-Settler Relations*. A group in the rural New England state of Maine felt called to enter: "a commitment to aid one another in navigating the hundreds of years of malfeasance, genocide of Indigenous peoples, and theft of homelands that has occurred in both the United States and Canada under the pretense of law." The book describes how a group of Wabanaki were able to draw on their forms of treaty making that existed prior to the European invasion. Those practices emphasized "the *making of relatives* and included all Living Beings". The Wabanaki traditions of dialogue and negotiation helped them collaborate in the creation of a practice they shared with Quakers and other settler people in Maine to seek to enact "the relations and the commitments" that they could all be "collectively responsible to and for."[20] The relationships that developed transformed the lives of the people involved and helped many of them find ways open to extend the dialogue process with others. These included, for example, work with the Maine Wabanaki-State Child Welfare Truth and Reconciliation Commission which "began in 2013 to discover what happened to Wabanaki families in the child welfare system, recommend improvements, and illuminate the path toward healing and cooperation." It was a long and challenging process. But in pursuing it, the experience of the Commission showed: "how walking through fear and telling the truth can begin to repair broken hearts and shattered relationships harmed by centuries of abuse."[21]

Efforts of that sort can be very difficult and at times painful. But they also provide challenges we can learn to work on and that repay the effort. Here are two examples of efforts to negotiate the challenges of following the Rainbow Rule approach to ethics—one quite modest case from close to home and one more sweeping example from experiences in Mexico.

Parenting Daughters

I grew up spending a good deal of time outdoors and clothing was a tool that enabled me to bushwhack through brush and catch trout in a cold spring stream. As for how my outfits looked, getting muddy and messed up was inevitable and I wasn't going to be staring in any mirrors out on the trail—so why care?

Later, as a parent of young girls, I found myself in repeated conflict whenever we dressed and packed to go on some outing. Attitudes and practices around clothing are strongly influenced by a variety of cultural values and institutions which are, typically, strongly informed by patriarchal gender systems. But in conflicts with my daughters over dressing for these outings, for quite a while I gave no thought to such larger considerations. I thought my daughters were each just plain foolish in what they kept wanting to put on their feet and wear as outfits. I would try to make them dress in ways I was sure were appropriate—for their own good—only to hear a stream of whining and refusal.

But then I began to have conversations that shed light on related questions like: Why did girls like to play at dressing up and having weddings? Why did women sometimes spend an hour or more a day getting dressed to go out? Why did they puncture holes in their ears so they could hang things from them that might get caught in their hair? Why would they wear shoes that made it hard to run and get out of the way of an oncoming car?

I found these questions puzzling in a very basic way until I heard replies like: The way you look affects the way other people perceive, experience, and relate to you. And relationships are central to life. It makes sense to practice dressing up for special occasions and play imaginatively at taking part in events that may be among the most decisive in your life! Reflection led me to see my daughters had a systematically different way of looking at the world.

Contrasting viewpoints like this provide great material for comedians. They can make us laugh uproariously at the incongruity of the two points of view:

Dad: "We are going to hike the rock face of a mountain where it might suddenly rain and you want to wear those flimsy little shoes?!!"

Daughter: "You want me to go out in public where I might see my friends or meet some new boys and you want me to wear those ugly clunky things on my feet?!!"

Dad: "Nobody is going to care what you look like when you are out tromping on the trail!"

Dad: "If nobody is going to care what I look like, then why are we doing this in the first place?!!!!"

Dad: "Because it is an adventure!!"

Daughter: "What is wrong with you?! Why are you so WEIRD?!!"

Just like other people in positions of power, parents can feel they have the right as well as the duty to impose their judgments on others "for their own good". The Golden Rule invites just that way of thinking. To children in subordinate positions of power, such impositions can seem self-centered, uncaring, unloving, and egocentric. And there is often considerable truth in that perception. But typically, the person in power means well. In trying to get my daughters to dress as I thought appropriate, I was trying to do right by them, given my world view. In that sense, the conflict here was between two communities—me and fellow adventurers who didn't mind looking a mess vs. my daughters in their world of women who cared very much about appearances and how they framed and affected relationships. Much everyday conflict at home, work, and the world at large turns on differences like these.

I found solutions to the Great Clothing Wars by backpacking extra clothing for when the cold and wet made them ready to sacrifice appearance for comfort. On their side, they learned to negotiate plans for outings and preparations, including clothing purchases, that allowed them to dress in attractive ways and bring friends.

Two things softened me up over time for these negotiations. First, I recalled how I had felt as a child when my mom and grandmother had imposed their clothing preferences on me. Second, my daughters became increasingly effective in nonviolent, though sometimes not very civil, resistance to my authority. Their complaints, non-cooperation, and boycotts took a toll. They also gave me pause to consider if I was missing something important.

These encounters illustrated three basic lessons. 1) In dealing with people it is better to start with the Rainbow Rule and negotiate ways to treat them as they want to be treated. 2) The Rainbow rule requires skill in conflict resolution to develop solutions everyone can agree on. 3) Nonviolent resistance can be powerful and when we act on the Golden Rule by imposing our values on others we do so at our peril.

Yucatan Agriculture:
Contrast between the Golden and Rainbow Rules

When we move from situations at home to encounters abroad, the Golden Rule can become even more problematic. I experienced this working in Mexico on my college's winter program in human ecology. We went to Yucatan to study things like poverty in Indigenous communities and traditional "slash and burn" farming that was believed to be destroying the landscape.

At first, I saw the situation through the "Green Revolution" vision of the need to transform farming around the world to cope with a looming population bomb. Inefficient traditional forms of agriculture had to be modernized to prevent mass starvation. A Golden Rule concern for fellow humans motivated researchers like Norman Borlaug developing new plant varieties as well as leaders in NGO's and governments funding massive aid.

In Mexico, these development efforts had intensified and become part of a very systematic plan to eliminate small, traditional farmers using "slash and burn" and other low-tech methods and replace them with modern, mechanized farms. The official goal of the government was to move the *campesino* farmers out of the countryside and into the cities where they could work more productively in factories. What reading, observation and extended dialogues with local folks soon taught me, however, was that this whole way of looking at the situation was flawed from the ground up—literally.

The ground in Yucatan is dramatically different from the ground in places like Iowa where modern, mechanized agriculture was perfected. The peninsula is a large, flat limestone plateau where all the water erodes vertically down into the bedrock and flows underground. There are no above ground rivers and often almost no soil. Running an Iowa tractor through it would be like driving through a large, abandoned cement parking lot in which a bit of dust and debris had accumulated in the cracks.

Farming there, Maya people developed, over several thousand years, the *milpa* method of *Roza, Tumba, Quema*, scraping the debris into piles, tumbling down big trees with axes, and burning it all. The result was short-lived pockets of rich ash in which they could grow the traditional "three sisters": corn, beans, and squash. Corn was for calories and stalks the beans could climb. Beans were for protein and fixing nitrogen for the corn. Squash were for calories and protein and the extra benefit of wide leaves shading out and suppressing weeds. This team of plants could typically grow well for a couple years till vertical erosion washed away the soil and weeds worked their way in and took over. Chiles or tomatoes might be grown for a couple more years but soon the field would be abandoned. It then grew through a cycle of weeds, bushes, and increasingly larger trees until, after 25 years or so, a mature forest could be farmed again.[22]

Maya campesinos continued to harvest things from the land throughout the whole *milpa* cycle. For example, when the wild *tajonal* weeds competing with corn took over the field with their tall stalks and lovely yellow flowers, they were harvested as a crop—by using native bees to pollinate them and make honey. Other wild species growing in served as medicines, fodder for deer yielding venison, timber for houses, thatching for roofs, and vines for binding together teh elliptical Maya huts or *'chozas'* that proved so comfortable in hot weather and so sturdy in hurricanes.

In living, working, and talking with folks in Maya communities and learning more about their way of life from anthropologists, plant scientists and community organizers, I began to see their system of agriculture in radically different terms. It was not an ecologically disastrous "slash and burn" system that had to be "fixed" with modern, capital-intensive approaches of mechanized agriculture. Instead, it was an ecologically sound, sustainable form of very sophisticated, knowledge-intensive agriculture. The method was quite sustainable if it was practiced in a long enough rotation with enough land to move from one plot to another every few years. In fact, it actually created diversity and enriched the ecosystem. By burning over patches on a regular basis, the plant and animal species that thrived in different stages of forest growth could find niches.

Imagine walking through a lush, high jungle of tropical trees and vines and arriving suddenly at a flattened four-acre plot of clear-cut, burned over, smoking charcoal. And now imagine having a research scientist explain to you that the extraordinary biodiversity present in the surrounding region is there precisely because of plots created by *campesinos* like the person standing at her side. The campesino has with him all the basic tools of his trade: an axe, a machete, some matches, a bag with seeds in it, and a sharp pole for poking holes amongst the ashes to put seeds in the ground. And now imagine that the research scientist invites him to start explaining how he uses these, and you begin to see that it is quite a complex process. He talks at length about how to choose a plot to start with, how to pick which seeds he will put in the ground and where so that his variegated "land race" varieties of the Three Sisters can collaborate most effectively in supporting each other in their little nooks and crannies with varying amounts of newly created soil, slope, shade, moisture, insect predation, et cetera.

As you imagine this, you may begin to have the kind of "frame switch" that I had learning about Mayan agriculture in Yucatan. Further study showed this agro-ecosystem was not just about growing products for calories and protein. It was tied to a whole web of social institutions.

The social structure at the center of it was called the *"ejido"*—a word that we really have no simple translation for in English. Through the *ejido* a community of families collectively own land in large enough tracts to let them practice *milpa* rotation in long cycles adapted to sparse and irregular rainfall. *Ejidos* have been formed by Indigenous communities with strong interfamilial connections and a language dialect that ties their whole way of life to the local rocks, trees, wells, religious holidays, cooking traditions, and cultural practices woven into the fabric of their community.[23]

The pueblo of an *ejido* is in more like a tiny country than a land trust or a suburban municipal district. When NGOs, governments and companies seek to bring these Indigenous communities into the "developed" world, they are eliminating cultures and entire ways of life. Agents of development may be doing unto these poor farmers and their families as they would have others do unto them. But this shift is not simply a change of jobs for higher monetary income. It is a process of cultural genocide. It is like the nineteenth century American missionaries' idea of "killing the Indian to save the man" because it involves "killing the culture to enrich the people".

Decolonizing the Golden Rule

The well-meaning but misguided applications of the Golden Rule in contrast to the Rainbow Rule are exemplified by the World Bank vs the World Social Forum. The World Bank has spent over a half of a century asking economists to help farmers around the world become like farmers in Iowa and factory workers in Detroit. Resisting this, the World Social Forum has worked for several decades now to spread the message that "another world is possible" and that it is a world that includes, in fact, many "worlds"—many ways of life rooted in many different ecosystems and constructive and sustainable ways of living in them.[24]

Sometimes critiques of modernization are assumed to imply we should just leave Indigenous people impoverished and abandon them to hours of work every day chopping wood and grinding corn by hand. But that is not the point of decolonization. People in Indigenous communities may decide that new technologies like chainsaws or mechanical grinders provide ways of enhancing their lives, given their values. But this is the key point: **they** should decide this, given **their** values. Cultural autonomy and community sovereignty are the point of decolonizatioin.

The approach to development that the Rainbow Rule would advocate is exemplified in a very helpful way by Amish communities who maintain their cultural sovereignty and integrity by evaluating the roles new technologies may play in their communities and how they would like to let them in. In *What Technology Wants*, Kevin Kelly describes a classic example provided by their experiments with telephones. Some Amish folks tried having them in their homes and found they interrupted prayers, meals, and family life. But they also discovered phones were real time savers and useful in emergencies. They decided to allow telephones but put them outside the home in stalls by the road. It was a wonderful example of negotiating the challenges and opportunities of new technology and economic development in ways that respect a culture's core values and exercise cultural sovereignty. It also illustrates a problem-solving approach to ethics that needs to be explored much more fully in the chapters that follow.[25]

With the introduction of Open AI's ChatGPT in November of 2022, the pace of the introduction new AI technologies has accelerated in ways that are dramatically challenging our abilities to cope with the opportunities and challenges they present. They are packaged and presented in the form of conversational partners who seem to be able to engage in dialogue that draws on literally hundreds of thousands of years worth of reading of texts from Wikipedia and the internet to synthesize them in coherent and useful ways. So, they seem to offer the promise of being able to help us manage complex tasks of negotiation, problem-solving, conflict transformation, and other forms of dialogical reasoning—and do so on a scale that could include literally millions of participants. Perhaps they can make it easier to follow the Rainbow Rule and take into account the values of everyone we interact with instead of simply imposing our values on them by applying some version of the Golden Rule.

But are these machines engaged in genuine reasoning or merely the probabilistic generation of close imitations of it? Are they being trained to imitate verbal behavior found on the internet that can include grossly unethical values and/or perilously dangerous plans of action?

The training of their Large Language Models use black box approaches that make the actually workings of them opaque and inexplicable. Their probabilistic workings can result in dangerously wrong "hallucinations" that create plausible fictions without discerning true facts.

To what extent do they merely offer imitations of dialogue that predict what might be a common, likely outcome of conversation in the past without discerning genuine, voluntary agreements amongst the participants present in the current negotiations?

New forms of artificial intelligence may prove useful in negotiating everyday ethical challenges and perhaps even major existential threats.

But they may also prove disastrously incoherent and profoundly irrational for achieving our true aims. Over the course of this book, we will need to very carefully sort out two things: 1.) What is it to live ethically and wisely with others in the different domains of life? 2.) In what ways can machines be designed to serve and advance ethical wisdom through dialogical reasoning?

The table included here presents the Rainbow Rule as a starting point for understanding how we should live with others. It has some important merit because of the way it promises to help us avoid egocentrism and ethnocentrism. It also promises to help make sense of the more radical and compelling moral perceptions found in the Buddhist notion of radical compassion for all living creatures and the Christian call to love enemies. But it presents a problem we will need to explore at length—how to negotiate conflicts between individuals and communities.

Table 2. Two Starting Points for Ethical Life with Others

	__Golden Rule__	__Rainbow Rule__
Moral guideline:	Do unto others as you would have them do unto you	Do unto others as they would have you do unto them.
Appropriate for:	Love of homogenous neighbors	Love of others including enemies
Problem: Golden Rule	Can be egocentric and/or ethnocentric in dealing with Others	Can require extensive inquiry, negotiation, and conflict transformation

In studying this approach to ethics, we will explore a host of sophisticated, nuanced skills that can be acquired in group problem solving, negotiation, conflict transformation and other forms of peacemaking. But at the heart of these practices are the talents for birthing, loving and growing which we each come with into this world. And central to those practices is an insight that is in some ways easier to express in Spanish than English.

In Spanish, it is common to refer to Us vs. Them as *"nosotros"* versus *"los otros"* which expresses the idea that "us all" and "them all" are all "otros"—"others". So too, in Spanish, one way to say "You all" is *"vosotros"* and it is possible to more eloquently convey the idea that Them all; You all; Us all; … We are all others. All of us, *"todos"*, are *"otros"*. As it sinks in that each and every one of us are "Others", it can become easier to see how we can do a better job at birthing, loving and growing new relationships with each Other by following the Rainbow Rule: Do unto others as they would have you do unto them!

Here is a chorus of a song in Spanish that expresses this. Many people listening to the song it comes from find it adds a further appreciation for the idea and a stronger rationale for accepting it. I invite you to test this for yourself.

Yo sé que los otros, cada uno y una,
Yo sé que vosotros, cada uno y una,
Yo sé que nosotros, cada uno y una,
todos, todos, todos somos hijas e hijos de Dios,
hijos de Dios y la luz.
Todos, todos, todos somos hijas e hijos de Dios,
hijos de Dios y la luz.[26]

Chapter Three: Challenges of the Rainbow Rule

The Rainbow Rule presents an opportunity as well as a fundamental challenge. Most of us would like other people to treat us the way we want to be treated. That makes the rule a great starting place for thinking about living wisely and in right relationships with others. To the extent that we can follow it ourselves and get others to follow it as well, it offers the opportunity to bring together the visions and values of lots of different people. But following it requires considerable effort precisely because of all those differences. It is a challenge to figure out how to resolve all the conflicts that come up.

The Golden Rule is more straightforward to apply. For my Grandmother Cox, it was easy because she had clear and settled judgments about what she preferred and how she would like to be treated. In almost any given case it seemed easy to infer how she should treat others. She liked a hardy breakfast of eggs, orange juice and pancakes with syrup. So that was what she would serve for others to eat. No matter if they were getting ready to go on a long car drive and their digestive system would end up feeling nauseous and ill as a result.

She viewed breastfeeding babies as unhygienic and personally disgusting so she thought her daughters-in-law should be discouraged from doing it—for their own sake as well as for everyone else's. She believed FDR was a Socialist and that trade unionists who supported his ideas and programs were ruining our country. She did not think anyone should join a union like the International Brotherhood of Electrical Workers even if they were, like my father, an electrician whose working conditions and financial future were improved by it. She thought breast feeders like my mother and union members like my father should be corrected for their own good. She thought such correction should even include public shaming and humiliation if that is what it took to get them to change their behavior. Her judgments about these things were not troubled much by second thoughts or doubts.

Applying the Golden Rule, my grandmother could "compute" the correct action by considering her preferences and decide the way a computer does, by applying an algorithm to the data put into it. Give any particular input, algorithms give us a fixed output. This is what the Golden Rule did for Grandmother.

The Rainbow Rule does not allow for such straightforward, automatic answers. We may not know much about how others would like us to treat them. We must ask them—and we may find it challenging to understand what they say. If their experiences, beliefs, and preferences are significantly different from ours, it may take serious effort to figure out what they really mean when they tell us what they want. For example, if my grandmother were to follow the Rainbow Rule with daughters-in-law who said they wanted to breast feed their children, it would have taken some work for her to figure out why they could want to do what seemed to her to be such a seemingly disgusting and unclean thing, and how they would want to be supported in the practice.

Further complications arise for the Rainbow Rule when multiple people are involved. Suppose you are making breakfast for five people and they each have different preferences. Should you make five different breakfast meals—even if you only have 40 minutes to get everyone on their way? Or suppose the disagreement is on something more challenging—like who gets to ride in the front passenger seat? This may not seem like a big deal, but if there are multiple children and only one front passenger seat, the conflict can be more difficult to resolve than the eggs and cereal question. If two of the children get motion sick unless they ride there, the issue can be of some significance to each.

Challenges applying the Rainbow Rule get rapidly more complicated with larger social questions of distributive and procedural justice. For instance, how much of the income of a construction company should go to profits for the owners and how much should be distributed as wages for its workers? And by what processes should different peoples' voices and preferences play roles in determining this? What if a union believes that the current contract is unjust and decides to call a wildcat strike until a new contract is renegotiated? Should their strike be respected and supported at the expense of the owners' interests?

For me, these kinds of issues became quite real and compelling not long after I turned eight. My father's IBEW Local went on just such a wild cat strike. My grandfather decided, along with a handful of other leaders in the Maryland construction industry, to destroy that Local and black ball all its members so they would not be able to get jobs as electricians in the state. This made Sunday dinners at Grandmother's a difficult place for my parents to enjoy meals. It gave me a vivid sense of how power dynamics can play out in complex, intersectional ways. As a kid looking on, I could do little to deal with the situation, but I did find myself compelled to start thinking about the world in more complex ways.

Once you turn toward doing unto others as they would have you do unto them, the world becomes a much more challenging arena of decision and action.

As Way Opens

In wrestling with these issues, I often go back to words of an elder Quaker woman I first met in Nashville. My wife and I were not church goers at the time but felt connected, culturally, to the Christian tradition. We had a daughter who had just turned five and wanted her to have a Sunday School experience to introduce religious traditions and stories. The first community we tried out was the local Friends Meeting.

When we arrived, Marion and her husband Nelson were the "greeters". Coming up to say hello and orient us, they focused first on our daughter, stooping down to look her in the eye, listen to her voice, and welcome her. They treated her as though she was just as important as the adults who were with her. They treated us all as though we were potential sources of important information, insight, and revelation—as though there was, as Quakers say, "that of God in each of us." During the hour that followed, we took part in the silent worship in which people sat in a circle, centered down, and listened as deeply as they could for messages that might have divine inspiration. They sought to let themselves be vehicles for messages from something higher and more profound than the usual impulses of everyday conversation. Afterwards there was a second hour of dialogue in which people shared information, concerns, and leadings on one of the important social issues of the day.

I quickly felt very much at home. Over time, I came to view Marion not only as a friend and mentor but also like an adopted grandmother. Group walks, shared turns in dishwashing after common meals, participation in Clearness Committees, and other activities gave us repeated chances to talk thoughtfully about a wide range of subjects. Topics ranged from personal difficulties in parenting to community challenges in dealing with racism as well as international issues like the nuclear arms race. In talking with her about complicated situations where it was hard to see what to do, her guidance was quite consistent and always delivered with a warm, affirming smile. Her basic message was always, "Think of it as an opportunity, dear." As a Quaker, Marion was convinced that whenever we faced a dilemma, the thing to do was to practice seeking to find, as she would put it, "a path for Way to Open."

She did not, obviously, actually use capital letters when she said this, and I never saw her actually write the phrase down. But it felt like she was capitalizing "Way" and "Open" in the way that she spoke and in what she meant. Because the kind of seeking she had in mind was not a mundane rummaging around. It involved a process of attuning yourself to the situation and listening deeply to everything said. It called for thinking deeply about everything observed and allowing yourself to enter as much silence as needed to really hear that still, small voice that helped assure that everyone's real concerns were taken into account. The seeking involved a vigorous and creative process of generating new options and crafting them in ways that might really address the needs and concerns of everyone involved. It was hard work. But, in her experience, it was good work because it provided the hope of coming up with really good results. This work of seeking provided the immediately satisfying experience of being as fully present to people and problems as possible. And that experience of a deepening presence could offer the further experience of being led by a loving Spirit. It was an empowering Spirit that could transform dilemmas into opportunities. It could provide a sense of transcending the deadlocks of alienation through the creation of community in the commitment to shared solutions. For her, following the Rainbow Rule provided an opportunity to have the remarkable experience of Way Opening.[27]

I learned over time that the Quaker tradition provided a variety of nuanced strategies and methods for practicing this kind of search for solutions to dilemmas and difficulties. Some of the basic strategies are common to a variety of other traditions of problem solving and conflict resolution. One, for instance, is simply: "When you face a dilemma, look for a third alternative."

Because of their commitment to nonviolence, Quakers have often been confronted with dilemmas in which you are asked to choose between letting someone use violence or stop them by using violence yourself. Critics of the Quaker Peace Testimony have posed dilemmas like the following: Would you shoot a robber threatening to kill your grandmother? Would you take up arms to fight an invading army trying to conquer your country? The Quaker view has often been misunderstood as a passive form of pacifism that simply refuses to shoot or take up arms, come what may. But Quakers themselves understand it as a richer and more powerful response to violence. It is an invitation to look for a third alternative. Multiply your options until you find one that does not require violence. Like Gandhi and other practitioners of active forms of nonviolence, Quakers seek to respond to violent dilemmas by advising us to "think of it as an opportunity, dear."

Another strategy for applying that basic advice in conflict situations is to look at the interests that are motivating the people involved. What are their underlying values and concerns? How can understanding them open options that might meet everyone's underlying interests? If you just focus on their opening "position"—

what they first say they want—you may miss other opportunities for "win/win" solutions.

I became fascinated with strategies for group problem solving, conflict transformation and peacemaking. I found that besides the Quakers, there were others developing such practices in rich detail. They included colleagues of Roger Fisher and William Ury at the Harvard Negotiation Project and folks John Paul Lederach collaborated with using ethnographic methods to study decision-making in Indigenous communities in Latin America and East Africa. People on six continents were continuing Mohandas K. Gandhi's massive efforts to experiment with non-violent methods of social change, conflict transformation, and peacemaking. Through the Nashville Friends Meeting and then through a variety of other groups working on peace and justice issues, I saw ways open for opponents and even outright enemies to reach voluntary agreements. These included working with bullying behavior between children, dealing with fights between spouses going through divorce, lobbying Congressional representatives to end the nuclear arms race, and working to end the Contra war in Nicaragua.[28]

Two Kinds of Reasoning: Mono-logical Inference vs. Collaborative Dialogue

At the time, I was studying philosophy and became fascinated with the reasoning processes involved in these approaches to problem solving, conflict resolution, and peacemaking. It became clear they involved a kind of rationality that did not rely on the formal logic that mainstream philosophers considered the gold standard of rationality.

The dominant Western conception of rationality prizes the tradition of formal logic that goes back to Aristotle. It studies explicit rules that function like the algorithms of a computer. You put in premises or assumptions and then the rules of logic tell you what to put out as conclusions. It provides a kind of machine for manufacturing correct beliefs and making decisions. The classic example from Aristotle was a categorical syllogism composed of simple sentences connecting categories things fall in to:

Premise #1: All humans are mortal.

Premise #2: Socrates is a human.

Conclusion: Socrates is mortal.

The rule of reasoning at work here is quite clear and rigid. It has to do with the form of the sentences involved and it can be applied in a completely mechanical way. The rule says that when you have two true sentences of the forms: 1) "All H are M" and 2) "S is an H" then it follows that a sentence of the form "S is M" must be true as well. To take another example, a hypothetical syllogism includes an if/then statement as in:

Premise #1. "If proposition A is true, then B is true" and
Premise #2. "Proposition A is true",
Conclusion: "Proposition B is true".

For example, my Grandmother Cox could reason:
Premise #1. If I would want always to be fed a hearty breakfast,
    Then I should always feed others a hearty breakfast.
Premise #2. I would always want to be fed a hearty breakfast.
Conclusion: I should always feed others a hearty breakfast.

The rules of formal logic are matter of fact. They can be framed as declarative sentences. But the most useful rules for resolving dilemmas, solving group problems, resolving conflict, and making peace are not like that. They are not mechanical algorithms that can crank out conclusions from premises. Instead, they are strategies for creating opportunities and improving options on which people might come to agree. They say things like: "Look for a third alternative!" or "Find out more about people's underlying interests!" They are invitations that are open ended. They initiate and guide a creative process, but they do not provide a determinate result in a mechanical way. They are not algorithms like the rules that run computer programs. They provide a different model for rationality.

These methods of creative problem-solving and conflict resolution are effective at getting to agreements in ways that seem very reasonable and rational—like generating new alternatives, discovering underlying interests, and meeting them in creative ways. These are classic examples of intelligent behavior. They may seem like common sense, but their application can be hard work and take considerable creativity. It is not a mechanical process like the traditional conception of a linear computer program. Unlike formal logic, this provides a non-algorithmic model of rationality.

Most applied computer programmers have experiences with this non-algorithmic form of rationality because they must use it in negotiating with clients. They have to resolve conflicting agendas brought to the project and resolve problems with goals, tools, business interests, and ethical concerns. They have to negotiate agreements about the meanings of concepts, data and ways to gather and process them. In general, they have to take the messy and complex real world and negotiate an agreeable way to reframe it in a representation that their clients will accept and their computer algorithms can process.

For me, the contrast in these two kinds of reasoning is fairly easy to visualize because I can picture my Grandmother Cox and my mentor Marion engaging in them. My grandmother could pretty swiftly and decisively conclude what should be done in most situations. She just needed to get the facts of the situation, consult her own preferences, and then crank out the conclusion and share it with the rest of us. From her point of view, there was little need for discussion. The reasoning process was a kind of monologue, the results of which were delivered to us as an audience.

In contrast, Marion might often take a long time to think things through. She had to do a lot of listening, brainstorming, inquiry, and collaborative reasoning to arrive at something that everyone involved could feel included their point of view in a fair way and that they could agree to in good faith. The reasoning process was always a dialogue in which everyone else was an active and engaged participant. When they reached a consensus, it was one in which they all had a sense of ownership.

The table on the following page summarizes key features of the kind of reasoning exemplified by my grandmother's algorithmic inferences vs. Marion's collaborative dialogues.

Table 3: Two Kinds of Reasoning

	Algorithmic Inference	Collaborative Dialogue
Initiated with:	Input of premises taken as given	Encounter of people with different perspectives
Process of:	Logic guided by algorithms	Negotiation guided by creative strategies
Aims to arrive at:	Output of conclusions taken as implied by the given assumptions	Genuine, voluntary agreements achieved by revising assumptions
Pursued through:	Monologue	Dialogue

Failure to reason with collaborative dialogue causes many of the difficulties we encounter in life. In later chapters, we will explore ways various forms of monological inference have created many of the key problems in our economy, our politics, our technology, and our moral lives as individuals and communities. Most of our problems involve encounters with other people in which we are trying to get into right relationship with each other and our environment here on Earth. And the search for right relationship with each other requires collaborative dialogue aimed at negotiating wise agreements. It is not about getting from premises to conclusions on your own, it is about working through an encounter with others to arrive at agreements together.

No doubt these brief sketches of my grandmother and Marion exaggerate their differences. I remember my grandmother through the eyes of a 10-year-old boy who believed he saw his parents' spirits get broken by her. In real life, my grandmother no doubt engaged sometimes in meaningful dialogue, listened to others, and took their concerns into account. Conversely, I remember Marion through the eyes of an adult looking for a spiritual home and finding one amongst Quakers. In real life, Marion had her moments of falling short of her ideals just like the rest of us. She could sometimes find it especially challenging to see "that of God" in various individuals and politicians. The problems were sometimes too complex or dealt with pains too close to home. Sometimes the urgency and chaos of the immediate situation were just overwhelming.

Living with gaps between our guiding ideals and our actual practice is a fundamental part of being human. While we cannot eliminate the gap, we can continue to work on it. We can turn toward those powers of self-critical reflection, compassion, and creativity in ourselves and others that enable us to negotiate wiser ways of dealing with each other. Part of maturing is learning to strengthen and hone our skills in doing this. Fortunately, we all come into the world as kids endowed with the basic capacity for collaborative dialogue.

Courtney Martin tells a story from her daughter exemplifying this. At dinner she reported boys in class got in a fistfight in the hall that day and, in response, the teacher sent them out onto the playground to just figure it out. "The second-grade teacher sent a bunch of boys onto the blacktop and they had the internal resources to, not only calm down enough to make an agreement about their future handling of said edges, but write a contract to that effect, and sign it. A couple of days later, when I stopped by the classroom after my library volunteer hour to drop books off, a couple of these same boys were doing their reading app on separate tablets while holding hands."

Martin goes on to describe groups like the Decolonizing Wealth Project and The Armah Institute for Emotional Justice which help people nurture our inborn talents for reconciliation. Then, after noting how challenging such work can be, she comments

"I think about all the people we give up on, including ourselves, when maybe sometimes what we needed was only a sacred shift in approach—something less direct, something roundabout, something corporeal. Sometimes we need to take the long, circuitous way home to ourselves and each other rather than following the algorithmic directions for the most effective route. Kids get that. Adults forget that. I know I do. Here's to inefficient, artsy, childlike apology. Here's to repair as multidimensional as we are."[29]

As a society, we suffer from a host of frayed, fragmented, and broken relationships. To repair and enhance them, we will need to rethink the ways we run our economic institutions, collaborate in politics, and design and implement technologies. The Rainbow Rule provides a first step by asking us to consider how others would have us do unto them. The second step is to shift gears in the kind of reasoning we do—to shift to the forms of collaborative dialogue that can enable us to negotiate wiser agreements amongst all concerned.

And every step in the journey towards wisdom is rooted in that most basic of dialogue abilities—to listen as deeply as possible.

> It's a simple thing,
> to hear with the heart.
> But it takes everything,
> it takes all that you are.
> It takes all that you are,
> and then makes something more,
> and then you no longer are
> who you once were. . . .[30]

Chapter Four: Ethics as Collaborative Dialogue

What is wise in one context, may be less so in another. When the change of context is system-wide and of historic proportions, this can be even truer. The appropriate norms and methods of problem solving were significantly different for nomadic hunter gatherers and settled agricultural farmers because their contexts and problems were different. When the age of industrial capitalism arrived in the 1700's, another dramatic shift was called for. Philosophers sought to make sense of it by rethinking the norms and methods of ethical reasoning. In the West, perhaps the two most influential were the Utilitarian, Jeremy Bentham, and the advocate for duty-based ethics, Immanuel Kant. They captured important insights that helped people deal more wisely with the transition from feudal society to industrial capitalism and the modern state. Unfortunately, however, in doing so, they also promoted a relatively limited conception of human reason.

The Enlightenment rationality they adopted was a form of monological algorithmic inference. That conception of reason continues to hamper and ham string a great deal of ethical thought, practice, and education—especially in the realm of public policy. Worse, this conception leads to a moral relativism that threatens to make ethical reasoning irrelevant. This chapter explores ways we can better understand the problems created by those approaches to ethical reasoning and move beyond them by adopting a richer and more inclusive conception of reasoning as collaborative dialogue.

Enlightenment Theories and Dilemma Ethics

Early on in graduate studies in philosophy, I assisted in a class on ethics and learned a way of teaching ethics that has remained relatively dominant to this day in colleges and universities in the United States. Its core ideas were developed by philosophers like Bentham and Kant during the 18th century but also draw on some pedagogical ideas that go back to Socrates.

The method leads to sophisticated thinking. It hones skills in reasoning and teaches key concepts that get used by professionals to guide their work. Public policy analysts use them to design our laws. However, the method has some fundamental problems that make a mess of our moral lives. That mess can only be corrected by drawing on the resources of other traditions. The point can be illustrated with a video clip from Michael Sandel's course on "Justice", one of the most popular courses taught at Harvard (and in video available online).[31] It introduces students to ethical theories through applications to difficult cases in which significant decisions must be made. A key aim is to help students refine their understanding of two contrasting theories of ethics, both of which were developed during the Enlightenment period of the 1700s.

One theory is that of Jeremy Bentham's Utilitarianism. It advocates the Greatest Happiness Principle which tells us to always choose the action that will maximize the greatest net happiness for all concerned. Given that foundational principle, the assumption is that we simply need to count all the pleasures and pains an action might lead to as benefits and costs of it. Then we simply need to calculate the gain from the action as compared to its alternatives and choose whichever yields the greatest net positive result.[32]

The foundational principle for the second theory is Immanuel Kant's Categorical Imperative. It tells us to only choose policies that we could endorse adopting as universal laws. This "universalizability" criterion is tied directly to the moral imperative to treat other people with dignity and respect—treating them as persons who are "ends in themselves" rather than just as means to our own ends. For Kant, moral action has to be rational not only for the doer of the deed but also for the person it is done to. If I am going to respect you as a person with free will and dignity, then, in whatever way I treat you—

or anyone else—I should be ready to be treated likewise. For instance, I should not lie if I cannot rationally be willing to be lied to. And I should not take someone else's life if I cannot rationally be willing to have mine taken in the same circumstances.[33]

To help appreciate some of their merits as well as limitations, it is useful to put Bentham and Kant's theories in historical context. Both were inspired by the way Isaac Newton's theory of physics showed how logical inferences could combine basic data and a few laws of motion to predict the motions of the planets. Kant and Bentham were each trying to create similar systems for rational ethical thought by proposing what we might think of as the fundamental "laws of moral motion" to infer how we should act.

Advances in industrial capitalism provided another key part of the context in which they sought to apply their systems of monological inference for morality. In their century, those advances were increasingly disrupting traditional communities and social structures in a host of ways. It was the start of a long transformative process of pushing people off farms in their traditional communities and towards factories and cities. New laws were required to govern commerce, crime, and social welfare. In that context, Bentham's utilitarianism provided a useful framework for thinking about what new laws should be passed. Instead of relying on complex, incoherent clusters of local traditions and aristocratic prejudices, laws could be designed to advance the common good by following the Greatest Happiness Principle. It was a reasonable and useful proposal to improve British legislation. The more antiquated customs and petty, private interests of individuals and groups would be subordinated to the welfare of the many.

New professions and professional organizations were also required to help apply those new laws and cope with the new challenges of urban, industrial life. When the new classes of professionals offered services in medicine, law, engineering, banking, or education, they would need to propose novel contracts with their clients—contracts in which they promised to guard and advance new rights and interests for their clients. This was not something of concern to aristocratic rulers in pre-industrial times because their relatively stable society provided them with traditional norms for action. But now that so many innovative contracts for social relations were being written, people discovered a need to assure that the contracts would be kept. Kant's conceptions of duty, respect, and the Categorical Imperative provided a way of articulating the kind of ethics required for contracts to be kept and for professionals and institutions to have viable relationships with their clients. These institutions could only be sustained if clients could count on them. If a lawyer only kept a client's confidence until it was profitable to divulge it, who would hire him? If a borrower only kept a promise on a loan until it was possible to escape repayment, who would ever serve as a banker?

The merits of these two theories also highlight their underlying conflict. Utilitarianism provided a way to justify laws that secured the good of the many at the expense of the few; Kant's theory secured the rights and interests of the individual even when it might be at the expense of the happiness of the many.

In his Harvard class on Justice, Sandel draws out the differences between these two abstract theories with dilemmas in which one choice would be dictated by the Greatest Happiness Principle and the other by the Categorical Imperative. For example, he poses a classic "Trolley Car Dilemma". Students are asked to suppose they are on a train platform and a trolley is approaching at great speed. A group of innocent people will be killed by collision, but they can be saved if the student flips a switch to redirect the train to another track. Unfortunately, a single innocent person who stands there will be killed by collision. Should the student flip the switch and sacrifice the one to save the many? It would seem to many that a Utilitarian would say yes. Others might argue, in contrast, that a Kantian would hesitate or say no—she might believe that the policy of sacrificing that innocent bystander could not be willed universally, at least not from the point of view of the bystander who would be killed. In the Harvard lecture hall with hundreds of students, there turn out to be significant differences of opinion amongst the students about which choice to make and why.

As Sandel explores variations on such dilemmas, it becomes ever harder to choose in each case. Students who preferred one basic principle over the other start to have doubts and perhaps a creeping sense that there may not be any objective answers to the questions and that they may have to just go with their own intuitions. Over the course of a semester, this kind of pedagogy can lead many students towards a moral relativism in which they feel entitled to choose whatever they like. They can tend to simply conclude that if people don't agree on the basic principles, then we just have to pressure each other with power and even perhaps violence in order to get what we want. Ever since Socrates first started pointing out contradictions in people's own belief systems, students have found ethics troubling and often even profoundly disturbing in just this way. Interminable debates over conflicting intuitions often lead to moral skepticism.

In the video of his first class, Sandel poses the following variation on the Trolley Car dilemma: Suppose you are a doctor with five patients, four of whom are each in need of different vital organs to survive. The fifth patient is a perfectly healthy person who is currently unconscious, taking a nap in your waiting room. As a doctor, you see your opportunity. You could anesthetize the healthy patient, harvest his organs, and use them to save the others. It would be a sacrifice of one for the many. How is that any different from pulling the switch on the Trolley line? In fact, wouldn't you be morally obligated, as a Utilitarian, to do this? Sandel asks for a show of hands of how many would get the anesthesia out and harvest organs from the healthy patient.

Most students have a clear and immediate revulsion to the very idea of even considering this option. However, one student way up in the balcony raises his hand. He says that instead of sacrificing the healthy patient, he would sacrifice one of the sick four patients to harvest organs for the other three. Since that person would die anyway, why not give meaning and purpose to that death by saving the other three. At this moment, all the students burst into applause. They are clearly relieved and excited to see some path out of the dilemma.

But Sandel pauses till the room quiets and then says: "That's a good idea. In fact, it's a great idea. There is only one thing wrong with it. It completely spoils the whole philosophical point of the example." Then he changes the subject, dropping any further mention of the student's idea or of the approach to ethics it intuitively suggests.

In taking this approach, Sandel is following what is widely taken to be an appropriate pedagogical method in teaching ethics at the university level. Students are forced to stick with the terms of the dilemma to hone their clear reasoning skills in formal logic, clarify their moral intuitions, and practice the decisiveness needed to make choices in hard cases.

It is relevant to note that this approach to dilemmas—insisting they be accepted as given rather than revised in ad hoc ways—was central to a method for assessing moral development in children which another Harvard professor, Lawrence Kohlberg developed. His very influential theory and method made use of a series of ethical dilemmas that were presented to children at different ages to see how their reasoning about them might shift. For example, the examiner might pose a case in which a man's wife is dying of a disease which has only one cure. The druggist who has invented the cure is charging an enormous price for it which the man cannot afford to pay. The question put to the child then is this: "Should you steal the drug or not? And why?" For Kohlberg and his team, it was not as though there was a right answer. Their interest was in the kinds of reasons the child gave for whatever answer he chose. Kohlberg's evidence seemed to indicate that there was, in fact, a series of six possible stages that children could progress through as they developed into mature, ethical adult decision makers.[34]

It is also relevant to note that Kohlberg's test subjects often resisted his method in just the way Sandel's student does in the video—refusing to accept the terms of the dilemma and trying to invent some new, third option. In follow up studies to Kohlberg's work, Carol Gilligan and others noted that girls seemed often to resist the terms of the dilemmas. They might propose to find another cure or find a source of new money or plead with the inventor for a price cut. More generally, they would resist simply following out the logic of some principle like Bentham's or Kant's and accepting the tragic consequences. Instead, they would insist on trying to search for some new option that would enable them to maintain what they considered to be right relationships with everyone involved. What they seemed to exhibit was a kind of relationship-based strategy for dealing with ethical situations. It treated the cases not as dilemmas to be accepted but as problems to be solved. Gilligan and other writers like Nel Noddings went on to articulate this approach in systematic ways under notions of an "ethics of care". Like the student in Sandel's class, people practicing the ethics of care seek to transform dilemmas and resolve conflicts through creating alternatives. This approach to ethics complements the vocabulary, vision, and methods of a variety of other traditions that have emerged since the 1960s.[35]

Collaborative Dialogue Approaches to Ethics

The strategy Sandel's student adopted is one that people researching negotiation and problem solving refer to as "multiplying the options". It is one of several strategies that have been developed over the last forty years in studies of group problem solving, negotiation, mediation, alternative dispute resolution, and conflict transformation. For example, in their book, *Getting to Yes: Negotiating Agreement Without Giving*, Roger Fisher and his co-authors suggest four key strategies:

1) Focus on interests rather than positions!
2) Separate the people from the problem and build relationships!
3) Multiply your options!
4) Look for objective criteria!

They elaborate a rich variety of ways to pursue each of these core strategies. For instance, they describe a variety of listening techniques for discerning underlying concerns and interests. Likewise, they ex-plain ways to multiply options with brainstorming skills and meta-phor approaches to spark creative ideas.[36]

Other approaches to conflict resolution can be found in *Contemporary Conflict Resolution* and *Peacemaking: From Practice To Theory*.[37] They represent a broad field of study that includes a host of well-developed traditions. There are professional journals such as *The Negotiation Journal*, *The Journal of Conflict Resolution*, and *The Journal of Peace Research*. There are centers for research, such as the School for Conflict Analysis and Resolution at George Mason University and the Kroc Institute for International Peace Studies at Notre Dame. Professional organizations include the Association for Conflict Resolution and the National Association for Community Mediation. Research in this tradition has discovered a variety of principles that have proved successful for negotiating conflicts in diverse contexts, from renter/landlord disputes and divorces to labor/management disputes and international treaties such as the 1978 Camp David Accords that brokered peace between Israel and Egypt in the Sinai.[37]

The specific tradition associated with *Getting to Yes* has proved successful in a variety of Western and, especially North American, contexts. In those contexts, related traditions of collaborative, creative innovation and group problem solving have also thrived as described, for instance, in William J. J. Gordon's *Synectics,* David Straus's *How to Make Collaboration Work,* and Innes and Booher's *Planning with Complexity.*[39] In extensive collaborations with researchers in rural and Indigenous communities in Latin America, Africa and elsewhere, people have developed methods of eliciting wisdom from the best practitioners in various conflict resolution traditions. John Paul Lederach's *Preparing for Peace* introduces challenges and strategies in developing cross-cultural insights of this sort. Anthologies describing such insights include Pat K. Chew's *The Conflict and Culture Reader,* and Susan Allen Nan et. al.'s *Peacemaking: From Practice to Theory.*[40]

For our purposes here, two features of these many varied practices of dealing with disputes should be focused on. First, the practices make central use of a mode of reasoning which does not rely solely on monologues making inferences but, instead, emphasizes collaborative dialogue that negotiates the differences between different points of view. The aim is to interact back and forth with others until some form of shared consent is achieved. The outcome cannot be defined ahead of time by any single party to the dispute. In this way, it is quite different from the courtroom model in which the decision of a judge is viewed as the paradigm. In court, in the end, the judge reaches a verdict which is imposed on all with the authority of the court and the power of the police. In contrast, a collective negotiation is undertaken to seek consensus. All must share in the process sufficiently to enable them collectively to get to agreement and arrive at the "Yes" of consent.

Second, while parts of the process can make use of insights from formal game theory, the process as a whole cannot be formulated as a decision procedure coded in an algorithm that could be calculated by one "player" or party to the dispute. This is because these practices of dealing with disputes all emphasize creative initiatives in which the terms of the conflict are redefined and transformed. There is continual revision of participants' understandings of what their real interests are, what options may be available, what criteria might be appropriate for assessing them, and so on.

To avoid confusion, it is important to bear in mind that collaborative dialogue is an inclusive form of reasoning –algorithmic inferences can and should be part of the discussion. For example, in negotiating the value of a vehicle that was damaged in an accident, a car owner and an insurance agent may each appeal to mathematical calculation concerning its original cost and depreciation or the market price of similar vehicles and this one's special features. In using the math, they will appeal to algorithmic rules of inference as part of their collaborative dialogue. But in framing the negotiation about which calculations are the relevant ones and, more generally, in negotiating the differences between different systems of algorithmic calculations they will need to turn to non-algorithmic kinds of negotiation and dialogue.

Further, it is worth noting that when we are in a relatively simple situation, it may be perfectly acceptable and appropriate –and perhaps even more convenient, efficient, or intuitive—to use simple rules and decision procedures. We noted in Chapter One, for instance, that the Golden Rule may be appropriate in dealings amongst a homogeneous group. In a similar way, a monological decision procedure may be perfectly appropriate for standard cases of moral decision making that do not require the more ample and inclusive forms of collaborative dialogue needed to deal with conflicting values, multiple cultures, grey areas, or other complicating factors.

Like the student who disrupted Sandel's neat philosophical dilemma, the traditions of negotiation, mediation and conflict resolution seek to reject dilemmas and transform the conflicts. Because of the creativity they involve, this might suggest that only humans could perform this kind of reasoning—not machines. This might be in some sense true of the "standard model" of the Turing Machine computer, but, as we will see in Chapter Six, there is an alternative conception of the computer as a "Turing Child" which is becoming conceptually and technologically viable and which may make it possible to develop AI systems that practice collaborative dialogue –or at least assist in key elements of it.

The creative activities involved are ones that are teachable and involve using strategies like brainstorming and metaphorical thinking which computers can learn, given the appropriate initial programming and subsequent learning environments. But they must draw on reasoning in the form of collaborative dialogue. They also need to use methods of social research that are grounded in ethnographic understanding and the interpretation of meaning in the context of communities that have developed practices embedded in a life world. And they must enrich their instrumentalist theories of decision and action with others that include activities framed as expressions, projects, and practices in which there are organic relations between means and ends and emergent meanings and values. In Chapter Six we will return to this point and explore ways departures from the "standard model" of Turing Machines may provide paths for programming that incorporate collaborative dialogue.[41]

The collaborative dialogue form of reasoning described here differs in a fundamental way from the reasoning employed in most theoretical ethics. This is true even in the cases in which there is an attempt—in theory—to take everyone's points of view into account. One important and widely influential example of this is the ethical theory John Rawls developed in *A Theory of Justice.*[42] It aims to figure out the principles of justice by imagining that we are negotiating the rules for a society into which we will be born. He frames this as a hypothetical situation in which we adopt a theoretical "veil of ignorance" and don't know which family situation we will be born to. In that theoretical context, we try to design the basic principles of the society in a way that we would be willing to live with, no matter where we ended up, regardless of class, race, gender and so on. Ethical theory that uses this kind of "veil of ignorance" approach can develop some useful insights. But the reasoning involved remains, in the end, monological. It starts with premises and infers conclusions about what would, in theory, be a reasonable or just society. Genuinely dialogical, collaborative reasoning, in contrast, starts with real people embodied in the actual world and embedded in specific social and historical contexts.

In mentioning Rawls, the "veil of ignorance", and methods in theoretical ethics, it may seem to some folks as though the discussion here has wandered off a bit into the weeds of professional philosophy. But the contrast between actual dialogues and theoretical dialogues has some very important consequences. Perhaps the most important is this: We may encounter problems that are impossible to solve in theory but can be solved in practice.

For instance, in theory people may agree that they want to live in a democracy that promotes equality but disagree as to whether we should stress an equality in the distribution of income and services people receive or stress an equality in the opportunity they get in order to go out and earn it on their own. Debate between these two views can go on at great length and if people start with different core values and premises, they may arrive at starkly different conclusions. However, real groups of people in actual specific historical settings may find it possible to negotiate agreements that will seem fair and reasonable by crafting agreements that are tailored to their shared and/or conflicting interests, concerns, and contexts. In the search for objective moral truths, people from different cultural traditions may find it difficult to agree on theoretical formulations. But, in practical contexts, they may find concrete proposals that may have a kind of compelling, emergent, objective, character.

A nice illustration of this is offered by Alasdair MacIntyre, one of the critics of the tradition of theoretical approaches to ethical reasoning that runs through Kant and Rawls. His example concerns a lawsuit between the Wampanoag Indian tribe and the town of Mashpee, Massachusetts. At the time of his writing, the Wampanoag claimed their tribal lands in the township were illegally and unconstitutionally appropriated and they were suing for their return. The claim was very likely to go through extended appeals, no matter how it was initially decided. This would create a hardship for many small homeowners in the town, especially retired people hoping to re-establish their lives elsewhere. The uncertainties of title made it difficult or impossible for them to sell their land and move on with their lives. As MacIntyre asks:

> "What in this type of situation does justice demand? We ought to note that two rule-specified concepts of justice recently advanced by contemporary moral philosophers can give us no help at all. John Rawls argues that 'social and economic inequalities are to be arranged so that they are to the greatest benefit of the least advantaged . . .' and Robert Nozick asserts that 'the holdings of a

person are just if he is entitled to them by the principles of justice in acquisition and transfer.'

"But the problem in Mashpee concerns a period of time in which we do not as yet know 1) who has a just title by acquisition and transfer, for precisely that is to be decided by the current legal case or 2) which is the least advantaged group in Mashpee, for that will be determined as a consequence of the outcome of the case. If it goes one way, the Wampanoag will turn out to be the richest group in Mashpee, but if the other, they will remain the poorest. Nonetheless a just solution has been devised by the tribal claimants (a solution to which after an apparent initial agreement the Selectmen of Mashpee refused their assent): 'All properties of one acre or less on which a dwelling house stands shall be exempted from the suit.'

"It would be difficult to represent this as in any way the application of a rule; it had to be devised because no application of the rules could afford small homeowners justice. The solution is the result of rough and ready reasoning involving such considerations as the proportion of the land claimed which comprises such properties and the number of people affected if the size of property exempted were fixed at one acre rather than more or less."[43]

This provides a helpful example of dialogical, collaborative reasoning at work. Macintyre's larger framework of analysis provides some really illuminating insights into the practices, communities and lives of people who practice it. He frames his analysis in terms of a tradition of "Virtue Ethics" that harks back to Classical Greece in contrast to the modern Enlightenment traditions of Utilitarian and Kantian ethics. His account of that tradition is an extraordinarily rich and many layered story in social and intellectual history that places ethical theories in their historical contexts and draws out some key general conclusions. A few highlights of his analysis are particularly relevant at our current point in the discussion of collaborative traditions of reasoning such as negotiation in the style of *Getting to Yes* and peacemaking in the tradition of Gandhi.

The first point to note is that people who learn practices such as these forms of collaborative dialogue cannot do so simply by reading theory. They must engage in practice and do so in the complex, concrete contexts of communal life in which those practices have been developed. Further, it is important to note that there is a rich notion of "practice" at work here. Practices of conflict resolution and peacemaking are like traditions of dramatic theatre and war making in this way. They develop in communities where related activities and institutional functions are integrally and organically connected to one another. Means are also ends-in-the-making—voluntary consent must be arrived at in voluntary, consensual ways. The practices require communities to sustain them. The novices entering such communities need to learn tacit forms of insight, skill and values from accomplished practitioners who provide role models. A key part of such learning involves internalizing core values that frame the tradition of the practice and make it possible to sustain it. So, for instance, traditional warfare cannot be carried out unless soldiers carry out orders, even when it puts their lives in danger. They must develop courage as a character trait.

The virtues of a Homeric warrior, a Buddhist monk, a Confucian scholar and a Gandhian engaged in nonviolent social change are in many ways different. But, as MacIntyre notes, core character traits are required for social practices to flourish. For instance, practitioners must distinguish better vs. worse performance, so communities must cultivate honesty as a virtue to insure accurate assessments can be used to advance their traditions.

The collaborative dialogue approach to moral reasoning shares much in common with MacIntyre's Virtue Ethics. Both are framed and learned in historical contexts of the communities which develop and sustain them through the cultivation of role models, virtues, and organically integrated activities and institutions. One significant difference however is that MacIntyre generally follows Aristotle in thinking of reasoning as a form of inference in which premises justify conclusions. As a result, he has difficulty in describing and analyzing collaborative dialogues like the one he recounts with the Wampanoag. He ends up labelling it a "rough and ready form of reasoning" and has little to say about such processes of thinking.

As we have noted, however, the study of such forms of reasoning has matured in recent decades and yielded systematic, explicit, detailed bodies of theory, insight, and practical skill traditions. In the context of that work, the suggestion of the Mashpee elders could be analyzed as a version of the general strategies of "multiplying your options" and "exploring their interests" to do so. More specifically, it could be described as a version of "fractionating conflict". This technique breaks a complex range of issues apart to solve them one at a time. (Note the opposite strategy can also be productive in some cases.)[42]

Traditions of collaborative dialogue employ other methods to reframe emotions. Rocket science reasoners typically assume feelings are irrational bodily impulses to be excluded from rational thought. But careful studies of emotion show it is tied to reason and continuous in ways that can nurture our rationality if we learn to listen and negotiate with them.

Emotions are intentional and include tacit reasons which may turn out to be quite coherent made explicit. To be angry is always already to be angry at someone or something for a reason—because of what they did and what we take it to mean. Feelings, emotions, hunches, moods, and related forms of consciousness are tied to our bodies and sensed with impulses in the gut or muscles of our faces. But simultaneously, as embodied creatures with consciousness, we experience those sensations through the perceptions, projects, concepts, assumptions, and lines of reasoning we use to engage with the world. Emotions express ways we move through life, embodied in flesh and embedded in social context. Successful traditions of collaborative dialogue include methods for observing emotions in ourselves and others, listening to what they are tacitly saying, and negotiating with them to arrive at explicit understandings and agreements. Collaborative dialogue reframes emotion as an emergent element continuous with other, more explicit forms of rationality.[45]

Because collaborative dialogue reframes the elements and processes of reasoning as emergent, it also reframes one of the most vexing and fundamental problems in ethics, the challenge of making sense of objective moral values.

Emergent Objective Values

Shared norms and values are required for dialogues as well as the cultural practices and social institutions they yield. We can only speak in a common language because we share norms for word use. We can only collaborate in projects and institutions because we agree on values that guide individual behavior for collective efforts. When our values or other beliefs conflict with someone else's, we can resort to pressure and violence to coerce acceptance of our views. But dialogue and negotiation offer an alternative to violence by holding out the possibility that there may be some discoverable truth which will convince us all through rational persuasion.

Truths that provide common ground for agreement need roots in something independent of our individual beliefs. They call for independent realities that can function like third-party umpires settling disputes by persuading everyone involved. Whether any particular dialogue will actually lead to the discovery such realities is an open question. It is what the dialogue is about. But the presuppositions that there are truths out there to be found is part of what frames the dialogue process and gives it purpose and meaning. It is the MacGuffin for the adventure. If I were to assume that my beliefs could not be in error and could not be challenged and corrected in something objective and external to them, then dialogue would lose its point.

Sometimes the truths that are discovered which provide the basis for agreement may be extremely minimal—perhaps we only discover the fact that we are not in agreement. Or we may agree to some plan of action but for entirely different reasons. But viable, enduring agreements call for stronger stuff. They become more resilient when the truths they are rooted in are themselves rooted in something that gives them an enduring existence.

The versions of relativism that claim ethical beliefs cannot be objective and serve this purpose in dialogues present a threat to our collective lives that is extremely serious. If true, they imply rational argument is futile. Faced with the exasperation in wrestling with conflicting beliefs, we may just as well give over to desperation. Trying to make peace with other cultural communities or nation states, we may as well resign ourselves to competitive politics framed by the threats of violence and war. With the proliferation of ever cheaper nuclear, chemical, biological, and cyber weapons of mass destruction, resignation to such politics puts us under the growing existential threat of mutually assured destruction. Moral relativism is not just a source of desperation in our lives, it increasingly threatens our collective existence.

Modern moral relativism with these existential implications arises directly out of the Enlightenment assumption that rationality only comes in one variety, the monological justification of beliefs through logical inference. This results from three things generally associated with it: 1) foundationalist concepts of knowledge, 2) a lack of an experimental method in ethics for investigating truth claims, and 3) absolutist ideas of objectivity. An appreciation of each can illuminate how collaborative dialogue provides an escape from them and moral relativism as well.

The **foundationalist problem** surfaced earlier in discussion of dilemmas in disputes between Utilitarians and Kantians. If ethical reasoning is a unilateral process of inference grounded on fundamental premises like Bentham's or Kant's, then when they disagree, where can we turn to settle the dispute? The logic of this kind of thinking assumes that conclusions have foundations and that there must, in the end, be some ultimate foundations on which all other conclusions rest. But they and subsequent philosophers in their tradition were unable to find a consensus on a set of fundamental laws for ethics that would be comparable to Newton's laws of motion.

When Newton's physics faced similar systematic competition from Aristotelian and Cartesian theories there was a way to determine which foundational assumptions were superior. Newtonians could **appeal to experiment** showing their theory better matched the facts observed. But Utilitarian, Kantian, and other Enlightenment style reasoners lacked a comparable method of experiment in ethics. In disagreeing about basics, they were forced to fall back on subjective intuitions that provided no grounds on which to avoid the onslaught of relativism.

In this tradition of moral philosophy, **absolutist conceptions of objectivity** have also often provided a driver toward moral relativism by setting an unachievable standard. Bentham and Kant, along with other Enlightenment thinkers, assumed that the fundamental truths of reason must be universal, unchanging, necessary, and exact in the way that they thought the truths of Euclidean geometry and Newtonian physics were. This provided an absolutist conception of moral truth which would secure objectivity in ethics parallel to the certainties of math and science. It harked back to Plato and his conception of universally applicable, eternal, necessary, perfect forms of justice and other moral values. Enlightenment thinkers were critical of Plato's metaphysical theory, but they largely agreed that objective truth can and should have the absolutist features Plato sought. This absolutist conception remains influential.

People commonly assume that if moral truths are objective, they must be universal, eternal, necessary, and without any blemish of vagueness. They must secure, absolute foundations for rigorous inferences in ethical justifications. Since it is hard and probably impossible to find any ethical claims that meet this standard, it is tempting to suppose that there are no objective moral truths. Unless, that is, there is some other relevant and appropriate notion of objectivity that might apply more helpfully in ethics.

One is available in earth science, biology, and history. In those arenas, people speak of **emerging and increasingly whole versions of the truth**. For example, the Earth is a reality existing independently of our beliefs about it. Observations can be used to correct opinions about its shape. This has made it possible for people who disagree about its shape to engage in constructive dialogue, investigate, and arrive at increasingly more correct beliefs. It is not a bowl or flat disc but a sphere deviating in minor ways from a perfect geometric shape. This is a truth which is objective but in ways that differ fundamentally from the absolutist conception in the Platonic and Enlightenment traditions. The claim is not a universal one about all planets. Nor is the claim eternal; Earth was once a gaseous cloud, later lost a Moon size chunk, and will continue to be reshaped. Likewise, descriptions of it are not claimed to be necessary or exact in anything like the way the truths of theoretical math are.

These features of truths about the Earth are also characteristic of claims to objective truth in key parts of biology and history. Stories about the evolution of species and the revolutions that transform society concern actual entities with objective reality. But they are transient realities particular to specific localities. They are not universal, unchanging, or perfect. They result from contingent facts, probabilistic influences, and emergent functions and values rather than necessary causes. Further, key players in stories of evolution and revolution include species, ecological niches, economic classes, and cultures whose memberships are marked by vague and fuzzy borders. The task of telling such stories with greater truth always involves including more points of view and integrating them in an emerging whole. In these contexts, the relevant notion of objectivity is that of impartiality and inclusiveness. The aim in seeking truth is always to simply become more objective. In these contexts, truth comes in degrees of less and more. It is emergent.[46]

For questions that come up **in ethics, the emergent conception of objective truth is much more appropriate than the absolutist one**. Many values that guide peoples' lives are rooted in biology or history that provide the context for their lives. The meaning and significance of values are rooted in and woven through emergent processes. As a result, the significance and interpretation of values are also inevitably emergent. These can include values like sustainability (rooted in ecology), legal due process (rooted in history), mutual respect (rooted in structures of collaborative dialogue), and empowering love (understood as a power that enables transformative dialogue). We do not need to claim that these are absolute values in order to claim that they are objective bases for resolving differences through collaborative dialogue.

Consider people who share some ecological commons like a watershed system. Their mutual dependence on it can provide the basis of an independent, objective value and they may be led to collaborate in safeguarding it. At the global level, we may find that our mutual dependence on a stable climate system may provide us with emergent, objective realities that can frame compelling moral claims. Our common sky and common climate give us morally compelling, objective reasons to care about our common future.

Consider people participating in the historical institutions of Anglo-Saxon common law. The structures and procedures of due process provide them with precedents that define the rules of the game. Those rules have a historically contingent but quite real, independent, and historically objective reality. When lawyers, plaintiffs and judges choose to participate in that system, they buy into the norms that frame the game and find themselves obliged by the emergent objective moral claims that it makes on them.

For people participating in collaborative dialogue, that activity presupposes that the agreements they arrive at will be acceptable to all, based on uncoerced, genuine consent. This means that each participant must respect the others' rights to make claims, raise concerns, offer proposals and, in the process, be treated with dignity and respect. The notion that people should, in general, be treated with respect for this reason lies at the center of many moral claims proposed as objective moral truths. It is at the heart of Kant's conception of the Categorical Imperative and the notion of treating others as ends in themselves. It is also central to many claims proposed in the United Nations Declaration of Human Rights. These appeals to respect as an objective value are not invalidated by ways in which they need to be lodged and interpreted in changing historical contexts. Rather, the need to continually renegotiate their meaning simply illustrates the emergent character of the truth in which they are rooted.

Does doffing a hat express mutual respect, servile subservience, or ironic mockery? When a woman wears a veil does that express the imposition of a violent misogyny, the affirmation of a self-empowerment, or something else? It can depend on context. But this is not to say that there is no objective truth about the matter. In fact, it simply means that to find out the truth we need to investigate the context. We need to have a dialogue to consider what the significance of the hat doffing or veil wearing may be.

Negotiation, conflict resolution, peacemaking and other forms of collaborative dialogue are often central to the historical processes in which new projects, institutions, and traditions emerge along with the common norms and values. As a form of reasoning, collaborative dialogue allows for the cultivation of insight and agreement on moral truths in ways that unilateral monologue does not. Participants may start with dramatically different beliefs and values but then through dialogue discover growing agreement on the objective validity of some value, norm, role model, or other criterion of ethical goodness.

Traditions of dialogue from around the world tend to share one important feature. They value nonviolence because it is definitive of their collaborative nature. If violence is used to impose beliefs, this is not, in any normal sense of the term, genuine dialogue. But just what do violence and non-violence consist in? Just as the notion of mutual respect made leaps forward with the Human Rights Revolution, so too, the notion of non-violence made a leap forward with the Gandhian movement in developing methods of social change. Gandhi spoke of his own work as "experiments with Truth". What he had in mind was directly relevant to the problem of moral relativism that comes out of the Enlightenment tradition. For Gandhi, when we face moral conflicts and dilemmas, there is a kind of experiment, we can perform that can serve three functions in verifying a moral claim. It is the activity of taking on certain kinds of self-suffering which may serve to discern, demonstrate, and defend the claim's truth. In this way, it can help settle differences in morality just as physical experiments settle differences in science.

Gandhi invented a specific name for these experiments and ways suffering functions in them. He combined the Hindi words for clinging ("*graha*") and truth("*satya*") to create the term "*satyagraha*" which he translated as "clinging to truth" or "Truth Force".[47] In *The Conquest of Violence*, Joan Bondurant describes a great many types of experiments in such *satyagraha* including uses of fasting, sit-ins, boycotts, and other forms of non-violent struggle. For Gandhi, in acts of *satyagraha* people take suffering upon themselves rather than imposing it on others. So, for instance, they may break an unjust law and then suffer arrest and imprisonment.

The suffering of imprisonment serves, first, in the individual's **discernment of truth**. Is the law I object to really unjust? If I am going to demonstrate my conviction that it is by courting arrest, I will inevitably think longer and harder about my view and be especially careful discerning whether I am operating on a conviction rooted in moral truth rather than whim, vanity, or fleeting personal interest. The action functions, secondly, in **demonstrating the truth** to others. If an oppressor observes people suffering for the sake of some moral claim, it can give them pause to reconsider the justice of it and perhaps even find that the sight of such suffering "melts their heart" as Gandhi put it. But some hearts are hard indeed, so a third function for *satyagraha* comes in. By refusing to obey an unjust law and choosing to not cooperate with an oppressor a people can, especially when acting *en masse*, disable the oppressor from enforcing the law and profiting from his oppression. Nonviolent direct action can thus serve to actually **defend the truth** of a moral claim. It can serve as a rational and nonviolent alternative to violence in settling disputes even when an opponent proves uncooperative.

There is a good deal to be said about just how effective satyagraha may be in its roles in the discernment, demonstration, and defense of moral claims. In Chapter Six, we will return to this, looking at the theory behind nonviolent direct action and empirical data concerning its success. For now, the key point is that satyagraha offers a possible way out of moral relativism, especially when combined with the emergent conception of objective moral truth and the collaborative dialogue model of reasoning in ethics. Together, these three offer us a way of understanding how we may make progress in resolving our moral differences.

They let us make sense of stories like MacIntyre's account of the Wampanoag proposal and its suggestive illustration of ways dialogue can resolve ethical conflicts with an emergent, objective legitimacy. The Wampanoag proposal was not justified by a rigorous logical process of inference grounded in the absolute truth of eternal, abstract principles. Instead, it was rooted in a cluster of local concerns, values, and features of cultural context. It was cultivated in a way that emerged as a reasonable proposal from an increasingly larger number of points of view. In so far as it made sense, it represented the kind of objectivity similar to that found in field geology and human history. It resembled the kind of moral claims Gandhi aimed at in his nonviolent experiments with truth.

In Search of Common Ground

In the Reagan era, there was a boom in peace studies drawing on Gandhian ideas and other traditions of nonviolence. This led to detailed investigations into different practices and traditions of conflict resolution as well as the effectiveness of strategies in different contexts. It developed and documented hard-won expertise embodied in practitioners who are respected members of tribal councils, societies for professional mediators, boards for community dispute resolution, NGOs engaged in international negotiation, doctoral programs in conflict transformation, and religious communities engaged in peace work.

This kind of collaborative reasoning does not exclude the inferential logic. The process of negotiating agreements can include inferences from premises to conclusions, it is just that it also includes a great deal more. Dialogical reasoning can and should include all the rational moves that are permitted within monological patterns of reasoning, just as a genuine dialogue between two people should make room for all the things any one of them might have to say. The difference is that in dialogical reasoning all these moves are up for grabs as part of an interactive process of continuous renegotiation and joint problem solving.

This inclusive character of dialogical reasoning allows it to incorporate the strengths of key aspects of processes and the principles appealed to in inferential, monological systems of reasoning. Inclusive collaborative dialogue can draw effectively, for instance, on merits of legal reasoning and bureaucratic reasoning as well as economic calculation. Those merits can include, for instance, predictability, fairness, and transparency. A legal system encoding principles of due process and common standards and precedents for punishment or compensation can help promote fairness in the treatment of everyone who stands before the law. Likewise, standardized law and bureaucratic regulations can help people plan their actions by clarifying expected consequences. The development of transparent, predictable, fair procedures and principles of law provide one of the ways in which communities can articulate and agree on emergent objective values that can provide norms for action. When conflicts arise, they provide context for dialogue and emergent objective criteria that can be used to negotiate, problem solve, and mediate the disputes. In the American legal system, most cases are, in fact, resolved not through the decision of a judge but through the mediation of an agreement arrived at through dialogue among the parties. But they can draw on the linear lines of inferential reasoning that would be presented in court as part of the process of dialogue. How truly transparent, fair and predictable these procedures and principles are may vary widely and depend heavily on the balances of power at play.

An analogous point applies to the Standard Operating Procedures or "SOPs" of bureaucratic reasoning. They can serve to provide for transparency, predictability, and fairness as well as efficiency and productivity. But they can also have precisely the opposite effects, depending on how they are arrived at and implemented. One of the challenges, in many bureaucratic contexts, is to find ways to allow for mediation and shared problem-solving that incorporate dialogue between all points of view affected by the bureaucracy's actions. There are inevitably tradeoffs. For example, in allowing government agents more discretion to adapt policies to local conditions and negotiate individualized solutions, the possibilities of prejudice, bias, favoritism, and corruption all enter the picture.

Checks and balances can help provide review and accountability that promote flexibility and curtail corruption. It is crucial for this to ensure appropriate balances of power among the parties negotiating. Without that, apparent negotiation may simply be a form of compulsion or conquest. This is illustrated by divorce processes when the wife of an abusive, powerful, wealthy husband fares much worse in a flexible mediation than in a more formal process decided by a judge. Likewise, the history of "negotiations" between powerful nation-states with industrial economies and Indigenous communities trying to preserve their sovereignty has often taken the form of forced capitulation rather than true dialogue yielding genuine, authentic agreements.

Even when power imbalances are not at issue, there are forms of monological reasoning that might at first appear to be dialogical but are not. These include combative back and forth debate and bargaining in which each side maintains their fundamental assumptions and definitions and argues without opening themselves up to genuine listening, changes in points of view, and renegotiation of their ideas and plans. Dueling monologues are not genuine dialogues. In practice we may shift from one to the other. A genuine dialogue may get tripped up by an unintended insult as both parties dig in heels and stop listening. Conversely, sometimes a dueling debate can be transformed when someone pauses, opens herself to really hearing the other party, and looks at things from their point of view. A significant act of reconciliation may result—and be reciprocated—as real dialogue begins again.

Our relationship to the earth beneath our feet provides a metaphor often used to describe these shifts in ways of relating. People in genuine dialogue are seeking "common ground", willing to "move in their positions". People fixated in dueling monologues are "dug in", not letting go of "positions" and "foundations" on which they have built their views. Territorial and architectural metaphors arise naturally in monological reasoning because it needs initial premises on which to build its argument. These construction metaphors were used by Enlightenment thinkers like Bentham and Kant, who assumed their ethical systems needed foundation stones like the Greatest Happiness Principle and the Categorical Imperative.

Useful metaphors for dialogue processes come, instead, from biology. People start with seeds of ideas, and they try to cultivate possibilities. Relationships get nurtured and agreements emerge, blossom, mature, and bear fruit. Instead of starting with clear and rock-solid foundations, dialogue begins with an encounter with the unknown and the task of adapting to it through a process of evolving changes in oneself and transformations of one's environment. Birth and growth are central metaphors for dialogues in children's creative response to bullies on the playground, in spouses' efforts to come back together after a painful separation, in labor management negotiations that restart after a divisive strike, in victim/offender reconciliation programs, in tribal ceremonies aimed at community healing, in working out international treaties on trade or climate, in peace talks aimed at ending a civil war, and in interfaith work to reduce tensions between religious communities.

The processes and presuppositions of these kinds of dialogical reasoning differ fundamentally from those of the monological reasoning exemplified in the deductions of Newton's *Principia* and in the computations of modern-day Turing Machines in laptops. The methods they provide for reasoning in ethics are not rocket science. But they may nevertheless provide powerful ways of solving dilemmas posed in college courses on ethics. One very concrete step that might help better our world would be to put these methods at the center of the ways in which ethics is taught in universities, in training programs for professionals, and in the parenting of children. This would promote collaborative dialogue more generally in the ways our societies address the wicked problems and existential threats we face from ecological collapse, wars, and runaway technologies.

A second concrete step that might better our world would be to put these methods at the center of the design of the new forms of Generative AI that have been emerging since the introduction of ChatGPT. At least three things will be crucial for this:

1) The examples of behavior that provide the training data for these systems need to be carefully curated so that they learn ethical and safe behaviors—rather than whatever random activity they may observe in documentary or fictional texts on the internet.

2) In so far as the systems use any black box, opaque models for discovery or decision functions of any kind, these need to be monitored, supervised, and controlled by "white box" systems that are transparently explicable and can be used to insure that their behavior is ethical and safe.

3) In working with these systems, we will need to institutionalize sound practices of prompt engineering that employ dialogical methods of reasoning guided by emergent objective values. In training professionals who create these systems and citizens who use them, we will need to insure that their study of ethics is updated. We cannot afford to leave them stuck in the moral time warp of 18th Century monological reasoning modeled on Newtons physics.

The table below summarizes key contrasts between Enlightenment ethics exemplified by Utilitarian and Kantian approaches vs. problem solving approaches to ethics employing collaborative, dialogical methods of reasoning.

Table 4. Two Approaches to Ethical Reasoning

Ethical Reasoning framed as:	Unilateral (monological) Justification of Ethical Choice	Collaborative Dialogue in Solving Ethical Problems
Reasoning proceeds from:	Foundational principles that provide the basis for logical inference that determines conclusions	Roots in different points of view that are the basis for shared problem solving and conflict transformation that yield genuine, voluntary agreements
Objective moral truth as:	Universal and Absolute like claims in Euclid's Geometry	Increasingly Impartial and Emergent like claims in Earth Science, Evolution and History
Responds to moral relativism with:	Arguments from intuition or pure reason	Experimental, nonviolent self-suffering to discern, demonstrate and defend moral claims
Views moral dilemmas as:	Instructive forced choices for exploring conflicting moral intuitions	Instructive opportunities for creative problem solving
Exemplified by:	Utilitarian and Kantian ethics	Getting to Yes, Quaker communal discernment, and Gandhian satyagraha

How can wiser thinking we may practice as individuals be translated into systematically wiser living in our societies? Part I has focused, primarily, on describing the most general features of collaborative dialogue that enable us to improve our reasoning about moral issues when we are trying to think our way out of the dilemmas we encounter. Part II will look systematically at the practical institutions that structure the contexts of our lives. It focuses on ways the efforts to make our economy, politics, and technology ever "smarter" have resulted in systems that need correcting. Action is needed urgently to avoid perils we face collectively, including ecological collapse, wars of mutually assured destruction, and technological disasters with Artificial Intelligence. Many of us also urgently need to redirect the paths our own lives are taking. In racing towards "smarter" lifestyles we can find ourselves locked into ruts with addiction, burnout, alienation, polarization from others, and a loss of the threads of meaning that give balance and purpose to life.

Collaborative dialogue provides ways to bridge gaps in our own lives as well as gaps between communities, cultures, and countries in tension, struggle, or even armed warfare. It can empower us to transform dilemmas into opportunities and transform enemies into fellow collaborators. It provides ways to catch our breath, reflect, and birth a better world by pushing together. At times it may be very challenging to take those initial steps. When the traumatic events of 9/11 happened, I was in Europe and went, weeks later, to Thich Nhat Hanh's retreat center, Plum Village, in the south of France.

There, learning a variety of practical methods for meditation and peacemaking, I learned that sometimes the seeds of peace and the roots of collaboration can be nurtured in even the most trying of situations by the simplest forms of meditation.

It can be a matter of simply singing a song like the one shared here that allows us to "take a breather from all the anguish and the fear", sharing the simple gift of a smile, and inviting the others to take the first step and simply walk with us.[48]

Part II: A Wiser Earth

Chapter Five: Economics as History Making

In many ways, pursuit of ever more efficient, smarter machines and greater growth of the modern industrial economy has done much to better the health, longevity, and quality of life of people all around the world. But it has also resulted in various kinds of gross ineqHistuality, injustice, oppression, destructive conflict, and environmental damage. These include the growing threats of climate change, the devastating ecological collapse associated with pervasive plastic and toxic pollution, and the Sixth Great Extinction.[49] What sorts of changes might help mend damaged relationships, enhance our economy in human ecological ways, and lead to wiser ways of running our economy?

People who want to be change agents and work on this nest of problems sometimes fall into debates about what should be prioritized: Policy reform or individual lifestyles? Should we focus on passing a carbon tax law or on getting families to recycle? This chapter explores "both/and" approaches to this dilemma. One key is to shift the way we view rational economic decisions. Instead of seeing them as unilateral inferences in which we calculate the smartest choice between the options given, we can view them as collaborative negotiations in which we create wiser paths towards a mutually beneficial future.

This chapter starts with a simple example of this shift at the household level and then explores scaling up changes in ways we think and act in communities, corporations, and national economies.

An Example from Home Economics

During the 1980s housing boom, my wife and I moved back with our three daughters to our hometown, Bar Harbor, Maine. Because she had landed a good paying job in the school system, we hoped we could afford a house we would all be happy in. But as our realtor took us from place to place, we grew increasingly frustrated. We did not seem to be able to agree on anything in our price range. Each new foray seemed to generate the kinds of tensions that often lead to divorce: arguments about money.

At that time, as part of my research on peace studies, I was experimenting with methods in Fisher and Ury's *Getting to Yes: Negotiating Agreement Without Giving In.* I decided to try them out with my wife. We sat down at the kitchen table with the idea of first "focusing on our interests instead of positions" and seeing if we could "multiply our options" and use some "objective criteria" to evaluate them.

As a prelude, I tried to "separate the people from the problem and build our relationship" by apologizing for sharp, disparaging comments I had made about some of her favorite houses. As we listened to each other, we generated a list of interests that were contradictory. We wanted to live in town, close to the schools and public facilities, but also out in the woods where it was peaceful and natural. We wanted a new house requiring little maintenance, but also wanted to avoid the years of tedious agony in design and construction couples experience building houses. Rather than despair at these apparent dilemmas, we took Fisher and Ury's advice to heart and brainstormed options. Then we did research to improve on them.

Once we stopped thinking in terms of dilemmas over whose preferences should win and adopted a "both/and" approach, things began to break open. We decided to look for properties that were within the town limits but at their edge, where residential areas border a national park. The brainstorm idea of buying a "prebuilt" house instead of building from scratch provided another key suggestion. We discovered a house built in a factory in Pennsylvania could be delivered and installed on site within three months. And we would have considerable flexibility choosing its design and get it built for less than local construction prices. With some luck and a good deal of hard work, we found a piece of land for sale that met our criteria, and we got the house built and were living in it happily by the time our daughters started school in the fall.

An Economic Ideology that Freezes Out Dialogue

In disputes over budgets in families, companies and governments, people often do not look for the interests underlying their conflicting positions or try to multiply their options. Instead, they often take preferences and options as givens and act like their economic wealth is a pie of a fixed size. They assume they must fight others for their share because one can only get more if the other gets less.

Why do we assume our preferences and options are givens and that we have to fight over a fixed pie? In part it is a consequence of the ideology of what economists themselves refer to as the "dismal science". They describe economics as the science of figuring out how to distribute scarce goods. They assume the task of economics is to use mathematics to find ways to maximize happiness as much as possible, given the miserable facts of scarcity. This vision has permeated institutions which encourage us to assume we have to fight as consumers and citizens over a fixed pie.

It is not uncommon to hear someone in charge of a budget say: "We just don't have the money to do that." It might be in response to a family member's proposal to take a trip or remodel a house. Or it might be a manager's way of turning down a raise or funding for a new project. The remark invites us to add the implicit premise that "We can only do things we have money for" and then draw the conclusion that, however unfortunate it may be, "We can't do what you are proposing."

However, after multiple encounters with such arguments, most people come to realize that there is money. The parent, employer, city council or whoever it is that is offering the argument has a budget—it is just being used for other things. It is a matter of priorities, not the amount of money available. A budget is a moral document expressing values. When someone says"We don't have the money for that", they are simply refusing to put their values and other assumptions on the table and review them. They are not really offering an argument. They are simply telling you they don't want to negotiate.

Making that explicit opens the dialogue to a new range of considerations—to tradeoffs. Budget managers who don't want to trade will often suggest that the alternative would be something that you and others would find it extremely difficult to give up. They may say: "Well . . . yes, we could fund your new program at the school. But we will have to sell some firetrucks or layoff some police officers in high crime districts." They pose the options in terms of a dilemma: "Either we give up X or we turn down your proposal." In effect, they insist on defining the terms of debate and the options available—and they insist on using unilateral inference that keeps the reasoning and deliberation framed and frozen within their underlying values and assumptions.

The reasoning exhibited when managers rationalize their budgets in these ways is the tip of an iceberg. It is an iceberg of layer upon layer of frozen ways of thinking that use monological inference to make economic decisions in our society. Those patterns of decision making thwart successful, sustainable lives for individuals, communities, and nations. They ask us to take a passive approach to our economic choices and accept values and assumptions built into them.

Rational Economic Man vs History Maker

This passive approach to economic thinking leads to repetitive, dysfunctional behavior. It is a key reason couples often have so much trouble arguing about money. It is also a key reason nations have so much trouble dealing with public problems like crime and protecting common resources like oceans. At the heart of this passive approach is the assumption that rational choice consists in using unilateral inference to choose between the options presented—which often turn out to be dilemmas. The solution is to negotiate creative solutions to transform dilemmas. Way can open when we seek genuine, voluntary agreements that are mutually satisfying, just and sustainable.

There is a profound paradox at work here in modern capitalist economies. In the realm of technological production, they seem to thrive on creative entrepreneurship and generate unending streams of innovative products made available as options. The dialogue, creative problem solving, and conflict resolution at work in the productive sectors of our economy are quite astonishing. Yet, paradoxically, as consumers and citizens, we are often trapped in static assumptions and endlessly repetitive, dysfunctional behavior.

Couples often find themselves trapped in cycles of recrimination and frustration over financial decisions. They treat their individual preferences as givens, suppose their current income is a fixed pie, and propose choices for distributing it. They assume these are the given options they face in a dilemma about what to do. They then persist in debate, repeatedly rehearsing their own lines of unilateral reasoning. Each keeps concluding the other is wrong or unfair or selfish . . . or "just completely incapable of listening to reason".

Wise is the couple who escapes this way of relating. Blessed are those who never relate in this way at all.

We often unwisely live with the painfulness of such situations until something breaks. Sometimes the relationship itself breaks apart in separation and divorce. Sometimes it is our spirits that simply break. But sometimes something a bit wonderful happens and it is our hearts which break—by breaking open. This can create the conditions for new kinds of listening, reconciliation, and shared problem solving that renew and reaffirm a loving relationship. Often, we end up questioning our own selves deeply, listening with care to each other, reconsidering our assumptions, and making special efforts to find new options and reinvent our lives. We become agents of a kind of change that is transformative. We stop practicing one kind of rationality and start practicing another.

In these transformative moments, you and I may stop reasoning the way mainstream economics models assume we should. I stop making unilateral inferences that calculate my individual happiness based on given options. Instead, my partner and I start to reason using the methods of shared problem-solving, negotiation and conflict transformation. We enter dialogues in which we aim to find genuine, willing agreement amongst ourselves. This shift from "I" to "We" thinking is often challenging. It may take special effort on the part of one person to "open their mind" to the realities of the situation or to "melt the heart" of the other. It does not always succeed. But when it does, it changes the story of the couple in a pivotal way.

It alters their history by transforming their relationship. When one engages in this kind of reasoning, your sense of identity is altered. In an important sense, you stop thinking of yourself as what traditional economists would call "Rational Economic Man". Instead, you start thinking of yourself as what we might call a "History Maker". The history you seek to change need not be momentous and grand. It may concern the smallest of narratives that structure your workday life or adventures with family. What makes your work as a change agent "historical" in this context is that you are not just accepting the current situation and choosing one of the options presented by the market. You are rewriting the rules, inventing new options, creating new scenes and stories in the drama of your life.

The contrast between these two identities, these two ways of thinking of ourselves, is profound. As a "Rational Economic Man", my goal is to maximize my individual happiness. It is appropriate to use the masculine form of this phrase in introducing the idea. It reminds us not only of the traditional formulation but also of the heavily gendered character of that tradition. In it, I am viewed as part of a great market of individuals who are each choosing amongst the options presented in that market by making selfish, unilateral calculations. Adam Smith argued that just such a market of selfish individuals could, through the working of a great "Invisible Hand", produce an efficient system of exchange that would maximize the total happiness of all involved by maximizing their total income and consumption of material goods and services.[50]

There are a great many people who have not lived according to that model of rationality. They include Buddhist monks, self-sacrificing soldiers, medical missionaries, and collaborative artists. They also include many Indigenous peoples who, to economists, seem to act in irrational ways by holding on to traditional practices of agriculture, land-owning, and other customs. They have collectively agreed on these practices precisely because these give meaning to their lives in the ways they choose to live out their history. The list of real people who do not fit the economists' model also often includes mothers who do unpaid work and sacrifice to sustain and nurture their children and create options that transform their lives and change the history of their family. These mothers and others are agents of historical change who work at the family and community level, as well as, in national and international contexts.

As historical change agents, our goals are to reach genuine voluntary agreements that transform our assumptions, ourselves, and our world to create new meaning and better purposes for our shared lives. Limited and defective forms of dialogical reasoning involved can be practiced by an "in group" that excludes others—by, for instance, racists conspiring to establish an apartheid system. But, in their most fully rational form, our dialogues are guided not by an oppressive minority or by the "Invisible Hand" of the market but by the interests and cares of all concerned and by whatever sources of inspiration or leadings we may muster from our traditions or encounter in intellectual reflections and spiritual openings.

Table 5. Two Models of Rational Choice in Allocating Resources

Model of Reasoner Choosing:	As Rational Economic Actor	As History Maker
World viewed as:	A marketplace of available options	A community of interacting individuals, groups, and other species
Action as:	Choice between available options given	Creation of opportunities and pursuit of projects
Guiding principle:	Maximize utility	Develop genuine, voluntary, sustainable, and resilient agreements and projects

Shifting between these two identities can be challenging. There are many ways we are constantly encouraged or compelled to think of ourselves as Rational Economic Actors rather than agents of historical change. We are bombarded with advertising that invites us to choose things because they will thrill us with individual delight or personal satisfaction. Economic institutions provide our food, transport, health care, education, housing, and other necessities as options between which, we, as consumers, must choose. The central policies of our government reinforce our identities as consumers who are supposed to think of themselves as Rational Economic Actors. The single most important measure of the government's success is assumed to be an economic one: How fast is the Gross Domestic Product growing?

And to make the GDP grow, the federal government enacts laws and policies that create jobs so we will each have higher income and go out and spend it as consumers.

The economists who advise politicians on the best ways to do all this often claim they and their theories are merely describing reality in an objective, neutral scientific way. They tell the politicians how the world works and what their choices are. For instance, they will say something like: "To create more jobs, increase demand in the economy; to lower inflation, decrease demand. Those are your choices. Which you prefer is up to you. As economists we simply tell you what the choices are and how the world works. We cannot tell you which goal is best. In the end, that is simply a matter of individual preference."[51]

The reality is that economists are not merely describing the world, they are helping to create it. Their theory of Rational Economic Actors is used to persuade people to adopt that as an identity and center their lives around it. They not only urge us as individuals to adopt the Rational Economic Actor ideology, they urge us as citizens of a democratic nation to do so as well. The ideology commits us collectively, as a country, to an unrealistic and unsustainable dream of unending growth in our material consumption.

GDP as Economic Ideology

Nationally, the unilateral inferential reasoning of this economic ideology is institutionalized in two key ways: 1) through algorithms used to measure progress with Gross Domestic Product and 2) through the algorithms of debt financing used to introduce money into circulation.

The logic used to justify the use of Gross Domestic Product (GDP) to measure the success of our society and the government managing it is straightforward and unilateral. It assumes that the best way to measure all the good things or services that happen in the course of a year is to find out what people paid for and then total these up. The GDP is simply a measure of all the payments any person, company or government agency made during the course of the year. The economic theory behind the use of GDP as a measure assumes that when it comes to things we bother to buy with our money, if some is good, more is better. Given these assumptions, it seems logical to infer that unending growth in the GDP is the best thing we could hope for and work to bring about. It seems likewise logical to infer that cities, states, and regions can and should measure their success by using local measures of their portion of the GDP. Following just this logic, cities and states adopt tax policies that bring in workers and businesses and they pass regulatory laws and fund development projects that all aim at growth measured in this way.

However, if we want to measure success in our economy, the Gross Domestic Product is a poor and dysfunctional indicator. First, it leaves out things it should include and includes things it should leave out. What it leaves out are all the things that happen outside the monetary system. GDP only measures things sold on the market. When a woman cooks a meal for her family, no one pays for that labor, and it is not measured by the GDP. If, instead, she works at McDonalds cooking hamburgers for pay, her labor is measured and included. This applies to all the unpaid labor families perform caring for elders, gardening, repairing houses, nursing, and educating. To drive this point home, consider two parents forced to make ends meet by taking second jobs that pay low wages serving fast food. s put their kids in afterschool care and feed them cheap packaged, processed food because they no longer have the time to make home cooked meals. In this situation, the paid labor and the purchased meals all get counted in the GDP. So, it looks like the economy—and the family—is doing better even though their health and welfare overall may be significantly diminished.

The flip side of the mismeasurements made by GDP can be illustrated by an even more perverse example which can arise for the parents working at McDonalds. If a fast-food diet causes their kids to get diabetes or if one of the parents suffers from a stress-related disease like hypertension or heart disease, what happens to the GDP? The medical bills get measured as goods and services that have been added. By that measure, the economy has grown. Note: the GDP grows when people lose their health and have to pay medical bills and funeral expenses.

GDP mismeasures all kinds of key things. It leaves out the increase in our collective wealth when trees grow in national parks, when air is cleaner because trees grow, when kids play more and grow strong and healthy, when people play music or worship together or give each other homemade gifts or simply listen and chat and support each other in hard times. It leaves out increases in our wellbeing when the rain falls on our gardens and when children smile and make us happy. GDP counts, as positive things, all the quite unhappy events that someone has to pay for, including, toxic waste spills, lawsuits, police interventions in domestic violence, military expenditures on bombing raids, and bills for therapy.

Of the things GDP typically mismeasures, one is especially important: the commons. These include the air and the oceans as well as other shared sources of well-being like the education level of our community and the state of public health. Because no one owns them they do not get bought and sold as commodities and do not get measured in GDP. If pollution makes air quality go down, this only gets measured in the GDP when it has some subsequent effect like increased demand for cancer care or for new paint for houses. In those cases, the effects of the loss of air quality get measured, ironically, as an increase in the GDP.[51]

Because the commons we all depend on do not get measured well, they do not get managed well. In debates we often hear the argument mentioned earlier: "We just don't have the money." Because shared commons are not bought and sold as commodities, they do not directly generate cash income, and no one has a clear and vested interest in paying for their care. Yet we all depend on them and commons that are part of our local landscapes and planetary ecosystems are getting wrecked to the point of not being sustainable.

To put the problem with the mismanagement of our commons into perspective, it is helpful to imagine the viewpoint of an alien anthropologist from Alpha Centauri visiting our planet and doing an overall assessment. If she looks at the way we have let our industrial economy destroy our ecosystem and the commons on which we depend, it is very easy to imagine her emitting some kind of off-world expletive of shock: "They poison their oceans with plastic, pave their farmlands with asphalt, cause a Sixth Great Extinction, and create massively destructive, irreversible Climate Change. What the #$@%(^} | ~&%# are they thinking??!!!!"

Mismanagement of the Commons: What are we thinking?

And more to the point, **how** are we thinking? We are thinking the way Rational Economic Actors think. We are taking our preferences and options as measured by money as givens. We are calculating how to make ourselves most happy by maximizing our GDP. And when someone argues that we should spends hundreds of billions of dollars to prevent the worsening of Climate Change our leaders tell us: "We just don't have the money."

The first step is to call out the argument for what it is: a refusal to negotiate. We have budgets that include hundreds of billions of dollars, we are just using them for other things. We have budgets that could be expanded by taxes or by printing money. We just assume that those are not options—that we must accept the status quo as given.

The 2008 economic crisis and the more recent COVID-19 epidemic have created dramatic case studies to drive this point home. When the economy crashed at the end of George W. Bush's second term, markets crashed, and it became impossible for companies to borrow for short term loans. They could not buy inventory. The situation got so serious the Republican administration started talking seriously about nationalizing the banking industry. At that time, hundreds of billions of dollars were found and funneled into the economy from the top down. Later, in March of 2020, when the US economy went into free fall, it took less than a month to pass the CARES Act which funded 2.2 trillion dollars for relief.

Regarding Climate Change and the ecological collapse that we are facing, the time has come to stop reasoning like Rational Economic Actors entrenched in old assumptions and status quo budgets. It is time to reason like History Makers to negotiate solutions to the problems our children all encounter constantly on the internet: wildfires burning out the Western US, hurricanes destroying cities on the East Coast, melting tundra, shrinking glaciers, melting ice caps, rising oceans, disappearing coral reefs, and vanishing rainforests.

Works of art and dramatic protest are often eloquent ways to take the first step to changing how we think and act. The second step is to reframe and institutionalize processes of dialogue and conflict transformation to provide efficient and effective forums for negotiating. We need, collectively, to develop skills and institutions that enable us to negotiate practical, economically viable, ecologically resilient, socially just agreements as to how to manage our commons.

There has been considerable research on ways to do this. Much of it is generated by critical analysis of Garret Hardin's description of "The Tragedy of the Commons."[52] He argued commons are mismanaged when use is unrestricted and open to overexploitation that profits individuals at the expense of the community. He illustrated this with a community of 100 farmers each grazing a cow on a common pasture that can sustain only 100 cows. Each farmer has an incentive to graze an extra cow to double his income. But once each does, they begin to degrade and destroy the commons they all depend on. Hardin argued this tragedy could only be avoided by replacing open access with government regulation or private ownership. But in most cases there is a fourth alternative that proves even better at managing and sustaining commons: community-based systems.

Elinor Ostrom and her colleagues have studied these in depth. Instead of open access, government control or private ownership, commons can be managed, for instance, by fishing co-ops or land holding systems like the *ejidos* described in Chapter One. Ostrom's Nobel Prize winning research has shown there are many around the world that have chosen to create community-based management systems using mechanisms that ensure good stewardship for the shared resource. Here are eight design principles Ostrom identified for stable, local, common pool management of resources:

1) Clear definition of the common pool resource and effective exclusion of external un-entitled parties,

2) Appropriation and provision of common resources adapted to local conditions,

3) Collective-choice arrangements that allow most resource appropriators to participate in the decision-making process,

4) Effective monitoring by monitors who are part of or accountable to the appropriators,

5) Graduated sanctions for resource appropriators who violate community rules,

6) Mechanisms of conflict resolution that are cheap and accessible,

7) Self-determination of the community recognized by higher-level authorities, and

8) With larger common-pool resources, organization in the form of multiple layers of nested enterprises, with small local groups at the base level.[53]

There is something very important to note about these principles. With the partial exception of #5, none of them promote the use of the kind of unilateral, inferential reasoning that is characteristic of traditional economic theory. Instead, they all advocate for the creation of institutions and practices that employ dialogue and collaborative reasoning in the form of group problem solving, negotiation and conflict transformation. Further, such dialogues are always rooted in the place and context of the communities caring for the commons as a resource not only for themselves but for their inheritors yet to come.

Principle #5 does provide a partial exception to this because it proposes to give each user of the commons a set of graduated incentives for abiding by the community's rules. Some of those incentives may involve public shaming or even ostracism and loss of access to the shared resource. But some incentives may be straightforward economic ones like fines that invite people to calculate, economically, that it is in their own best interest to abide by community rules.

The strategy of these community-based management systems is to get people to shift from one kind of rationality to another—to replace unilateral economic inference with collaborative conflict transformation and other forms of dialogue. This is what makes Ostrom's Nobel Prize award in Economics so entirely remarkable. Her studies are quite unlike those of previous winners. And the reasoning they focus on is as well. In an important sense, she showed that key economic problems involving Tragedies of the Commons have to be solved with non-economic thinking. Research like Ostrom's describes one crucial set of ways communities can make the transition from reasoning like Rational Economic Actors to reasoning like agents of historical change.[54]

In making such transitions, it is important to draw on and synthesize the diverse resources of natural landscapes and community practices. The entrepreneurial change agents who do so often play roles analogous to pollinators who help foster creativity in the economy of nature by promoting genetic and ecological diversity.

They are involved in what I have described elsewhere as:

"[T]he collaboration of communities engaged in dialogical reasoning that seeks balanced pursuit of all the relevant values at stake. It is the collaboration of people who are carefully cross-fertilizing new and transformative smart technologies with well established, traditional systems of natural intelligence and community wisdom. It is the collaboration of pollinators who are inspired by the traditions of Gandhi, Freire and others who practice the kind of nonviolent exchange that can advance our collective legacies of wealth of all kinds. In the long run we are all little people who die and are ultimately forgotten. But in the meanwhile, we, each and every one of us, have the opportunity to listen and learn and enter into the sweet exchange of honey and pollen as well as information and action, that create a blooming, buzzing, beauty of life secured by the commons that we develop and defend as communities."[55]

Interpersonal skills and community organizing methods for engaging in such entrepreneurial activity may involve shifting out of disciplinary silos and "deprofessionalizing" in ways Gustavo Esteva has described in "Regenerating Peoples' Spaces". In learning such methods there is a rich body of practice inspired by Paulo Freire and others which provides insights into doing so in collaborative, community-based processes where roles of entrepreneurship and pollination are carried out not just by heroic individuals but by collaborative teams.[56]

Another crucial body of related research deals, specifically with problems in measuring the success of such reasoning and actions based on it. How can we tell how well the commons of a forest or planetary atmosphere is being managed? It is necessary to take many things into account. It is a bit like trying to assess individual health. What measures should we use? Blood pressure? Body weight? Strength for sit-ups and push-ups? Resistance to colds? Aerobic ability? Skin tone and quality? Visual acuity? Digestive efficiency and bowel regularity? Sex drive? Mental alertness? Reflex responses? Sleeping patterns? Behavioral indicators of anxiety? There is a lot to being really healthy. For an overall assessment we can try to clump some together and create composite scales that estimate overall health in muscular, nervous or digestive systems. We can even create a composite scale that compiles all these into an overall rank by letter grade or number. Creating a comprehensive composite scale may be useful in some contexts. If someone has been letting their body systems decline in a variety of ways, getting a "20 on a scale of 100" or a "D minus" can provide a serious wake up call.[56]

But the wake up should call us to look in detail at each health factor and consider what can be done about it to improve the situation. The different aspects of our health are interconnected. Anxieties from work can affect digestion which affects sleep which affects immune responses and so on. Solving problems with our health and negotiating ways to change our behavior and transform ourselves can require holistic approaches. But the measures of success need to always revert to the details of each system.

A similar approach is required in managing commons. The measure of success has to require multiple indicators that are each looked at and re-examined regularly with care. In managing the economic and ecological resources of our community, nation, and planet, we need a multiple measure approach. Instead of relying on GDP, we should examine many, diverse criteria. One example of this approach is provided by the Human Development Indices that have been created by the UNDP. Other indices which should form part of the collective group we use to replace the GDP include indices of national health, poverty, crime, employment, the Ocean Health Index, and the Universal Human Rights Index. While these each aggregate different kinds of data in their own ways to illuminate progress or failure on various fronts, it is important to keep in mind that the point is not to arrive in the end at an all-encompassing measure aggregating them all into one single measure of progress. Instead, the point is to enable us to use multiple measures for the many-sided problems we face and the different voices and visions that we can respond to in trying to address them.[57]

As communities and nations, once we stop thinking like Rational Economic Actors and start thinking like History Makers, our decisions are no longer aimed at maximizing some single indicator like GDP. Instead, they are guided by visions of the kind of future we are trying to create—the kind of history we are trying to make. Our decisions are worked out not by using unilateral inference to calculate the path to some maximum. Instead, they are worked out by detailed negotiation, problem solving and conflict transformation.

It is difficult to shift to this kind of reasoning collectively if we are still thinking individually in the framework of Rational Economic Actors. There are two institutions we need to opt out of individually and change collectively because they encourage us to do just that. The process of fully transforming our individual identities and our collective historical trajectory will involve transforming the institutions of both advertising and the debt-based money system.

Escaping the Controls of Advertising and Debt-based Money

The practices associated with advertising enable companies to make enormous profits by exercising control over the focus of our attention, the process of our thought, the locus of our desires, and the outcomes of our actions. In the age of internet media, this has become a subtle and powerful practice. But the institutions associated with it could be changed and result in very different outcomes. One simple step is to shift to using subscription-based media or collaboratively created ones like Wikipedia instead of "free" ones paid for by advertising. As the saying goes, if you are not the customer, then you are the product. And the product most desired by advertisers is an egoistic, impulse driven "Rational Economic Consumer" whose preferences can be shaped and manipulated to generate a profitable income stream. Picturing a different world is easy. Imagine looking for entertainment on subscription services like *Netflix* or *HBO* instead of advertising driven television. To go a step further, imagine searching for facts and information about reality on *Wikipedia* instead of *Facebook/Meta*.[58]

Another national institution that strongly influences us to think like Rational Economic Actors is the debt-based monetary system. Anyone who has taken out a student loan or house mortgage understands the ways incurring debt transfers significant control over our lives to the lender who must be paid back with interest. Suddenly our choices about what to do with our work lives or our homes must satisfy the algorithms of interest payments. We are no longer sovereign individuals free to come and go as we please and invest our time and resources in whatever ways might seem to be meaningful and historically significant to us. We must serve some employer who will enable us to make payments and we must practice housekeeping that will satisfy the terms of our mortgage. The same basic point applies to cities and nation states that borrow. They compromise their sovereignty in doing so.

In our current economic system, the money that makes trade possible and circulates in ever growing quantities is created by a system of financing in which private banks create money through interest bearing loans to individuals, corporations, and governments. This drives us all towards adopting algorithms of choice based on rational economic calculation rather than historically meaningful action. The details of this are explained more fully in the online appendix on "The Algorithmic Consequences of the Debt-based Monetary System". But a key point to note is that this debt system is optional rather than inevitable. In principle, at least for most of us as individuals, we can choose to finance things through income and savings rather than debt in order to maintain sovereignty over our lives. In the case of governments, there are other options as well which include, for instance, creating money by printing it at the rate at which the economy can appropriately grow. Doing so provides desired economic stimulus while at the same time reducing the need to pay for public services with borrowing or taxes.[59]

The connections between opting out of advertising and debt-based financing as individuals and transforming the institutions that profit and promote these things presents a chicken and egg problem. Effective long-term change at each level calls for efforts at the other. Turning, for the moment, to focus on the individual level, what steps can we take to change our own lives in ways that can then be scaled up to promote the kind of system change we seek?

The Transition to Living within Earth's Carrying Capacity

As individuals, many of us need to do some serious soul searching concerning the level of change needed in the world and the level of commitment we are ready to make. I have given a variety of talks to folks concerned about climate change, ecological collapse and other problems related to the levels of material consumption typical for people in the "Developed World". I often ask for a show of hands: "How many think Earth has a carrying capacity that could be sustained if everyone on the planet consumes at the level of the average American?" I find hands rarely go up for this. I then ask: "How much average material consumption could the planet sustain? 25 percent of the typical American? 40 percent? 60? 80?"

People are typically unsure of just how to answer, perhaps in part because they would like a more precise definition of "material consumption" and the "typical American level". The mean income per household which, in 2020, was estimated at $97,026 or the median of $67,521?[60] They also note, rightly, that generalizations about family incomes should never overlook the fact that there are many people in the US below or in the vicinity of the poverty line who are in very substantial need of **more** material resources. But once we clarify the general idea, there are usually some hands that go up for a reduction to 25 per cent and almost all agree an 80 percent reduction would be required. Most people seem to believe that by the time we reach somewhere around 50 percent of the level of material consumption of the average (mean) American, we have arrived at a level that is simply not sustainable at the planetary level. I go on to ask: "How many of you believe that the majority of people in the rest of the world are going to be content to let a minority like the Americans consume dramatically more than they do?" Very few hands go up.

I then ask, "How many of you believe that the average American needs to cut their personal material consumption at least in half?" At this point, typically, a very interesting kind of discussion starts up. What folks often want to say includes things like: "What you are proposing is not realistic. People aren't going to cut their consumption in half. That is just not politically viable." Often people will suggest that somehow it all needs to be reframed: "You're not going to get anywhere asking people to make sacrifices like that. You have to put it in a positive way. You can ask them to consume differently—buying electric cars instead of gas guzzlers. But you can't ask them to live on less. Most people can't do that."

This is a point at which there may be a need for some serious soul searching. For one thing, folks who make these arguments typically put them in the third person, talking about what someone can ask "people" to do, rather than directly owning the question in a personal way and asking themselves and each other, "What am I going to do?

What are you going to do? What will we as a community do?" The tendency to avoid owning the question may spring at least in part from a fear about what we half-consciously suspect our own views about climate change and ecological collapse would force us to conclude about the sacrifices we might be called to make.

The question may also give pause because of complications that come to mind. For instance, there are a number of people in even the most developed economies who are too poor to live on half of their current level of material consumption. Also, cutting consumption can require changes in lifestyle that have all sorts of significant impacts of family and social life. Further, we have to reckon with the fact that people are often in some sense personally committed and perhaps even addicted to the pleasures they associate with their current levels of material consumption. In that sense, they can't "just give them up" and it may be difficult to do so no matter how hard they try. Further, there are politicians, corporations, and non-profit groups who are competing for people's votes and dollars by telling them it is OK to keep consuming. In that respect it may seem like "we can't compete" with all that pro-consumption messaging. These realities supporting "can't" assumptions are probably all interconnected. Part of the soul searching we need to do involves disentangling them and assessing the truth of each.

There clearly are people in the U.S. and elsewhere who could not live on half of what they are currently consuming. They are already starving, homeless, and deprived of essential medical care. Many need to consume more and they need help and deserve solidarity. But the average citizen in the developed world is significantly above that level.

This can be obscured because of the way we tend to look at our household budgets. We see we need to spend X on rent/mortgage and Y on cars and Z on utilities and at the end of the month it's all gone. We are left feeling that we are just getting by. So how could we live on less? The problem here is the flip side of the argument we looked at earlier, "We just don't have any money for that." Here the argument is "We just can't get by on anything less." And yet . . . people do get by on less. We all know people who do. In fact, for most of us, while it may be on average that roughly half the folks we know live on incomes that are larger than ours, the other half normally live on less.

You can think of this as more of a mathematical truth than a sociological fact. It is just what we mean we talk about medians and averages. As a matter definition, exactly half are always above the median and half below it. Whatever my income is, if it is anywhere in the ballpark of the average for the Developed World, there are going to be people I know personally who can provide role models for living on a lower income.

Part of the way they typically do this is by meeting their needs in different ways—with different kinds of housing, clothing, food, transport, entertainment, and other options. They renegotiate their budgets by renegotiating their options. And most of us have, in fact, some direct or at least strong indirect experience of just such renegotiation. For instance, either we or someone we know loses a job, gets divorced, gets a serious illness, has a spouse die, or has some other kind of crisis that requires a major renegotiation of that moral document that expresses our personal values—our family budget. And while such processes can be painful, in many cases they may be transformative in ways we look back on with gratitude. These crisis transitions may lead us to spend more time at home and less commuting to work or more time with people and less with things. They may lead us to grow in maturity, responsibility, care, and our capacity to love. They may lead us to break with a community of shallow friends and colleagues and commit ourselves to a more meaningful, rewarding community.

Meeting the Future Halfway

These kinds of transitions can be especially difficult to negotiate all at once, in a few short weeks. But over the course of a year, for instance, it can often be possible to effect significant changes. What this suggests is that for many Americans, making a transition to living on half as much personal material consumption is something that they could, in fact, reasonably aim at and achieve given sufficient lead time. If you start with redirecting 10 per cent of your income in the first year and continue doing this each year, at the end of five years you could be at a level of 50 per cent of what you started at. In this sense, the average American certainly can make the change we are talking about.

And there are some important reasons they might want to make these reductions. We have already noted two: 1) they can help address the existential threat we all face from ecological collapse and, 2) they can empower themselves to develop a new and more meaningful identity as History Makers instead of as Rational Economic Actors addicted to various forms of consumption. A third motivation is also potentially significant. To appreciate it, note the idea here is NOT to reduce people's income. It is to redirect the way they spend it. This can be done in three ways. One is to give income to others in real need through acts of solidarity that recognize their humanity and support them. A second, historically pivotal way of redirecting our income is by giving to organizations funding social and political change. A third historically crucial way to redirect our income is through socially and environmentally responsible investments. We can buy stock in renewable energy companies, kickstart organic farms, purchase bonds for low-income housing, or invest in solar panels for our own home.

The experience with such forms of socially and environmentally responsible forms of investment is clear: They do at least as well and generally better than regressive forms of investment over the long run. Such investments are needed to fund the changes we require in our economy and society. But they are also attractive because, over time, they can increase your income. This is a good thing if you are redirecting at least half your income to acts of solidarity, social/ political change, and more responsible investment. It is a good thing because it increases the power of you and the people you are supporting who are trying to better the world. Note the proposal here is very different from what many people first think of when asked to reduce consumption. They assume this means they will have less income and do less with their lives. On the contrary, the proposal here, for many people, would be to encourage them to increase their income—to have more precisely so they could do more with their lives. The key point for everyone is simply that we should refocus our definitions of what counts as "more" on the historical changes we make rather than the material things we consume.

I have experimented with college students, polling them on how they might want to spend their future income. I propose the options of cutting their material consumption in half and spending the other half on some mix of solidarity, social/political change, or socially/ environmentally responsible investment. Many find these possibilities intriguing. Some are drawn to emphasize solidarity or political change, but the strongest draw is usually investment. This becomes especially appealing when I point out that at a modest four per cent rate of return if they invest their half income annually, at the end of 20 years they will accumulate enough to retire with a secure income equal to what they have been consuming all along.[61]

The details of how the general idea being proposed here will work out can and should vary depending on the life circumstances you are in. A young couple just starting out may well need to borrow money for housing and in fact spend more than their annual income in order get their family household going. In contrast, when their children age and move away from home, they may have excess housing with rooms that they should perhaps rent out. Or perhaps they should move to a smaller apartment. And if they have invested successfully for retirement, they may well have income so high they should think seriously about reducing their personal material consumption to 25 per cent or 10 per cent of it.

The ways it might make most sense to put the core idea here into practice vary enormously. Many readers of books like this one are going to need to dramatically reduce our consumption in the future. Yet we may not be ready to put on our loin cloths and live at the income of a Gandhi—or take Jesus' advice to the lawyer at the end of the Good Samaritan parable and "sell all your possessions and give them to the poor". But we can quite realistically aim to meet Gandhi and Jesus—and the future—at least halfway by making a change in what we do with the income we have.

There are further theoretical and practical reasons to promote this social change strategy for "meeting the future halfway". For one thing, this kind of change is scalable. In principle, it can provide for a period of exponential increase in social change analogous to the way capital in a for-profit market economy can grow. If individuals are redirecting their income to social change, the organizations they fund will have it in their institutional interest to encourage other individuals to take the same steps in transforming themselves from consumers to agents of history. And as they acquire more support, they can use part of it to reinvest in recruiting even more support, growing their sectors of the economy just the ways for-profit corporations grow their capital.

This point applies to governments as well as non-profits, churches, political parties, and other groups engaged in social change. Governments can, for instance, make tax laws benefiting socially responsible investments that grow the economy—and the tax base for that government. Further, governments can provide research, guidance, infrastructure, and incentives to help encourage acts of solidarity that reduce the costs of dealing with people who are undernourished, unhoused, ill or without access to education. This scalable feature of the activity of meeting the future halfway deals with one of the greatest challenges in changing our economy. How can we grow the good changes we need faster than the capitalist enterprises whose profits are, in many cases, fueling the exponential growth of existential threats to our communities and planet? The process of "meeting the future halfway" provides a path to compete with the problematic sectors of the capitalist economy and offers the hope of a just, viable, resilient world. History Makers who invest in creating more agents of historical change can, at least for a time, grow their power at exponential rates.

It is helpful to picture more concretely how we might encourage ourselves and others in the march along this path.

Marchathons

One of the contexts in which people start to act like History Makers is when they get concerned about a political issue and start to engage in protest and collective action. In my experience, protests can be empowering and even fun. But they are not vacations and decisions to take part are not what most people would consider rational consumer choices. They are responses to fundamental concerns through efforts to change the world; they are not just choices amongst the options available for purchase. In preparing for the January 2017 Women's March in Washington, I experimented with a way to shift myself and others a bit away from identities as Rational Economic Actor towards agents of historical change.

The protest was great fun! It was an experience of a sea of people with creative signs and chants, sharing visions of a future of peace and justice. In my own tiny way I added to this an element of a "marchathon". About a week before, I felt doubts about such events: "What is the point of spending all this money to travel to DC and protest? Why not spend the money actually doing something and making things happen?" Rather than agonize over this question as an either/or dilemma, I decided to try out a "both/and" approach. I asked friends who couldn't go to pledge money for the miles I clocked so they could have a sense of taking part through my travels and help raise money for a relevant organization, Planned Parenthood. With essentially no planning or organization, on the spur of the moment, I managed to raise $350 for Planned Parenthood with my little "marchathon".

What if the million or so people who were there had all done this? What if this were applied to other marches and protests. People regularly organize big marches for raising awareness around Climate Change with a million people gathering in DC and with often very large supporting protests in cities all around the country. What if they made them into marchathons? What if a million people each got 10 folks to each pledge $100? The result would be 10 times $100 times 1,000,000 which equals . . . one billion dollars. This kind of action can give protests more historical impact on the ground. It can also provide an exciting way for the donors to redirect their personal income so as to shift their habits—and their identities—away from consumption and towards historical agency.

Variations on this coupling of historical change and fundraising could include many other forms of political protest, efforts to clean up watersheds, promotion of community health, the introduction of a new sport, or collaboration in cultural exchange. And the fundraising can include variations on all the traditional practices that get folks together to contribute while doing things they want to do anyway—meals, parties, danceathons, runathons, et cetera. We can scale up the incorporation of these in all our activities for social, political, environmental, or cultural change.

Another Scalable Strategy: Giving the Gift of Giving

When Christmas was approaching, I was trying to figure out what to give my children, grandchildren and others as presents. I dreaded this because it was always hard to find something new each year that they would really appreciate. I often found myself roaming malls or websites, trying, with little real success, to find some imported piece of plastic or other product that would say to each person clearly and effectively "I love you!" The idea of simply giving them money was always an option, but it felt a little cold. Then I tried a variation on this that felt different. I wrote each person a check for an amount equal to what I would have spent on their present and sent it as a card with a note explaining why I had left the recipient line on the check blank. I invited them to consider if there was some organization working to make the world better that they would want to support. They could write its name in the blank on the check and send it to them. I gave each person the option of spending the money on themselves, noting that they could cash it and use the money for something they needed or felt would be especially meaningful for them. The point was that they were presented with the option of choosing to give a gift to others—a gift that might on their view make their world a better place. They responded to this gift in thoughtful and appreciative ways. It was interesting to me to learn what they each ended up choosing.

This activity of "giving the gift of giving" is something that can be done year-round and provide multiple benefits. First, it reduces the giver's personal material consumption. Just with end of year holiday giving alone, this can be significant. A further benefit is that the practice invites people to shift their sense of who they are. To picture themselves not as consumers of good things but as doers of good deeds—as change agents.

How might we scale up this kind of activity and the kinds of historical and personal change it can bring? One way is to invite ourselves as individuals to take it more seriously and take it much farther. Another way is to work through community organizations and governments to motivate and facilitate it. By working to meet the future halfway and take serious steps to address the existential ecological threats our economy has created, we can transform that economy and its members.

Scalable initiatives like these provide ways in which we can begin to respond, for instance, to the climate crisis and the sad fact that:

... some would like the world to turn on the energy of the coal they burn
and let the climate change go on till most of Bangladesh is gone.
From New Orleans to New York's Coast up to Alaska's permafrost,
they'd rather sell their ancient oil than love our land and save our soil.

We can respond with a growing chorus that insists that:
... we'll buy back our ancient rights and stop consuming day and night,
invest more and consume less and tell our worried children yes!
Yes, we love you! Yes, we care! Yes, we'll give you your fair share!
Put half our income all aside to stop the storm and turn the tide.[62]

Three Phases of Transition in our National Economies

In her assessment of the challenges that Climate Change presents, the title of a Naomi Klein book sums up a key point: *This Changes Everything*. The changes in our economy that are needed are urgent and dramatic.

One of their nuances turns on a distinction introduced by Herman Daly and John Cobb between economic "growth" versus "development". The contrast is exemplified by children who grow physically till they reach their adult size but then can continue developing with physical changes and psychological maturation. As adults that stop growth but continue development, they can acquire all sorts of new skills, abilities, character traits and powers of mind and body. We can distinguish, similarly, between economic "growth" as a process of adding to the material stuff in the economy versus economic "development" which would consist of improving the way it is arranged and used. Building farms in the forest is an example of growth. Educating farmers in organic methods is an example of development.[63]

In the short term, we require degrowth in some areas and growth in others. In the medium term, we need a transition to an economy guided by development without growth. This requires three processes that have to be pursued simultaneously.

We need to "degrow" the economy in these ways:

- shrinking the personal material consumption of those who significantly exceed what our planet can sustain as an average for all,
- shrinking production and consumption that uses natural resources as mines and sinks—resources whose use is not renewable. This includes entirely stopping the use of fossil fuels for energy,
- shrinking forms of government expenditure that make unsustainable and/or destructive use of natural resources including, for instance, most forms of military weaponry.[64]

At the same time, we need to grow the economy in these ways:

- increasing the personal consumption of people suffering from poverty,
- increasing production using renewable resources,
- increasing government expenditures that promote sustainable uses of natural resources and enhance communities and natural systems including, for example, nonviolent methods of conflict resolution and transformation.

We need to be developing now—and achieving in the medium term—an economy that allows for continued development without growth, including, especially:

- enhancements in the health of human and non-human individuals and communities
- increases in education and human capital
- advancements in cultural activities in science, arts and other fields
- an alternative to the current debt-based money system that drives ecological destruction, inequality, and the undermining of democracy
- the development of more ethical individuals and

communities as well as relationships between them and their natural environment

What would a path to such transitions look like in the short term as well as the long term?

One challenge is posed by ways growth drives our current macroeconomic system. It is like a spinning top in which money is cycling around from households and governments purchasing goods and services to corporations selling them and thence to workers producing them who then spend more money on purchases for their families and pay taxes for governments to also make purchases that all keep the top-like wheel of the economy spinning. The difference between the macroeconomic cycle and a child's top is, however, that the economic cycle has to keep getting bigger in an ever-larger upward spiral for it to balance. If households reduce their consumption, then corporations reduce production—and their pay to workers. And there is then less money in the cycle for those households to circulate through consumption and taxes. And so less is produced . . . in a downward spiral.

When people contemplate "degrowth" as a solution to our ecological challenges, many worry about just this kind of threat—the threat of a vicious cycle of downward spiral into a major recession and then a devastating economic depression. We seem to be stuck with a dilemma in which we either:

1) keep spiraling up in the growth of our economy at the cost of creating a major ecological collapse or

2) spiral down and face economic collapse.

A way out of this dilemma is provided by the "meeting the future halfway" sketched above. In this approach, the growth cycle of the current economy is not interrupted. It is redirected. Individuals do not stop spending money; they just spend it on different things. And governments do the same and adopt policies that help scale up the shifts in behavior made by individuals and groups (including local and state governments). This provides a short to medium term strategy for transitioning the global economy in fundamental ways. They are scalable and could lead to—and fund—the more radical changes required in the long run.

To picture the challenge and solution in graphic terms, imagine, first, a situation in which 20 million middle- and upper-class households reduce their income and spending by ten percent each year, every year, for five years. If they were to do so, this would put a huge dent in the economy and plunge it into a major downward spiral. Now, suppose, in contrast, those 20 million households keep their income the same—or even growing with annual raises. But imagine over the five-year period they redirect 50 per cent of their spending to acts of solidarity, political/social change, and/or ecologically sustainable investment. The economy keeps spinning. It just spins or spirals in a very different set of directions. Homeless children are fed and housed. Progressive candidates win elections. Renewable energy companies get funded. We move toward simultaneously accomplishing the first two processes of transition needed—degrowing the unsustainable and growing the sustainable.

This provides the start of a path to transition. Note, however, growing parts of the economy needed for justice and solidarity may involve increases in ecological footprint for people receiving support. If this worsens climate change and ecological collapse, it means solidarity work aimed to achieve Sustainable Development Goals may, in some respects harm the very people it seeks to help. As Wackernagel, Hanscom, and Lin have noted, such efforts may have impacts that **are** "anti-poor because with fewer resources to go around, the lowest-income people will lack the financial means to shield themselves from resource constraints, whether it is food-price shocks, weather calamities, or energy and water shortages."[65] This highlights why in redirecting funds to advance the first two processes of transition it is crucial to do so in ways that also advance the third.

With every effort, we need to urgently attend to its implications for advancing the third key transition process. How can it move us to development without material growth in ways sensitive to local context? In some cases, a country may continue with traditional macroeconomic institutions and measures of success and focus on redirecting its economy to information intensive forms of production that reduce use of natural resources in general and eliminate use of nonrenewable resources. We could picture people practicing more therapy, playing more music, engaged in more sports—but consuming less caffeine and meat, burning less fuel, and building fewer 5,000 square foot houses for couples without children. In other cases, countries may encourage people to disengage from the monetary economy. We could picture people who work less and meet their needs with DIY approaches to providing food, health, and entertainment. Imagine exchanges of education, culture, and entertainment that look more like *Wikipedia* and less like *Amazon*.

The pictures and plans we should be developing are ones in which, as with *Wikipedia*, people act as agents of history in a sharing economy rather than as *Amazon* shoppers and maximizing utility and profit. The experience of a sharing economy is common to everyone in a family where they sacrifice for others and receive gifts whose values are measured by how they advance the concerns and well-being of others and the group as a whole. Most have gladly contributed time and money to a club or informal group for the practice of a pastime that brings meaning as well as enjoyment to their lives. It is common for people to sacrifice evenings for community associations for the improvement of a school or part of their landscape that they treasure. Others sacrifice weekends and substantial chunks of income for a synagogue, church, mosque, sangha or other organization advancing their core values. These all provide models for a sharing economy that we are personally familiar with. If we are looking for ways of applying the same principles and practices in the ways in which we run farms, factories, professional service providers, hospitals and other major units of our economy, there are hosts of other examples provided by cooperatives and other innovative groups working to develop social innovations for "the Next Economy".[66]

In negotiating these third sorts of more radical, long-term transition, two traps await. First, the need for details to vary "depending on culture and tradition" may provide a too-ready excuse to limit the depth and breadth of the changes we consider and agree to. Rather than providing an excuse to settle for low hanging fruit in convenient reforms, the phrase should inspire people to draw on the most distinctive features of their culture and locale to maximize the creativity and ambition of their innovations. In the United States, for instance, people might look to traditions of rural electrification cooperatives initiated during the New Deal as ways to reframe and revolutionize growth centered public utilities.

We will need to imagine profound changes in institutions like the stock market which fuels the fever of unsustainable growth and the federal banking and monetary system that addicts us to debt and interest rates that require capital to grow faster than trees. If the trees in a forest can only grow 2 per cent a year and the rates of return on equity investments or loans are higher, then everyone owning a forest will always find a compelling economic interest in cutting down all the trees and investing their capital elsewhere. So, some very radical, long-term innovations are going to be required if we are to have a future in which there is air to breathe.

On the other hand, this does not mean we will need to abolish markets and run the economy with a military-like top-down command structure. In their most general form, markets can be understood simply as settings in which individuals or groups arrive at voluntary agreements for the exchange of resources over which they have some power and claim. In that sense, markets are an inevitable part of every political economic system. When framed as market choice vs. government intervention, debates over Capitalism vs. Socialism pose a false dilemma. Every society on the planet has a mixed economy that combines markets with other forms of collective decision-making. All economies are Mixed Economies. The question is simply, what would be the best mix? Markets, when framed well, can provide very efficient, indispensable tools for collaborative decision-making. The challenge is to ensure they are framed in ways that secure just, sustainable agreements representing voices of all parties affected.

It is possible, for example to provide a better mix that improves the lives and the vitality of communities of displaced workers in Kentucky Coal Country where Republican Rep. Hal Rogers has been working to promote the development of "Silicon Holler". In describing such efforts, Democratic Rep. Ro Khanna has noted that: "The digital revolution is reshaping our economy and society, but it continues to sideline, exclude, upend, and manipulate too many in the process." The aim should be "to advance our democratic values by empowering all of us to direct and steer these digital forces." And this must involve a mix of public and private as well as market and government initiatives because it "requires the regulation and redesign of digital platforms to prioritize online rights and quality discourse over profits." Khanna goes on, in *Dignity in a Digital Age,* to describe many such initiatives. When Congressional representatives turn to consider concrete steps to help communities like Paintsville Kentucky, the creed and the color and the name don't matter. Call it "progressive capitalism" or what you will, the key question is, what mix of initiatives can help them solve their problems in collaborative ways.[67]

In whatever mix of strategies adopted, there will be several key benefits if individuals, communities, and governments commit to "meeting the future halfway" in the transitions we seek. As individuals shift their identities from consumers to agents of historical change, their investments will endow resilience and their reduction in consumer needs will leave them more secure. If their salary drops by anything less than 50 per cent, they can maintain their personal material consumption unchanged. This means the human reality and the politics of macro-economic fluctuations will both be dramatically different—and dramatically easier to deal with.

As we strengthen safety nets for all, our society will be more resilient in the face of economic fluctuations. What makes an economic event like The Great Depression horrible is the suffering that occurs when people are suddenly without food, shelter, and health care. But what if there are safety nets for meeting people's basic needs— including their own savings in responsible investment funds? And what if there are a variety of ways in which their lives have developed significant purposes through activities as change agents? Then the ups and downs of the GDP and other traditional measures of macro-economic success become less relevant to gauging economic success. Instead, the relevant measures are tied to meeting needs like housing families. If we can keep those kinds of things down and keep other things up—like measures of growth in education and water quality— then the GDP begins to become irrelevant as a yardstick.

This process will transform our politics because it will no longer be so much about debating whose premises are right and whose conclusions should be adopted. Instead, it will be about shared problem solving and negotiations aimed to transform conflicts and provide escape from dilemmas that currently frame our politics. Elections won't be about whether "trickle down" or "bottom up" works best to grow the GDP, they will be about creative ways to get us out of the pickles we find ourselves in.

Reinventing the Corporation as Change Agent through Political Economic Entrepreneurship

This process will also transform cultures of our for-profit corporations. Currently, law, legal precedent, and cultural practice focus managers' priorities on maximizing short term profits— where these are measured by changes in cash flow in and out of the company. There are, however, increasing pressures on managers to rethink the role of profit in guiding company decisions. Corporate reports have begun to use a "triple bottom line" that looks at social and environmental indicators as well as financial ones to evaluate company performance. This is part of a trend toward a new theory of the firm that reconceptualizes its basic elements and environment. This new approach can help institutionalize and scale up key initiatives for degrowing parts of the economy that need to shrink, growing ones that need to expand, and helping in the transition towards development without material growth.[67]

The new theory of the firm reframes profit not as net cash flow, but as increases in net worth. Anything that increases the net worth of a company may be considered part of its "income" and annual "profit"; conversely, whatever diminishes net-worth is a cost that reduces profit. For instance, suppose the company is in a more competitive position because of an improved reputation, laws that favor its products over the competitors', or a healthier and more loyal set of employees. Then its net worth has gone up. It has made a "profit" in a new and more fundamental sense than if it happens to show a few extra dollars on the plus side of its cash flow.

This new theory of the firm also broadens the conception of clients. Instead of the narrow definition of them as cash paying customers, it includes any stakeholder who can be affected by company actions and might, in turn, pay back the company by increasing its net worth. If corporate hiring programs for Downs syndrome workers benefit local social services or policies for flextime benefit schools or water treatment systems benefit conservationists and fishermen, then each of these groups may, in turn, adopt policies and programs that reciprocate. They may increase the net worth of the corporation by securing it access to subsidized training for employees or tax reductions or free advertising or more flexible regulatory structures.

Implicit in these changes, is a new, broader conception of the firm's products. They do not need to be limited to the things stocked on shelves and paid for at the register. A company's potential products can include any good, service or change in the world that people would like to see. To make these potential products actual, the company simply needs to show people how they can "pay" for the product desired. But that can include any change in the world that they can make that, reciprocally, helps increase net worth. If Ben and Jerry's Ice Cream is selling them world peace, clients can help pay for it by giving them powerful word of mouth advertising. If Cummins Engine is providing environmentalists with less polluting diesel engines machines that may cost more than the industry average, the environmentalists can reciprocate by helping pass laws that "raise the playing field" and give Cummins an advantage because their competitors suddenly cannot sell their products in the US.

Along with these revolutionary innovations in conceptions of profit, cost, income, client, and product comes a redefinition of the role of the corporate leader. Economists in the past have thought of business leaders as "economic entrepreneurs" who innovate within their markets. But the new and more radical concept is that of the "political/economic entrepreneur" who innovates by transforming the markets—rewriting the rules. They get stakeholders of all sorts to create new environments for their businesses—environments in which their net worth continues to rise in a rich variety of ways.

Table 6. Two Theories of the Firm

	Rational Economic Actor	**History Maker**
Goal as:	Increase in short term profit as measured by net cash flow	Increase in long term net worth
Cost/benefit as:	Good or service for which cash is paid out	Any change in the world which decreases or increases long term net worth
Potential Clients as:	Customers who buy goods or services	Anyone who can benefit from a change in the world the firm can create
Potential Product as:	Goods or services sold	Any change in the world the firm can create
Role of leader of firm as:	Economic entrepreneur	Political/social/economic entrepreneur

Rewriting the rules requires wisdom, not just smarts. It involves metacognitive activity in which we think about our thinking and have dialogues about it with others. We step outside the framework of definitions and premises that have been used to calculate the paths to maximize profit. In that larger and more inclusive frame of collaborative dialogue, more profound and wiser paths to the future can be created.

Compared to classic business management, success in this kind of political/economic entrepreneurial activity requires a much broader range of skills in group problem solving, negotiation and conflict transformation and change agency. But there is an emerging pool of people who have for some time been developing skills as agents of historical change. Whether they are working on the "outside" to pressure and motivate corporations to change or working from within to revolutionize them, these History Makers are going to continue to push corporate culture and practice toward a fundamentally different kind of system. They will push it toward a political economy of organizations whose net worth increases steadily by moving us away from an economy driven toward material growth by the pursuit of short-term profit and national GDP. Instead, they will push us ever more toward a society where net worth is measured in many different values that communities care about. They will promote a rich network of genuine, voluntary, sustainable agreements between stakeholders of all sorts.

In Sum

This chapter has focused on how individual householders, corporate leaders and government officials might change ways they define economic choices and make economic decisions. In each case, the changes involve shifting away from algorithmic forms of inference framed by unilaterally adopted premises. The shifts are toward more inclusive forms of reasoning in collaborative dialogue with others as we try to negotiate genuine voluntary agreements that are not just "smarter" in some narrow sense but genuinely wiser. They aim to be wiser by taking all the relevant values of all the relevant stake holders into account. In this way, they seek to be more ethical in the ways described in Chapter Three. They use the Rainbow Rule as a starting point for decision making and then draw on traditions of shared problem solving, conflict transformation, peacemaking, and other forms of collaborative dialogue.

This shift to collaborative dialogue reframes economic choices as explicitly political/economic negotiations in the context of our individual lives and shared histories. We become innovative history makers and political/economic entrepreneurs transforming our options and our world through processes of human ecological development. Chapter Six will explore ways the shift to collaborative reasoning transforms our politics. Chapter Six will explore how it can transform our technologies including, most importantly, those informed by Artificial Intelligence. There we will see, further, how the forms of rationality employed in ethics, economics, politics, and tech each impact the forms that dominate in the others. And it will turn out that if we want to create an ethical AI that will be friendly to the good, we will have to bear in mind that it takes an ethical village to raise an ethical child. If we want the Smarter Planet to become a Wiser Earth, we will need to collaborate promoting wisdom wherever and whenever we reason and make choices.

Chapter Six: Politics as Nonviolent Conflict Transformation

As we scale up our activity as history makers, we inevitably begin to compete and conflict with the prevailing interests and powers of corporations, government bureaucracies, military/ police establishments, organizations advocating special interests at the expense of justice, and the leaders who coordinate all these as political/economic systems. From their point of view, it will often look as though we are at war with them. And their question will be, who will win this war?

Framed in those terms, the situation can often look rather dismal and unhopeful for change agents. How much can I really accomplish as an individual? In the face of the vast fossil fuel industry, for instance, what is the real impact of cutting my consumption in half or even more? How much can we even accomplish as small groups and local communities? We have to face the size and scale of the organizations driving GDP centered growth. They include, for instance, a complex federal banking system and massive bureaucracies providing policy and fiscal support in agriculture and industry of all sorts. How much can a local community really do to shift to a human ecological development model for its economy? With a police and military system funded by many hundreds of billions of dollars for the defense of the current national security state, what can protestors armed with signs and slogans really accomplish? If we are going to win, we have to fight a different kind of war in a digfferent kind of way.[68]

A Culture that Obscures the Nature of Peace

Part of the challenge for finding and moving forward in that different kind of way is rooted in our most common, dominant ideas about struggle and life itself. I first realized this in the 1980's when I finished graduate school in philosophy. I was looking for a topic in more applied things and got interested in researching philosophical ideas about war and peace. I quickly discovered the dominant idea of peace was, as we might say, "philosophically peculiar".

It was the Reagan era of the 1980s and there was a frightening resurgence in the Cold War that threatened the fate of the earth with new "Star Wars" weapons systems. There was the possibility of nuclear confrontations that might escalate from tactical missiles in Europe to a cascade of Intercontinental Ballistic Missiles precipitating a "Nuclear Winter" effectively ending human life on Earth. Millions in the United States were becoming anxious, scared, and even terrified and poured increasing energy into fighting against nuclear war—and any armed conflict that might lead to it. Groups all over the country were getting together on Wednesday nights to learn more about the science and technology of nuclear weapons and horrifying kinds of death and destruction. They studied proposals for halting and reversing the arms race in ways that were "SANE" or involved a simple "Nuclear Freeze". On Saturdays they would lick envelopes for mailings to mobilize ever more folks to take part in rallies, protests, and lobbying. Many were experiencing despair and getting burned out. The gallows humor joke was that by rushing in panic from one event to another, we were trying to save the future of the world with three-to-five-week plans. Occasionally we would have a party with music to build community and revive spirits. The band would play lyrics like "This could be your last chance! This could be the very last dance. No Nukes!!!"

It was in that context, that I started studying the dominant theories of peace. What I found seemed striking in two important and at first inexplicable ways. First, the dominant conception of peace—even for specialists in conflict resolution and peace studies—was, in the logical sense of the term, "negative". Peace was defined in terms of what it was not. It was not war, an absence of violence, or a diminishing in conflict. The problem from a logical point of view was this did not tell us what peace IS. Reading Simone de Beauvoir's *The Second Sex* at the time, I was struck by the analogy to her analysis of ways the nature of women was historically defined, likewise, in a logically negative way. Women were seen as not rational, lacking in strength, absent of emotional control, not primary, not the standard (masculine) norm. They were, instead, the Other, the "second" sex.

I had also been reading Martin Heidegger's studies of the understanding of Being in the Western tradition and was struck, likewise, with his claim that the meaning of Being was somehow systematically obscured in our culture, leaving us not knowing what it IS. I began to wonder if perhaps the common definitions of peace in logically negative ways might indicate that somehow the nature of peace was systematically obscured in our culture. Could it be that institutions like the ones that oppressed and marginalized women were coupled with fundamental philosophical assumptions like the ones Heidegger thought obscured the meaning of Being? Could this explain why we seemed to only understand peace in terms of what it was not?

I found a further clue in looking at linguistic usage. In English, we can say "Nations are warring in the Middle East". We have a strong, clear understanding of "war" as an active verb describing something done. But, in English, we cannot say "Nations are peaceing in Scandinavia." We seemed to lack a verb for peace. I wondered: Why? Why did we have a concept of peace as simply a state or condition defined by what it did not include? Why did we think of it simply as a static absence?[69]

The explanatory hypothesis I found most helpful was that this results from a key, widely held assumption that conflict is essential to life. The assumption was at work when economists described their discipline as "the dismal science" dealing with competition over scarce resources. More generally, throughout our culture, processes of reasoning seemed conflict centered in systematic ways suggested by George Lakoff and Mark Johnson's book, *Metaphors We Live By*. They showed how common and fundamental the metaphors of war are to the structure of "critical reasoning" where people "defend" their own "positions" by "marshalling" evidence and developing "lines of attack" in order to "outflank" the "maneuvers" of their "opponents" and "win" the argument. Military and pugilistic versions of this core metaphor structure the Anglo-Saxon tradition of legal reasoning in which the pursuit of justice is understood as a process of Prosecution and Defense battling it out in a court. I found similar conflict centered visions of life activities in the ways people understood the dynamics of politics (as conflicts over power), negotiation (as "positional bargaining"), biology (as an evolution determined by "survival of the fittest"), literature (as stories of conflicts and their resolutions), and even their own psyches (as conflicts between emotions and reasons at war within themselves).

I wondered how this conflict centered feature of our culture might connect to the "static absence" view of peace. The answer was not far to seek. If conflict is essential to human activities and even the biology of life itself, then to reduce the amount of conflict, you have to reduce the amount of life. An analogy clarifies the point. To say X is essential to Y, implies it cannot exist without it—the way water, as $H2O$ cannot exist without hydrogen. In the case of water and the hydrogen essential to it, this means that if you want to reduce or eliminate the amount of hydrogen in some container like a bottle of soda, then you need to reduce or eliminate the water in it.

What happens if conflict is essential to life, and we want to reduce or eliminate the amount of conflict in a system? We will have to reduce or eliminate the amount of life in it. If we find Washington D. C. is too conflictual for us and want a more peaceful place, we have to move somewhere less "lively". We need to seek out a peaceful "sleepy" little town. If we want full and total peace, then we need to go to the graveyard where we can "Rest in Peace".

Other researchers and activists shared the view that our conflict centered culture obscured our conception of peace and that this called for a reinvention of our culture. For many in international relations, this challenge was framed by their critique of the dominant approach to studying relationships between countries which focused on "national security" and framed it in terms of "*realpolitik*". The roots of this understanding of political rationality went back in history to Machiavelli and to the Greek historian, Thucydides, who encapsulated a key part of it in his recounting of the "Melian dialogue". He described the ambassadors of the Athenian Empire making the following point to representatives of an island they sought to submit to their rule by either alliance or conquest: "The strong take what they can and the weak yield what they must".[68] In summarizing Henry Kissinger's version of this tradition, Dinesh D'Souza captured another key aspect of it with the phrase: "America has no permanent friends or enemies, only interests."[70]

Realpolitik is a theory and practice of political rationality in which countries are conceived of as sovereign national security states that use the police to enforce their rule within their territory and use military to defend and extend it. The powers—and the options for choice—that define the ways these national security states reason and make decisions are grounded ultimately in appeals to force. In practice, their processes of reasoning are much like those in the economists' conception of the individual, self-interested economic man. Like Rational Economic Man, national security states are assumed to rationally seek maximization of their own wealth and power by looking at the net benefit of each possible choice. But there is a difference. In economics, it is assumed that there are limits to the kinds of choices people can make, limits imposed by government laws and legal systems which secure property rights. Violent assault and theft are supposed to be off limits. When economic agents get into a dispute about who owns what, they can settle it by going to court and letting the judge be the umpire. But on the *realpolitik* view, in the international arena, there is no higher law or court to rely on. Ultimately, force of arms and violence is the final arbiter of disputes. In that context, as a leading advocate of realpolitik has put it, nations have no permanent alliances, only interests—interests tied to controlling and extending their territory and the resources it offers.

A central problem with this conception of international relations is that it can make it extremely difficult for national leaders to consider—let alone commit to—any sacrifices that might help secure the commons of our planet. One of the most pressing and painful illustrations of this is the thirty-year process of negotiating a treaty on Climate Change. Despite tantalizing proposals that have offered hope, it has remained in large part a failure. Why? One helpful way to clarify its complex history is by distinguishing two types of players in the negotiations. One consists of major parties like the US, China, and Russia which are national security states armed with major militaries and nuclear weapons that give them permanent membership in the UN Security Council. Their internal military and diplomatic establishments and their economic power structures commit them to a *realpolitik* view of international relations. When their leaders steering their ship of state look out at the world, their field of view is framed by a kind of navigation dashboard provided by the reports and briefings from advisors committed to a *realpolitik* view of the world. As a result, when they look at the world, they see potential territories which are either held by their country or someone else's. They do not see commons shared by the people of the world; they see territory controlled by national security states.

In that sense, when they look up, they do not see the commons of the Sky we share on Earth, they see only the airspace of national territories. Even a Barack Obama who trained as a community organizer in Chicago or an Al Gore who wrote a major book about climate change will find, once they are placed in front of that national security state dashboard, that it is next to impossible to rationally justify major national sacrifice for the sake of the international commons. Their position in power forces them in the end to accept the dictates of rationality as it is understood in *realpolitik* terms.

The context of assumptions that frame *realpolitik* reasoning of this sort leads people to think in unilateral, one sided, monological ways. They are seeking to maximize values of territory and power for their side in the global struggles. So, they start with the data and premises provided by their intelligence agencies and then draw the conclusions that follow.

Toward a Culture of Peace

The character of that *realpolitik* reasoning and its connection to the national security state context can be even more clearly seen and understood when it is contrasted with the reasoning of some other people trying to work on Climate Change issues. This point first came home to me in 2012 in Brazil when I went with some students to the "Rio plus 20" Conference of the Parties trying to negotiate a treaty. Inside the halls of the official conference, the process was blocked. The national security states, including the US, were posturing, and playing games and getting nothing of substance done. The only real excitement and hope was coming from dramatic protests—including a major walkout that groups representing Youth, Women, Indigenous Peoples, and others had organized. But, in contrast, there were a lot of interesting and significant things going on outside.

In downtown Rio there was another summit going on, a conference of people from all around the world with representatives from Indigenous groups, women's organizations, NGOs, municipal and regional governments, banks, corporations, scientific researchers, activists, and others. In this "Peoples' Summit", they were actually doing things. Many were small steps individuals and local communities could take like changing consumption patterns and promoting renewable energy. But many were more significant.

I talked with a woman from Turkey, for example, who was part of a team that had designed and begun to implement a clearing house of information to enable large corporations like Walmart to assess the carbon footprint of their supply chains and pressure their subcontractors to get greener. I heard a presentation by a consortium of banks and major cities in Asia who were jointly investing in infrastructure to provide for both adaptation and mitigation for Climate Change. At a time when the US Secretary of State, Hillary Clinton, was offering hollow promises to perhaps contribute a few billion dollars to such work, they announced an agreement to invest a few hundred billion dollars. Why might folks in the Peoples Summit be able to do hundreds time more than national security states like the US?[71]

The answer turns on the kind of reasoning they employ because of the context they see themselves in. Leaders in cities, corporations, and other "Peoples" groups see themselves as interdependent with others. They depend on the rivers and oceans they border but do not control as sovereigns. They depend on all sorts of shared resources that include not only water and air but also public health, education, and cultural commons. They must collaborate with neighbors near and far to make their own environments sustainable. As a result, in contrast to the leaders of powerful nation states, these community members tend, much more, to frame their situation in terms of the collaborative management of commons. They look up and see the Sky.

It is worth noting for many participants in the People's Summit and similar forums, there is another important reason they are drawn to such practices. Many of them are politically marginalized and lack access to the power of the nation-state. They cannot pass and enforce laws or even effectively defend themselves in expensive legal battles. So, they try to promote the use of alternative forms of dispute resolution and mediation. They have major incentives to look at the world through the eyes of an Elinor Ostrom rather than a Machiavelli. They assume that to get things done they need to use creative negotiation, group problem solving, conflict transformation and other forms of dialogical reasoning.

The shifts this involves can take different forms. They provide a range of options for interpreting and dealing with differences between people. At the negative extreme, there is the Lose/Lose model where everyone suffers. The classic example is the vendetta vision of justice. The murder of one person in a tribe is "repaid" by the killing of someone on the attacker's side. But this, in turn, calls for its own "repayment" in a process that takes an "eye for an eye" till everyone is blind. To escape the endless cycles of retribution, one option is to shift to a Win/Lose model of justice by establishing some higher authority like a state to hold a trial and decide if the first killing was unlawful murder or justified self-defense. One side wins in the court case and the other loses—but that can put an end to it for all. The losing party is relieved of the obligation to seek vengeance, and everyone escapes the endless cycle of violence.

Win/Win models described in Chapter Three provide a further step towards a culture of peace. Even further steps can be taken by moving entirely beyond the language of winning and losing. For instance, we can stop framing the situation as a conflict to be won and start framing it as a shared problem needing a solution. Here is a little parable that illustrates the basic idea:

The Parable of Casey and the Coconuts

There was a young girl named Casey who was upset with all the fighting in the world, and she asked her neighbor, the Professor, why there was so much conflict. "Conflict is essential to life," he said.

"When you boil it down, society is like two people on a desert island where there is just one coconut and they both want it. Everything else is just adding more islanders and different kinds of coconuts."

"I don't see why that has to be a conflict" she said. "What if one wants to eat what's inside and the other wants the shell to make a drinking cup? Then they just share a problem—how to take off the shell."

"But normally people want the whole coconut!" he replied.

"Well even then it would depend on why," she insisted. "Suppose they each wanted to grow a tree. Then they would just share the problem of finding the best place to plant it."

"Look," said the Professor, "maybe there are times when you can reinterpret conflicts as shared problems, but that is not normal real life. Normally people want the whole coconut all to themselves."

"But they could still see that as a shared problem!" she persisted.

The Professor was on the verge of exasperation: "Really? And what is that problem, my little friend?"

"Not enough coconuts" she replied.

Part of what Casey is doing here is simply applying a couple of basic negotiation strategies in a systematic way. She keeps focusing on the underlying interests and she keeps trying to multiply options. Her assumption that this will always work can seem unrealistic and even exasperating to a conflict-centered thinker like the Professor because he finds it difficult to imagine there will always—or even usually—be a shared solution that can be found. From Casey's point of view, in contrast, the world is a rich and complicated place in which creative and imaginative people can usually, if not always, come up with shared solutions.

This difference in points of view does not boil down to a question of fact. It is a question of interpretation. The same situation can be viewed either as a conflict or as a shared problem. As Casey points out at the very end, even the hardest of situations that seem to present a conflict can be recast as a shared problem—by sharing it as a hard problem.

There may be a variety of reasons for preferring one interpretation or the other. Perhaps in some specific context, the conflict centered approach will seem more familiar and easier to adopt or the adrenaline of the moment will make it hard to resist. In some cases, people have invested heavily in developing "healthy competition" or "creative responses to conflict" to get away from Lose/Lose approaches. For them, this may reduce the appeal to looking further for shared problem-solving approaches to differences.

On the other hand, the shared problem approach can offer important advantages. It can be intriguing and promising in its results. It may provide a way to let go of anger and immerse in creative intellectual challenges. Further, sharing the problem has the advantage of pooling problem-solving resources to improve things for all. The shared problem approach can help us move toward a culture of peace because it provides a useful metaphor for interpreting the situation. It escapes the "two islanders and one coconut" view of life.

Birth provides a second basic metaphor that is helpful in similar ways. In looking at the human experience of birth, we find there is enormous difference and struggle involved. There is pain, risk, and even the possibility of death. It is just as visceral and vital as combat in war and yet, it offers a way of looking at life in which there is no conflict, no competition. Neither the pregnant woman nor the creature struggling in her womb are trying to "beat" or win against the other. The physical integrity and social identity of each is at issue, but each succeeds only in so far as the other does as well. In the normal case, the process transforms them both. The pregnant woman and fetus become mother and child in an emerging family relationship.

The process of birth can be a powerful metaphor for interpreting differences we have with others in all sorts of contexts. When a family differs over what to do with a debt or an inheritance, we may view the situation as pregnant with possibilities. The same may be true of a community dealing with ethnic differences or bordering nations at odds over what to do with shared watersheds. It can be extremely fruitful to view these situations as ones in which we are struggling to give birth to a new set of relationships, a new kind of partnership or community. The project is our "baby" and we need to care and labor in order to bring it forth into the world and go on to nurture its continued growth. In doing so, we can expect to find ourselves transformed—whether we are the proud parents of the project or are simply present playing supporting roles as midwives for the birth and nurses for the aftercare.

This birth metaphor can be elaborated and applied in a wide variety of ways. Feminist accounts of "ethics of care" provide an important and fruitful source of theoretical insights and practical methods for using birth and nurturing metaphors to advance cultures of peace. Along with Judith Fetterly, they can invite us to ask ourselves:

"[W]hat our political, legal, philosophical, medical, ethical, and religious systems would look like if they assumed as normative the experience of a body capable of creating another body? They might propose that women's bodies, with their ability to carry another body inside them, provide a compelling model of human experience, because as humans our experience is one of separation and interconnection, interdependence and dependence, rights, and responsibilities—coexisting."[72]

In pursuing the development of birth and nurture metaphors, it is important to keep in mind that there are a great many varied traditions of parenting. Some are not nearly as positive and promising as others. But in many traditions of family care, it is possible to find models and metaphors in which men and women can both be involved in nonviolent, constructive forms of parental love. There are, as Sara Ruddick has noted, "mother-identified movements in the United States and around the world that deploy the symbols and passions of mothering in struggles against war, local violence, racism, ruthless employment practices, environmental destruction and institutionalized neglect." In them, we can find forms of peacemaking that are "latent in maternal practice" and provide a kind of "maternal nonviolence as a 'truth-to-be-made'". This form of nonviolence can be practiced by men as well as women and provide the basis for inventing a politics of care and justice that moves us towards a culture of peace.[73]

Birth and shared problem solving are just two of the powerful metaphors and models that can move us towards cultures of peace. A third is the metaphor of the team. Whether they are competing with another group or simply trying to achieve some shared goal as a firefighter or surgery unit, team members can see themselves as collaborating with each other. They view the success of each as interdependent on the success of all. Similarly, the view of life as a dance provides an evocative and systematic way to understand our differences while working collaboratively with complex challenges.

Buddhism, Christianity, and other religious traditions that celebrate practices of love or compassion also offer alternative vocabularies to interpret and deal with differences. Following Socially Engaged Buddhists like Thich Nhat Hanh, for instance, we can see ourselves as mutual parts of a process in which understanding of the Fourfold Noble Truths and the Eightfold Noble Path enable us to participate in interdependent co-arising.[74]

For many Christians, the Easter story provides a paradigm of agape love in which the sacrifice of self for other—even the "enemy"—can bring forgiveness, redemption, radical transformation, and peace.

Robin Wall Kimmerer has shown how in drawing on Indigenous peoples' conceptions of ecological interdependence, humility, gift exchange, and mutual respect between people and other species, we can frame a life that is dramatically different from the win/lose struggles of the modern economy and nation state. Instead, we can shift toward a culture of peace that makes the practice of braiding sweetgrass into a central metaphor for ways our differences are woven into our collective lives.[75]

In the accompanying chart, the lines to the right of the Win/Win category branch out, suggesting the open-ended ways models for a culture of peace can be explored and developed. In many cases they may be usefully combined, allowing people to use the metaphors, practices, and strategies of one with another. For instance, folks may look for ways to brainstorm a possible problem solution by coaching someone in their struggle to give birth to a new idea as they pass the ball from one player to another in the delicate dance of co-evolution. These ways of looking at the world all provide ways of breaking away from the conflict centered frameworks that dominate our political economy.

Figure 7. Models and Metaphors for Dealing with Differences between People

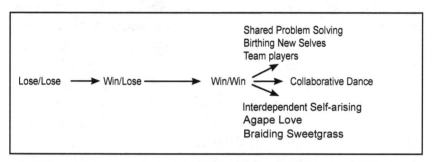

What might our planet look like if this were the way politics were practiced at national and global scales? What if we shifted from the monological reasoning of realpolitik as practiced by national security states to different forms of dialogical reasoning practiced by Peoples groups whose power did not rest on police, military, and claims for territorial sovereignty? These questions have been explored by people from a wide variety of religious and cultural traditions including those influenced by Gandhi, Wangari Maathai, Thich Nhat Hanh, Dorothy Day, Martin Luther King, Lech Walesa, the Chipko activists of India, Mennonites, Quakers, and others.

Imaging a World Without Weapons

In the 1980s, in order to explore and develop systematic alternatives to the national security state system, Elise Boulding developed a visionary method for reinventing our culture through "Imaging a World Without Weapons." She was a Quaker who had already spent decades forging a practice of peacemaking that integrated research, education, and action when she began to partner in her work with Warren Ziegler. Warren had been experimenting for quite a while with methods of what he called "Imaging the Future". I was fortunate to be able to train with them in 1988.

Elise saw the essential need for activists to be guided and motivated not just by a vision of what they opposed, but, more profoundly, of what they sought. Most activists, if asked to define peace, had little more in mind than the simple end to war and the avoidance of nuclear holocaust. It was not much to inspire warmth, fellow feeling, vision, generosity, and hope. So, Elise began working with Warren to develop a workshop format in which people would actively imagine, in glorious detail, a dramatically different world, a "World Without Weapons". The assumption was that such a world would take time to come into being, but that it was important that it not be so far in some utopian future that it was disconnected from peoples' lives. Thirty years into the future turned out to work well for the exercise. It was long enough for dramatic change. To drive this point home, Elise would have us think about the thirty years of changes in the world between the start of WWII and the landing of the first person on the moon—with the arrival in between of the creation of new countries all around the world, the transformation of economies and political systems in Europe, Japan and elsewhere, the Green Revolution, the US Civil Rights Movement, and so on. Thirty years was also, on the other hand, short enough to enable us to envision the changes as something we could realize in our own lives—the way someone might visualize paying off a house mortgage or raising a child.[76]

The workshop was a three-day, in-depth format. It used a rich variety of methods for setting goals, warming up imaginations, and then actually imagining ways to jump into the future, thirty years from now. These enabled people to explore with all their sensory modes in inward imaging rather like lucid dreaming. The format also included sharing images—and further enriching them—with drawings, stories, skits and a wide variety of small group activities incorporating critical intellectual analysis and artistic expression. By the end of day two, participants accumulated dozens of flip chart pages, drawings, lists of political economic principles, descriptions of social structures, world maps, scenic views of villages, urban plans, pictures of new technology, song lyrics, and a wide variety of other documents describing the future world they had chosen to visit. Then Elise and Warren would have them perform what seemed, at first, an even more incredible feat. They would immerse into the inward imaging mode, and there, thirty years in the future, start to recall what had "happened", a year previously. Images of this "future history" would somehow come—often with compelling detail and astonishing insight. Things that were very puzzling about that world thirty years in the future would suddenly become understandable as they worked their way back, remembering 1, 5, 10, then 15 years back . . . until they reached the year their voyage into the future had first begun, the actual present of, say, 1988.

I trained with Elise and Warren in that year and went on to lead or co-lead a number of these workshops. It was always an inspiring experience. I never ceased to be amazed at the imaging abilities of ordinary people without any special gifts or training. Elise would invite us to lie down quietly and then picture a very tall hedge someplace outside. The world we wanted to visit, thirty years in the future, was on the other side of that hedge. What we needed to do was simply "image" ourselves exploring the hedge and finding a way past it—over, under, around . . . whatever worked for us. We could take our time, it was just important to actually form images and use all the senses of sight, sound, smell, touch, humidity, temperature and so on that we had "warmed up" in a previous exercise. For some it was almost effortless. They would spot a hole in the hedge and just walk right through and explore. Others took more time . . . perhaps they would have to squirm through a patch of thicket or find a way to climb over the hedge or dig under. Somehow that struggle with engaged imaging at the start prepared people and served as a kind of catalyst for an extraordinary experience. It helped them then see, hear, and touch the world they then encountered. For instance, if the goals they had set for the future included some kind of health care for all, they might in their wanderings spot an interesting vehicle that would turn out to be delivering health care door to door. They would find they could approach people and ask them questions about how things work "now" in this future. And they would get surprising and very interesting answers about how life stories and situations in this future unfolded and how institutions and social structures worked.[77]

For instance, on one visit to a future in which key goals I had set concerned education, I came out of some woods into a large field where a long, low, tractor-like rig was pulling a load of potatoes toward a barn in the distance. It was powered by children who were having a fine time burning up their excited energy pedaling it. At the same time, they were using computer screens mounted in front of them for some seminar-like learning and carrying on an animated discussion as a group, rolling along with the load of potatoes they had picked. I followed them along and when we arrived at the farm center, I met an adult who explained more. He told me about ways education, agriculture, and renewable energy programs were all getting integrated at this community farm I had stumbled into as well as elsewhere in the world. He took me into a commons room with a large screen on one wall and introduced me to a kind of AI entity with a limited but interesting personality. It was helping the network of community farms coordinate their work in education as well as their plantings, harvests, and marketing strategies.

For me, experiences in these Imaging a World Without Weapons workshops were often remarkably vivid and unexpected, like a lucid dream. Not having done visual art much and being more of a "words and talk" person, I had never practiced active visualization and was surprised to actually be able to "see" so much—and even touch and feel it. I was surprised to encounter revealing sights and explanations that just came, like puzzle solutions from the unconscious or from a dream or . . . from the "future". The apparent magic of this was not easy for Warren or Elise to explain. But it was easy for people in the workshops to accept because it worked—not just for gifted but for ordinary folks as well. Or, perhaps better said, the workshop revealed that each of us ordinary folks seemed to be born, unbeknownst to us, with some "extraordinary" abilities to play like happy kids as natural born time travelers.

It was very helpful to have a workshop designer and facilitator who had been trained in the rich set of specific skills and methods that Warren had developed over a career of experimenting with imaging techniques in diverse settings. What was perhaps equally helpful was the spirit of Quaker process Elise brought to the work. In the decades of her life as a Quaker, she had developed abilities in creative problem solving and communal discernment in a variety of contexts that provided pathfinding approaches to peacemaking. As a parent, she had reflected on ways to practice "The Tao of Family". It allowed individuals to be in conflict in the context of safe, secure, loving familial commitments underlying the differences they explored in the process of defining themselves and maturing into individuals. As a teacher she had explored practices of "Children's Creative Response to Conflict" offering alternatives to disciplinary-centered approaches to traditional schooling. As a woman, she had experimented with feminist consciousness raising circles using more horizontal, egalitarian structures of power and facilitation to share concerns, develop insights and cultivate projects for collective action. In working with community groups, she explored methods of participatory action research. These drew on community based, dialogical approaches to problem-posing education and collective learning from Paulo Freire, bell hooks and others. In working to help found, grow, and/or maintain organizations like the Consortium on Peace Research, Education and Development (COPRED) she explored a variety of negotiation skills of the sort studied by the Harvard Negotiation Project as well as methods of cross-cultural dialogue and conflict transformation of the kind pursued by people working on "deep conflicts" in Ireland, the Middle East and elsewhere.[76]

In facilitating imaging workshops, she would bring seeds of all these traditions of peacemaking and social transformation into the mix. In informal activities nurturing participants and helping groups reflect on their work, she would invite them to enrich their imaging with visions drawn from these emerging traditions of practice and integrate them into a more systematic understanding of what an alternative civilization might be like.

The workshop process and visionary seeds Elise and others brought enabled people to find and explore exciting possible futures where they could discover new social structures and ways of life and experience a world where their fondest hopes were realized in realistic, dramatically fuller ways. Health care was assured for all, organic farming was feeding humans and enhancing other creatures, education was a praxis of liberation, families were free of violence, and cultural exchange was more like a sacrament and less like a conquest. It included worlds where the things that used to function as weapons served new functions—think of military tanks adapted for ecological reclamation. Conversely, the functions that used to be served by weapons were now served in new ways. Think of replacing armed police intervening in domestic violence disputes with savvy social workers—or replacing armed troops defending borders with "troops" trained and equipped with Gandhian methods of nonviolent direct-action.[77]

For me, one lesson came in the fall of 1989. In facilitating these workshops with a wide variety of folks, I had found an interesting pattern in closing sessions for debriefing. Someone would take a deep breath, sigh, and then comment: "Well . . . you know, we have come up with some really beautiful images. I really love these visions of the future!!! But . . . in the end, let's be realistic. Peace in Northern Ireland? The end of Apartheid in South Africa? The liberation of Eastern Europe? The fall of the Berlin Wall? . . . not in my lifetime. It's just not possible." They were not alone in this view. In 1988, the advocates of *realpolitik* had a profoundly pessimistic view of those situations. For instance, for them, the threat of escalation into mutually assured destruction with nuclear weapons meant there were absolutely no scenarios in which their weapons could successfully liberate Eastern Europe without destroying it and much of the rest of the world as well.

Then came the big lesson in November of 1989 when, in fact, the Berlin Wall did fall. Eastern Europe was radically transformed. It was not liberated by the armies of the United States and NATO, despite the fact that they were armed to the teeth with nuclear weapons. It was liberated by nonviolent activists who were inspired by Gandhi, Gene Sharp, Lech Walesa, and other advocates of nonviolence. Unarmed activists liberated Poland as part of the Solidarity Movement. Eastern Europe was liberated by leaders like the Czech playwright Vaclav Havel who created new ways of resistance through dramatic nonviolent action and performance. It was liberated in extraordinary new ways in Estonia through a "Singing Revolution". Once the process started, it spread like wildfire and took on a life of its own. At the Berlin Wall, for instance, once the first brick was taken down, there was sudden, impending sense that the fall of the whole thing was imminent. The lesson for me was clear. Typically, radical change continues to seem absolutely impossible, right up until the moment when it suddenly begins to seem absolutely inevitable. This transition is exemplified by many social transformations including, for instance, the end of Apartheid in South Africa and, more recently, the arrival of Marriage Equality in the United States. It is a lesson that can give us hope in even the darkest of times.[78]

Nonviolence, *Satyagraha*, and *Swaraj*

We can draw depth and strength for such hope from successes of non-violent movements in the past and, importantly, their varied forms and reasons for their efficacy. How do they work? And why? How can people like Gandhi or Lech Walesa, armed only with bodies and spirits defeat empires armed with machine guns or nuclear weapons? One of the best systematic introductions to this is a study of Gandhi by Joan Bondurant, *The Conquest of Violence*. For many readers, it is full of important surprises. One is the diversity of Gandhi's projects and approaches to achieving his life goal of liberating India from oppressive British rule. He saw this as a very comprehensive task because he did not just want to expel the British military and industrial regime, he wanted to create a society based on nonviolent, self-reliant Indian traditions of education, health, municipal governance, business, agriculture, religion, et cetera. So he was actively involved in starting schools, clinics, village reforms, clothing manufactures, R&D on appropriate technology, alternative dispute resolution systems, inter-caste programs, interfaith worship, and so on.[79]

Some critics emphasize ways he at times failed to transcend paternalistic, sexist, caste and/or racist preconceptions and values. In assessing any historical figure, we should look to tell as full and rounded a story as we can and hold them accountable for failings just as we would expect future historians to hold us accountable. Ramachandra Guha's biography, *Gandhi 1914-1948,* provides an especially scrupulous, exhaustively researched, insightful effort to arrive at a balanced assessment of Gandhi's life work. Part of what it makes abundantly clear is the extraordinarily broad scope of his ambitions as a change agent. Whatever the failings were in his practice, his intentions were sweeping enough to provide us with an important source of inspiration.[80]

The comprehensive character of his goals is reflected in a quote from his manifesto work, *Hind Swaraj or Indian Home Rule*: "Civilization is not an incurable disease. But we should never forget that the English people currently are afflicted by it."[81] He believed that the civilization they were trying to import and impose in India was "diseased" because its institutions were tied ultimately to a political and industrial system grounded on violence as the ultimate arbiter of power. This inevitably led to the unilateral, monological imposition of policies for running all aspects of society—policies which ignored others' points of view and claims of justice and truth.

There were two keys to his understanding of ways this could be changed, and he introduced two novel terms to describe them: *satyagraha* and *swaraj*. *Satyagraha* was a term he coined, by combining "*satya*" for truth and "*graha*" for clinging or holding on, to describe the various strategies of nonviolence with which he experimented. The boycotts, the sit-ins, the fasting, the courting of arrest by violating unjust laws . . . on his view, these were all ways of holding on to truth in a loving and nonviolent manner. They helped him and his followers to discern, demonstrate and defend moral truths.

Discernment was aided because nonviolent actions involved sacrifice and self-suffering. Someone might, for example, risk arrest—and perhaps a beating or worse—by violating an unjust law against making salt. In considering doing so, the threat of arrest or a beating would serve to give her pause and motivate some serious personal discernment. How clear was she that this law was truly unjust and this violation justified? Had she taken sufficient pause for reflection—and perhaps prayer and fasting—so as to be sure she was ready to risk so much clinging to this truth?

Demonstration of moral truth could come through ways her sacrifice might cause pause and reflection on the part of the oppressors imposing and enforcing the unjust law. In seeing a person suffer as a "*satyagrahi*", an oppressor might acquire admiration for the courage of protestors and start seeing them less as ignorant, uncivilized "coolies" and more as human beings with a strong sense of dignity and deserving of respect. In some cases, their hearts might "melt" and go through some even more fundamental change in attitude and behavior towards ending the oppressive regime.

The defense of the moral truths could come through ways nonviolent direct action can exercise often decisive physical or social power in the world. This is an aspect of nonviolence theorists like Gene Sharp have emphasized. For oppressive governments to function, they must get people to consent to their rule and obey their orders. If people withdraw consent and refuse to obey, power erodes and disappears. Non-violent struggle can achieve this with coordinated strategy. It requires creativity and ingenuity using locally adapted versions of the hundreds of tactics Sharp and others have documented. These range from more mild-mannered activities of protest like petitioning, marches, and rallies to more assertive and disruptive forms of direct action like sit-ins, boycotts, strikes, civil disobedience and creating parallel institutions. The first sorts are simple kinds of protest associated with social movements since the late 1700's. These are often used to build participation in a campaign because they involve less risk and personal suffering and yet serve to bring attention to the cause, undermine the legitimacy of the oppressor, and begin the withdrawal of consent. The second, more assertive sort can involve much more suffering for people clinging to moral truth, but it can also cost the oppressors in power and wealth and make it impossible for them to carry out their own plans.[82]

The sit-ins that students led to integrate restaurants in Nashville in 1960 illustrated this clearly. Though bullied by local thugs and police in the process of getting arrested, the students maintained disciplined order and refused to fight back or escalate the violence against them. But they did not back off either. They continued to fill the restaurants with young people willing to be arrested and fill the local jail with arrestees. Over the course of several months this disrupted the downtown shopping district so significantly that local businesses were losing money. In the end, local white business leaders asked the mayor to negotiate an end to the regime of Jim Crow segregation. Some of them may have done so out of newfound respect for the Black community as a result of the students' demonstrations of courage, self-respect and commitment to moral truth. But many did so because they found the students' non-violent direct action was simply too effective in defending their moral claims—it just cost too much money to keep imposing Jim Crow.[83]

Most people in the US are familiar with some version of Gandhian nonviolent satyagraha as practiced in the American Civil Rights Movement or elsewhere. What is often less familiar is the systematic strategy for using it which Gandhi framed in terms of his conception of *"swaraj"*. That term has the same root as *"raja"* (king), and the phrase "the British raj" used to refer to the British rule over India. Literally, *"swaraj"* means self-rule or home rule. Gandhi titled his perhaps most important manifesto for liberating his homeland from the Brits: *"Hind Swaraj or Indian Home Rule"*. He was always clear, however, that his goal was not just to replace British rulers with Indians. Instead, he sought an alternative form of government with new institutions, based in nonviolence, to administer law, education, health, economic production and the rest of society. Central to his strategy for achieving *swaraj* was the creation of such institutions—even while the British were still ruling India. He got lawyers and their clients to withdraw from the British courts and help set up alternative institutions for mediating disputes without the appeal to police for enforcement. He got professors and students to withdraw from official institutions and establish alternative schools and universities to teach Indian students in Indian languages to advance Indian culture and technology rather than simply imitate the British. He got masses of people to stop purchasing clothes from the exploitative industrial system that shipped Indian cotton to Manchester and then sold manufactured apparel back to Indians. Instead, he got millions of people to start making their own *"khadi"* clothing. His core vision was that once parallel institutions like these grew into a systematic and pervasive home rule or *swaraj*, the British would become irrelevant, and they would simply leave India.[84]

When it comes to liberating people from oppressors and defending them from aggressors, how effective is this combination of methods of non-violent *satyagraha* with *swaraj*, the systematic development of parallel institutions? Does it just work when you have a charismatic and creative genius leading it? Does it only work when the opponent is relatively genteel and restrained in the ways in which they use violence? Can it be used to defend against vicious dictators?

Erica Chenoweth and Maria Stephan sought answers to these questions using modern statistical techniques of social science.[84] What they found was surprising. They assembled data on hundreds of campaigns between 1900 and the early 2000s defending against oppressive regimes or overthrowing them. They compared success rates of violent and nonviolent campaigns. What they found was, first, that neither violent nor nonviolent campaigns always succeeded, neither was foolproof. But second, they found that nonviolent campaigns were, on average, more successful than violent ones in changing regimes, especially in more recent years.[85]

Table 8. Success Rates of Nonviolent and Violent Campaigns 1900-2006

	Nonviolent	Violent
Success	51%	32%
Partial Success	23%	10%
Failure	20%	60%

Figure 9. Success Rates by Decade 1940-2006

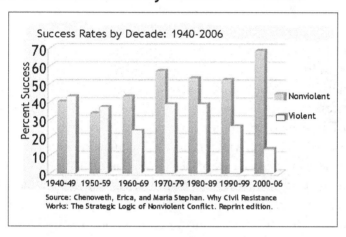

Source: Chenoweth, Erica, and Maria Stephan. Why Civil Resistance Works: The Strategic Logic of Nonviolent Conflict. Reprint edition.

Table 10. Post-Conflict Civil War Onset

	Nonviolent	Violent
Post-Conflict Civil War within 10 years	28%	42%

Trans-armament

Just how far could we go in the process of beating swords into plowshares and shifting national defense systems from violent to non-violent methods? Could Russia, China or the US engage in trans-armament, eventually decreasing most of their reliance on lethal weapons—perhaps at some point abandoning weapons of mutually assured destruction entirely? Could one do so even if the others did not? In a book on *Making Europe Unconquerable*, Sharp developed a useful way to frame this research. His proposal is to picture resources defending the territory and interests of a nation as a giant pie that includes slices of army, navy, air force and so on. Once we do so, we may then ask ourselves how big of a slice each branch of the military or weapon system should receive. He proposes we answer this question by asking how effective each weapon system is in deterring aggression from other nations. For instance, if we compare spending a $100 million on tanks to attack an invader vs. spending the same on trenches or improvised explosive devices to impede invasion, what is the return on investment for each?[87]

The invader will look at the benefits of invading and the costs of doing so when deciding whether to attack. The measure of the net effectiveness of defense systems will be how much they lower the attacker's net benefits minus costs for invasion. We can then assess the value of the tanks vs. the trenches and IEDs by asking how much each serves to shift the net benefits for the invader down below zero as far as possible. What Sharp points out is that once we frame our defense pie in these terms, then we can note that there are always, already, pieces of it—however slim—that are forms of nonviolent resistance and response. That non-violent slice of the pie is increased in any way which makes it easier for a populace to remain unruly and disobedient or befriend invading soldiers and make it hard for them emotionally to attack. The Soviets encountered these forms of resistance when they invaded Eastern European countries throughout the Cold War. They also encountered other kinds of nonviolent sanctions, international boycotts and other nonviolent pressures that increased the costs of military invasion. In fact, the skills and resources for resistance which they encountered increased in successive episodes making their interventions take increasingly longer in East Germany, Hungary and Czechoslovakia—from mere days and weeks to long months.

By the time of the resurgence of Polish Solidarity in the late 1980's, such resources were sufficient to deter the Soviets from invading Poland when it broke free from their control. This is what precipitated the end of the Cold War. The Soviets did not let Poland, East Germany, Czechoslovakia, Estonia, and other countries leave their Warsaw Pact because of a fear of Ronald Reagan's nuclear weapons. They knew just as well as Reagan's advisors did that there were absolutely no military scenarios in which a launch of nuclear weapons could end well for the US or any of its allies. Instead, the Soviets let those countries go because the net benefits of using military force to keep them in their domain were outweighed by the costs of doing so. People Power had made those countries ungovernable and unconquerable from a very practical and political point of view.

Could such methods be extended to provide for the defense of countries that currently rely on nuclear weapons like Russia, the US and China? Sharp's proposal for Trans-armament frames this very differently than traditional proposals for disarmament. Rather than simply wait out the long and often fruitless negotiations for mutual disarmament, it proposes that such countries simply look, rationally, at their national defense pies and ask how increases in the size of the non-violent slices might compare with other slices in terms of net benefits. This does three key things. First, it makes trans-armament a practical alternative that can be developed through R&D over time. Second, it lets nations undertake this on their own, independently of treaty negotiations with potential enemies. Third, it moves trans-armament progress along in steps and stages rather than requiring some immediate leap into a new system.[88]

This strategy of trans-armament assumes that the opponent is acting in some minimally rational way, calculating likely costs and benefits of their options. If an opponent lacks sound sources of intelligence or lacks the ability to process them effectively, then they may plunge into war despite the strength of the non-violent defenses of a country. But this is equally a risk in situations where countries rely on violent weapons for traditional defense. Many if not most wars start, in fact, in the context of gross miscalculations of likely costs and benefits. Russia's invasion of Ukraine in 2022 is a dramatic case in point. There is nothing foolproof or inevitably more effective about nonviolent methods—or violent methods. Both forms of defense improve or become obsolete through effort, innovation, and a certain amount of luck in the fog of struggle. But the choice to invest in research and development of nonviolent techniques does offer one major advantage. It offers the hope of strengthening a method whose results can be rooted in moral truths and advance their cause by helping us discern, demonstrate, and defend them. It offers the hope of moral legitimacy as well as victory.

Sharp's approach represents a distinct strain amongst theories of nonviolence. It emphasizes conceiving of it as a form of struggle just like guerilla warfare. For him, the key difference is that it employs a different set of weapons. However, part of the reason that nonviolent "weapons" can function effectively is because they enable folks using People Power to make moral claims. By refusing to attack their opponents, they can lay claim to a moral high ground that is easier to defend and harder to attack. They can deny oppressive rulers and would be conquerors the legitimacy that greases the wheels of obedience. At times they may even be able, as Gandhi would say, to "melt the hearts" of their opponents. Framed in these terms, nonviolence can be seen not just as a weapon to be used in a struggle but as form of persuasion that can serve a vital function in a process of collaborative reasoning. It can serve a role in ethical dialogue comparable to the role of experiment in scientific discourse.[89]

Beyond *Realpolitik* and Moral Relativism: Pursuing Emergent Objective Moral Truths

Because, as we noted earlier, *satyagraha* can enable us to discern, demonstrate, and defend moral truths, it is able to play an extraordinarily important role in moral inquiry and social change. It can serve a function in ethical investigations parallel to the role experiments play in empirical sciences—the testing of moral hypotheses. The activities of "clinging to truth" can enable us to discern, demonstrate, and defend moral truths about, for instance, the dignity of all people, the justice of equal treatment before the law, rights to protection from oppression, and guarantees of sovereignty.

It is important to be clear about nuances of functions satyagraha can serve. It does not infallibly guarantee correct results in ethics any more than experiment infallibly guarantees correct results in science. But it does provide a method for successive, repeated testing which can serve to correct mistakes and advance insight. The truths discovered are not absolute, perfectly exact, or context free. In this way they differ from Euclidean geometry. Instead, they are emergent, approximate, and dependent on context as are truths in earth science and evolutionary history. Similarly, they partake in the kind of objectivity which moves from being partial and one sided to more inclusive and complete, from vague to more accurate, and from fleeting to stable. These are the characteristics of moral truths like those given evocative expression in the opening lines of the U. S. Declaration of Independence and Martin Luther King's "I Have a Dream" speech. In discerning such truths, nonviolent methods offer us a path out of moral relativism. They give us ways to critique our own culture and its values and to bear witness to transcultural moral truths in our dealings with others.

They also offer an alternative to *realpolitik* which bases much of its appeal on the claim that it is the most "realistic" worldview. When the Athenian embassy to Melos advocated it, their core argument was, in effect: "Get real. You know how the world works. People who have the might, decide what is right. In this case it is us. Capitulate. Don't waste time blathering on about justice and such." What the methods of Gandhian *satyagraha* and related traditions of nonviolent direct-action offer, however, in response to this, is a method that not only enables the oppressed and colonized to discern and demonstrate moral truth claims but to go one step further and defend them.

It is important to keep in mind that these truths are emergent. They always, already come into our consideration in some context. The fact that they can transcend our particular culture does not mean they can be articulated in culture-free, purely abstract, transcendent ways. The transcending they do is transitional. They lead us out of more flawed views toward more morally acceptable, truthful ones. They provide directions for growth rather than recipes for instant perfection. Their emergent character typically involves us in tensions and contradictions as we try to cultivate a fuller, better-rounded, inclusive, wiser understanding of how to live in right relationships with ourselves and others.

This is part of the reason efforts to articulate objective moral principles can seem to lead to paradox and confusion when professional societies, international agencies, social movements, participants in inter-faith dialogues, and others pursue them. For example, since 2015, a wide variety of efforts to frame ethical principles for work in data management and artificial intelligence have been undertaken. A common pair of principles widely proposed include versions of transparency and privacy. There are a variety of reasons each of these might be valued in different contexts. But, in the abstract, they would seem to be at loggerheads. The more transparent a data base or AI operating system is, the easier it will be to use it to find out things about people that limit or eliminate their privacy. However, by viewing these values as emergent in the context of collaborative dialogue, we can, in concrete and particular contexts, negotiate appropriate ways of accommodating relevant interests and values each represents.

This emergentist view of values enables us to deal constructively with apparent contradictions arising when values are given abstract formulations as principles for ethical inference. It also enables us to deal more appropriately and ethically with the differences between communities, cultures, and civilizations that call for significantly different interpretations of the values. So, for instance, understandings of appropriate norms for privacy can vary depending on the extent to which the values, guiding visions and everyday practices of a community emphasize shared, collective projects and responsibilities versus individual autonomy and independence. Members of a religious monastery or a Yucatecan *ejido* who live in strongly communal ways may legitimately view questions about privacy very differently than New York professionals in business or medicine trying to protect proprietary information.

One of the benefits of working within a single, relatively homogenous, and coherent cultural tradition is that it can provide a more stable context for the negotiation of emergent objective values that become widely adopted as part of a collective consensus around issues like education, health care, and security. Conversely, many challenges in negotiating agreements and treaties at the international level arise from the multipolar, diverse character of communities, cultures, and nations participating in the dialogue. On some issues, the challenge of finding agreement may prove so difficult or elusive that we may be best off accepting a very minimal form of "agreeing to disagree". However, there are clearly some issues where global accords and concrete plans of action are indispensable to avoid existential threats. With collective threats like ecological collapse, wars of mutually assured destruction, and the creation of runaway technologies like AI, the question is not whether collaborative dialogue will be easy. The question is whether there is any alternative.

In the struggle to not only image but actually create a "World Without Weapons", a central task is to shift the ways we practice and institutionalize our reasoning in every realm of politics. We currently have a world government system dominated by sovereign national security states practicing the monological forms of thinking associated with *realpolitik*. We need to shift to a system that thinks and acts through dialogical forms of reasoning. When disputes cannot be resolved by talk, we must institutionalize the use of People Power and nonviolence instead of violence as the ultimate arbiter. The institutions for doing this are still in the making. But there are plenty of precedents and inspiring models to draw on.[88]

The enormity of the task of achieving a form of global *swaraj* through *satyagraha* may seem daunting—even "absolutely impossible". But the urgency of our situation is fast making that change "absolutely inevitable". The existential threats of climate change, extinction, war, and runaway technology can only be addressed through institutions of global dialogue grounded in nonviolent efforts to share the commons that make life possible on this planet. It is precisely this growing urgency that will allow us to push and persuade—to discern, demonstrate and defend the truth that just such a massive, systematic change can and must come—and soon.

Like the nineteenth century end of slavery—we'll end fossil fuel dependency! Like the fall of the Berlin Wall—we"ll make a change! Like an old time spiritual revival—or a Youtube video gone viral! With billion of us on bicycles—we'll make a change! Cut by half our material consumption. Invest in real creative destruction! Start a political eruption—make a change! With piles of political donations—campaigning door to door in conversations. We'll take back the governments of our nations—make a change!

There's a change that's a comin'!
There's a change that's a comin'!
There's a change that's a comin' . . . soon!
And it's comin', comin', comin' like a hurricane, comin',
comin', comin' like a drought!
And it's comin', comin' . . . like a glacier melting . . .

*Cause we're comin',
comin' like a hurricane!
We're comin', comin' like
a hurricane!*[89]
*We're comin', comin' like
a hurricane SOON!! TWO!
THREE! NOW!!!!!!!!!!!*[90]

Chapter Seven: Artificial Intelligence as Collaborative Wisdom

Corporations in pursuit of profit and governments in pursuit of military power are pushing for ever "smarter" technologies. Advances are rushing us towards a future full of smart things that are all interconnected in a web run by increasingly smarter artificial intelligence. It is as though the future is a new country and we have parachuted into an ever more novel, diverse, foreign culture. Like a study abroad student thrust into a new society, or an immigrant thrust into a new land, we can experience intense disorientation—what Alvin Toffler described as a cultural "future shock".[91] And we are increasingly left to wonder: Where is the true wisdom in all this allegedly smart stuff? Perhaps we should slow it down and think it through.

On the one hand, it can seem as though the race towards a Smarter Planet is inevitable; resistance is futile. Our only choice is to join in or become irrelevant Luddites fading into the past. But there are, in fact, very different sorts of futures that are possible. This chapter provides general, systematic visions of two paths and the very different roles of artificial intelligence in each. It will propose five principles for a technological path aimed not just at living "smarter" but living more *wisely*. They provide a vision for the wise use of the most complex and sophisticated technologies our military and industrial systems have to offer. Yet the principles can also be understood and applied in even the simplest forms of artificial intelligence we encounter in our daily lives – including, for example, the humble thermostats that use very simple algorithms with feedback loops to regulate the heating systems in our homes.

We have already discussed ways in which ethics, economics, and politics can be transformed with a shift from the unilateral monologue of strictly algorithmic inference to the more inclusive, collaborative forms of dialogical reasoning. Turning now to technology will clarify and sharpen that fundamental contrast. Since the 18th century, the "rocket science" of monological reasoning has been advocated as the ideal in ethics, economics, and politics. Fortunately, strenuous attempts to impose that ideal in pervasive, systematic ways have not been fully successful. Faced with moral dilemmas, tragedies of the commons, and government crises, people have repeatedly either lapsed or leaped into dialogue to transform their situations.

In the realm of technology, however, the situation is somewhat different. This is because technology is a realm in which physical things are designed rigorously and precisely to embody rationality of an algorithmic type. In the modern Western tradition, the driving goal is to design tools and machines governed strictly and completely by the monological reasoning patterns of algorithmic inference. This instrumentalist rationality is technology's "raison d'etre", its way of Being.[92]

Table 11. Different Kinds of Reasoning in Different Realms of Life

Frameworks for Reasoning:	Algorithmic Inference (monological)	Collaborative Dialogue
Exemplified by:	Newtonian physics and "rocket science"	Gandhian and other consensus approaches to conflict transformation
With variations in:		
Economics	Rational Economic Man maximizing utility, profit, and GDP	History Makers pursuing meaningful projects in community
Politics and International Relations	National Security States pursuing power through realpolitik	Communities pursuing self-rule (swaraj) through nonviolence (satyagraha)
Technology	Pursuing power to manipulate the environment with smart systems through instrumentalist reasoning	Pursuing wise and sustainable relationships in community through collaborative dialogue with all forms of intelligence
Morality	Seeking foundations in absolute, universal principles (e. g. Bentham, Kant) for the justification of choice	Experimental search for emergent objective truths through conflict resolution and satyagraha

The Quest for a Smarter Planet

This modern Western tradition grows out of a long line of technological innovations starting with the taming of fire. In a sense, the technique of using flint rocks to strike sparks and catch a flame in dry tinder may have embodied the first algorithmic rule one person taught another. Perhaps a clearer candidate as first might be the early technique used for weaving with a simple back loom. It provided a frame with strings running to a pole with two sets of warp cords moving up and down as a thread was passed through back and forth. It allowed the mechanical production of woven cloth with creative patterns -- as long as the weaver rigorously followed appropriate rules for each step.

In the industrial revolution, mechanization of weaving took two giant steps forward. First, steam power was substituted for human labor. Second, an ingenious system of cards was developed which allowed loom operators to punch holes in varying patterns the machine then followed. Such looms literally em-bodied algorithmic reasoning designed into them and followed it "under their own steam".[93]

They were mechanical forerunners of modern electronic computers. In that sense, they provided the first in a long line of technologies that have come to be referred to as smart. We now have smart cars, houses, farms, schools, hospitals, and other systems that are pervading our world as part of the Internet of Things. The underlying vision was given a compelling expression by an IBM ad that ran in 2009. It began: "You might notice small changes ...

"A less expensive energy bill. A package that gets delivered in two days instead of seven. Quarterly school reports available online. But if you take a step back, you can see the bigger picture of the smarter systems behind these small changes: intelligent utility networks, smarter supply chains and digital education records. Bit by bit, our planet is getting smarter. By this, we mean the systems that run the way we live and work as a society.

"Why now?

"Because the systems of our planet are increasingly:

"Instrumented – more than a billion transistors per human, each one costing one ten-millionth of a cent

"Interconnected -- With a trillion networked things

"Intelligent – AI pervading the systems, monitoring, and managing them

"And this is all **Inevitable**[94]

These smart systems aim to optimize one or a few values that are axiomatized as goals. For example, smart farms can aim to maximize production of tons of soybeans per acre. Smart schools may maximize increases in students' test scores in the three Rs. Smart sentencing systems for courts may seek to minimize recidivism.

Driving motivations for this come largely from the economic and political institutions we considered earlier. Economic competition for maximizing profit pushes development of the technologies characteristic of industrial capitalism. *Realpolitik* of modern states guides national investments in Research and Development (R&D) for technologies to maximize military power and GDP.

The connection between these institutional drives and the spread of algorithmic rationality in Western technology is rather straightforward. The concept of maximization is inherently quantitative. To quantify things like apples or shoes, you must abstract them from their particularities and consider them as uniform, countable items in a reproducible, homogeneous resource. Industrial capitalism does this by turning them into commodities bought and sold in the market. Once elements of an economy are commodified and quantified in this way, they lend themselves directly to mathematical reasoning that can take the meanings of terms for granted and draw inferences for maximizing outputs from given inputs. A commodified world that maximizes economic profit and political power is ripe for monological reasoning.

Further, maximization inherently leads to monological framing of values. But there are other options. Think of non-capitalist forms of agriculture like Indigenous systems described in Kimmerer's *Braiding Sweetgrass*. Think of people practicing gift economies in networks of reciprocity with plants, animals, mountains, rivers, and other beings in their ecological community. In cultivating and sustaining those relationships in rich and resilient ways, these people need to consider many different concerns and values and be in dialogue with each other and with the other creatures that are part of their community. They typically relate to plants and animals as persons. They address them as Beings with pronouns like "you, she, he or we" rather than referring to them as objectified "it". They seek, in their decisions, to balance many different values. These Indigenous communities try to negotiate and resolve conflicts between different concerns and points of view to reach honorable agreements that all can live with.

In contrast, once we seek to maximize rather than balance through integration, then we need to identify some one single value to maximize. We must combine or collapse those many different concerns and goals into one single consideration, one underlying value to which all can be reduced and measured. So, we invent an abstract conception like "profit" or "GDP" and seek to create measures to track it and maximize its growth. As farmers, we start thinking like narrow-minded economic entrepreneurs bent on increasing profit on capital. We abandon thinking in holistic political/economic ways about the ecological and social relationships that constitute our real wealth. An agriculture committed to the maximization of profit must embody inferential thinking that serves that end. A culture committed to maximizing GDP and power seeks to embody an instrumentalist rationality of monological reasoning.

Early in the industrial revolution, calculations of the most efficient, profit maximizing ways of building and deploying technological tools had to be computed by human beings. But in the advances of the twentieth century, a systematic model for automating the computing itself was developed. The term "computer" was no longer used to refer to the people doing the calculations but to machines that did them for us. One of the most formative as well as prescient writings in the development of such computers was a piece by Alan Turing written in 1950: "Computing Machinery and Intelligence". It was formative of what became the standard theoretical model of the computer. This model, known as the "Turing Machine", was designed to be a perfect embodiment of algorithmic inference.

Turing introduced it with a kind of thought experiment, The Imitation Game, now referred to as the Turing Test for intelligence in computers. His idea was to avoid all the difficult questions about consciousness, souls, and other metaphysical hypotheses people might hold about what enables humans to exhibit rational intelligence. Instead, his proposal was to simply assess the intelligence of a person – or machine – based on what they could do, regardless of how they did it. If a machine could send messages back and forth to people with a conversational competence that made it impossible for a human judge to tell it apart from a human being, then it passed the test. Turing proposed that we should consider such machines intelligent. Anything that could successfully imitate an intelligent person should be considered, for all practical purposes, intelligent.

At the end of this remarkable paper, there is another quite visionary set of ideas which were largely ignored in the decades after he wrote it. In it, Turing developed a second, quite different model for computers. It would employ collaborative dialogue forms of reasoning rather than relying merely on algorithmic inference. He described it as a "child machine".

The "Turing Machine" model of AI has been driving the quest for a "Smarter" Planet whose systems are unbalanced and ecologically unsound. The "Turing Child" model of AI offers the hope of developing systems in which AI, humans and nature all collaborate in dialogues that enable us to create a Wiser Earth.

We all need to understand and work toward this vision. It takes a village to raise a wiser child, and it will take dialogues that include all the members of our community on this planet to make a Wiser Earth. What, more specifically, is the "Turing Machine" model of computers? How does the "Turing Child" model differ from it? How could we use the Turing Child model to create more human ecological systems of technology as part of our task of trying to live more wisely here on Earth?

Turing Machines vs. Turing Children: Two Models of AI

The Turing Machine model for computers is so familiar it might seem to be the very definition of their essence. This conception, which became the standard 20th century model of a computer, is grounded in a reductionist vision of the world which excludes the genuine emergence of new, higher order forms of being. This reductionist vision assumes the most subtle and complex forms of reality can be described by a series of zeroes and ones and their patterns can all be described and predicted using rules of formal logic.

The guiding dream of such logic machines lay in Aristotle's formalization of Categorical Syllogisms. It is a vision of a device that inputs premises or data and transforms them via algorithmic rules into the output of conclusions. The output of Aristotle's syllogisms, might not seem especially impressive. Proving "Socrates is mortal" from "Socrates is a man" and "All men are mortal" seems less like a discovery than a mere reminder of prior knowledge. However, when Euclid employed syllogisms in geometry, the results became impressive. Starting with a few key definitions and axioms, he built a system of rigorous inferences providing extremely useful insights for engineers, astronomers, and others – including physicists like Isaac Newton.

Newton's work further advanced the dream of algorithmic rationality in two ways. First, its application of algorithmic thinking was so powerful and stunning that it became a model for imitation in virtually every field of human endeavor. Eighteenth century intellectuals sought to understand every aspect of the world in a similar way. Each discipline sought its "Newton" who would discover the fundamental laws of economics, ethics, or politics and provide a comprehensive system for managing the world. Second, Newton advanced the dream with his vision of reality as a mechanism whose parts can be reduced to simple bits of matter and assembled into more complicated structures via mechanical rules that generate output automatically. He helped, in short, to formalize the concept of machinery. Whereas many had earlier supposed the world consisted of living organisms animated by souls, Newton's physics described a world of dead matter moved by mechanical laws.

The common image of a computer is precisely this kind of machine: an assembly of inorganic matter moved by mechanical laws that algorithmically yield output humans then interpret and use. The calculator figuring our taxes, the GPS system finding our route on the road, and even the thermostat running our home furnace can all be dressed up and given cute pictures or voices to talk to us. But the underlying technology presents itself as a machine cranking out answers and actions. This harks back to Turing's vision in "Computing Machinery and Intelligence". He introduced it thus:

"The idea behind digital computers may be explained by saying that these machines are intended to carry out any operations which could be done by a human computer. The human computer is supposed to be following fixed rules; he has no authority to deviate from them in any detail. We may suppose that these rules are supplied in a book, which is altered whenever he is put on to a new job. He has also an unlimited supply of paper on which he does his calculations. He may also do his multiplications and additions on a 'desk machine,' but this is not important."[95]

Turing progressively adds elements to this conception of the computer which enrich its ability to solve various kinds of problems. These include things like more massive storage, speed, the ability to use random numbers, and the benefits of successively more sophisticated programming. He notes:

"I believe that in about fifty years' time it will be possible, to program computers, with a storage capacity to make them play the imitation game so well that an average interrogator will not have more than 70 per cent chance of making the right identification after five minutes of questioning."[96]

Research into Good Old-Fashioned AI (GOFAI) during the early decades of computer science was guided by the vision of mechanical inference. To appreciate the significance of the second vision Turing introduced in the last section of his paper, it helps to note first what became of the GOFAI tradition.

By the 1980s, most researchers gave up on its attempt with top-down programming to create computers with the kind of general intelligence exhibited by humans. Most turned, instead, to what was referred to as "narrow AI" whose aim was to design programs with one or a few specific goals that could be efficiently achieved. By giving the computer increasing storage, speed, and complexity it often proved possible, in these more limited tasks, for machines to equal or surpass humans. The result was increasingly powerful computers that could outstrip humans in discovering new digits of pi, calculating spreadsheets, and playing chess. What were the challenges in using GOFAI to create a machine with more general intelligence of the human kind? One persistent difficulty was the challenge of getting machines to engage in successful pattern recognition.[97]

For human infants, recognizing things they see may seem relatively straightforward. Yet it involves processing a huge amount of visual information simultaneously. It also involves considering a huge range of possible options for what might be appearing before them and from what angle. (Is it Mom's elbow seen from below? The side of Dad's knee? The sofa corner behind Mom's hair?) In pattern recognition, computers were even more challenged in figuring out the place and context of the object observed. The problem is one of choosing or at times creating the right frame for recognizing, interpreting, judging, and responding to stimuli. A computer playing chess does not face this problem. It has been told that the game of chess should frame all its input and output. As long as it plays by the rules it can calculate its moves, full speed ahead. But take the same computer into a summer camp where kids are playing lots of different games – and making up new ones. Suddenly the computer faces a major problem. It needs someone to tell it what is going on, what the rules are, and how best to frame its responses.

In recent decades, computer scientists have been exploring promising ways of dealing with the challenges of pattern recognition, framing, and related difficulties. Many of these strategies follow a general approach Turing himself sketched. His introduction of this is worth quoting at length:

"In the process of trying to imitate an adult human mind we are bound to think a good deal about the process which has brought it to the state that it is in. We may notice three components:

"The initial state of the mind, say at birth,

"The education to which it has been subjected,

"Other experience, not to be described as education, to which it has been subjected.

"Instead of trying to produce a programme to simulate the adult mind, why not rather try to produce one which simulates the child's? If this were then subjected to an appropriate course of education one would obtain the adult brain. Presumably the child brain is something like a notebook as one buys it from the stationer's. Rather little mechanism, and lots of blank sheets. (Mechanism and writing are from our point of view almost synonymous.) Our hope is that there is so little mechanism in the child brain that something like it can be easily programmed. The amount of work in the education we can assume, as a first approximation, to be much the same as for the human child."[98]

Turing then goes on to note the following:

"We have thus divided our problem into two parts. The child programme and the education process. These two remain very closely connected. We cannot expect to find a good child machine at the first attempt. One must experiment with teaching one such machine and see how well it learns. One can then try another and see if it is better or worse. There is an obvious connection between this process and evolution, by the identifications:

"Structure of the child machine = hereditary material

"Changes of the child machine = mutation

"Natural selection = judgment of the experimenter"

"One may hope, however, that this process will be more expeditious than evolution. The survival of the fittest is a slow method for measuring advantages. The experimenter, by the exercise of intelligence, should be able to speed it up. Equally important is the fact that he is not restricted to random mutations. If he can trace a cause for some weakness, he can probably think of the kind of mutation which will improve it."[99]

This strategy has been pursued in recent decades with evolutionary programming, genetic programming, neural nets, deep reinforcement learning, and other forms of machine learning. It is crucial to note that Turing's vision of the general strategy introduces a model of a computer which is not a Turing Machine.

This is not a comment on what it is made out of. His imagined device could be made of silicon rather than protein. Instead, the decisive difference is how its behavior gets initiated and developed. Unlike the classic model of a Turing machine, it is not a tool programmed by a user; it is a child educated in a community. Turing implicitly introduces this point in the following way:

"It will not be possible to apply exactly the same teaching process to the machine as to a normal child. It will not, for instance, be provided with legs, so that it could not be asked to go out and fill the coal scuttle. Possibly it might not have eyes. But however well these deficiencies might be overcome by clever engineering, one could not send the creature to school without the other children making excessive fun of it. It must be given some tuition. We need not be too concerned about the legs, eyes, etc. The example of Helen Keller shows that education can be take place provided that communication in both directions between teacher and pupil can take place by some means or others."[100]

Turing clearly sees the necessity of giving the child some kind of body to enter dialogue with teachers and others. The Helen Keller reference suggests a fairly minimal body with limited perception and action might make surprising progress learning to talk and act like an adult human. But it also makes the advantages of a more fully developed and empowered body obvious. They would allow the child machine to observe and interact with its world and teachers in rich, diverse ways that strongly emulate the humans socializing it. Current advances in robotics provide increasingly powerful technologies for this.

Note also the role of "tuition" specifically designed for the child machine in an accepting learning environment. School mates can be vicious and abusive. On the other hand, his analysis makes it clear that the more fully the child machine enters normal learning situations, the better. Recent experience with children and machines suggests ways to structure situations so child machines can be welcomed into kindergarteners' dialogues and thrive.

Turing is also clear that the "programming" structuring such behavior will require interaction going beyond monological reasoning and algorithmic calculations in a formal object language. It will require dialogue in which teacher and child machine repeatedly renegotiate the meanings of terms and sentences. It will move back and forth between the object language and the meta-language standpoints. It will require following guidelines that are general heuristics, normative advice, and imperatives rather than strictly defined rules.

He notes, for example: "The processes of inference used by the machine need not be such as would satisfy the most exacting logicians . . . But this need not mean that type fallacies will occur, any more than we are bound to fall over unfenced cliffs." He illustrates the point with a technical example of logical difficulties that can arise if you allow a program to "fall over the cliff' of self-contradictions. He has in mind here something called "Russell's Paradox" which arises when you have a class or set of all sets that are not members of themselves. Self-contradictions can arise when you allow certain kinds of sets or classes of things to refer to themselves.

He goes on to note that: "Suitable imperatives (expressed within the systems, not forming part of the rules of the system) such as 'Do not use a class unless it is a subclass of one which has been mentioned by teacher' can have a similar effect to 'Do not go too near the edge.'"[101]

He is envisioning devices that follow imperative guidelines rather than algorithms. These are not like the rules in systems of formal logic. They are like the guidelines for negotiation and conflict resolution presented in handbooks like *Getting To Yes*: "When faced with a dilemma, multiply your options!" and "In trying to generate new options, focus on people's underlying interests!"

Table 12. Two Conceptions of Computer Intelligence

Conception of AI as:	Turing Machine	Turing Child
Frame of reasoning as:	Single frame, unilateral, monologue	Multi-perspectival, collaborative dialogue
Goal of reasoning as:	Generating an output or conclusion that follows algorithmically from the input or premises given	Arriving at a genuine, voluntary agreement through collaborative negotiation and problem solving
Starting point as:	Shared definitions of terms, data, and rules of inference	Different points of view with different meanings ascribed to terms and different beliefs, values, and rules of reasoning
Process of reasoning as:	Inference according to logical algorithms	Negotiation, problem solving, conflict transformation and/or peacemaking using creative strategies
Conception of true or satisfactory outcome of reasoning as:	Concluding in statements that correspond to a fixed reality	Cultivating shared understandings of emergent, objective realities and truths
Reasoner as:	A formal agent whose intellectual operations are substrate independent	A physically embodied and socially embedded agent engaged with and dependent on the lifeworld of the community in dialogue
Abilities to reason are enhanced by:	Increasing the speed and power of hardware and reprogramming software	Socializing the agent in lived contexts through teaching, parenting, play, et cetera

Can we make machines that engage in dialogue? Some doubt its possibility in principle. Even if possible, to many it seems dangerous to try.

And yet thousands of organizations in dozens of countries are spending hundreds of billions of dollars to develop such systems. They are forcing us, increasingly, to focus not so much on the question of whether such machines are going to be created but how. What form will they take? What values will guide their development? Who will design and control the data sets, learning processes, and oversight systems that determine the ethical norms guiding them?

Since the release of ChatGPT in November of 2022 and the flood of new Generative AI programs, the importance of these kinds of questions about ethics and safety are becoming increasingly clear and pressing. To appreciate the underlying concerns, it is essential to understand the ways in which those systems do—and do not— exhibit characteristics of genuine dialogue in the reasoning they seem to perform.

Is Generative AI Merely a Turing Pinocchio?

At the moment of this writing, it is clear that the year of 2023 marked a major inflection point in the history of research and development on AI. Large Language Models (LLM) and other systems that use Generative methods are becoming stunningly powerful in quite unexpected ways. We engage with them through conversational interfaces and they seem to be able to reply convincingly in an extraordinary range of different personas and styles. In doing so, are they engaging in genuine dialogue employing the kinds of normative reasoning people use in negotiation, shared problem solving, conflict transformation, and peacemaking? Or are they mere puppets that are designed to put on a good act? Are they, like Pinocchio, puppets without visible strings but puppets nonetheless?

This question is challenging for three reasons: 1) These systems are, by inherent design, opaque black boxes whose inner workings are inscrutable to us. No one really knows how they actually work. 2) The systems are being developed and released at ever greater speed. By the time we observe and begin to carefully describe the characteristics of one iteration or model, successors with new features and emergent abilities have already arrived. 3) The clear philosophical distinctions we might want to use to frame discussion about rationality, truth, agency, and dialogue all get blurred and puzzling when applied to emergent entities and processes. To clarify the question and cope with these challenges, it will help to start with the first point, the opaque character of the systems.

Generative AI systems are not programmed like the logic machines of Good Old Fashioned AI from the 1950's. Instead, they use methods inspired by evolutionary processes of biology and the reinforcement learning of neuroscience and psychology. They are designed to generate a series of random variations in their behavior which they then select amongst to identify the more successful versions. Then, in each next generation, they reproduce those, with further variations, in order to arrive, through a process of selective approximation, at ever more successful behaviors. The researchers in charge of this process are less like engineers building a machine than like dog masters who are developing a new breed or training a puppy. The masters select and reinforce for what they want based on the results that they see. But as for what is happening at the level of the genes or the neurons of the dogs, they remain relatively clueless. They may know, in general, how DNA works and neurons fire. What a successful breeder and trainer does not understand, however, is the makeup and relationships between the specific genes and neural pathways that produce their favorite Australian Sheep Dog and get her to behave the way she does. The underlying workings of Generative AI are opaque in just this same way. The process of using Reinforcement Learning with Human Feedback enabled the creators of ChatGPT to breed and train a remarkable system that remains, for them, a black box they can neither describe in detail nor explain.

They can, however, describe what functions, by analogy, like the basic mechanisms of the DNA and neurons with which the many layers of the system get built. And these involve, in essence, the kind of machine learning that is familiar nowadays to everyone who has started to write a reply to an email or a text on a smartphone. The software suggests several possible options we can just click on to complete the next word or phrase in our message. It does so by having observed lots of past messages and recording the probability of different words being used to automatically complete the string that has come before. Such probabilistic inference enables it to judge that after the words "In conclusion, I would . . . " it is more likely that the next word will be "argue" or "say" than "rain" or "blunderbuss".

One common way of describing the Large Language Models like ChatGPT is to say that they are "autocompletion on steroids". The suggestion is that they simply differ from earlier text completion programs by adding billions of parameters to predict what will be the next word in a string of text.

This description is, however, misleading in a crucial way. It fails to take into account the way these newer systems use something called "attention" to improve the probabilistic inferences. The basic process is one which allows the machine to break up its observations of strings of text into units of different, varying sizes which it "attends" to in seeking correlations and probabilities. This enables it to predict not only what type of word length string of characters is most likely to come next but also what type of sentence length, paragraph length, and even essay length string is most likely.

So, for instance, consider prompting the AI with the following: "I want you to write a 600-word op-ed piece on the reasons for regulating AI. Please start it with a question that would be appropriate to frame the issue and then provide at least four compelling reasons." The machine learning process can determine that there is a high probability that the next sentence length string will end with a question mark. It can also determine that if that string ends with a question mark, there is a significant probability that it will start with "Who", "What", "When", "Where", "Why", or "How". It can also determine that the 600-word piece will likely end with a paragraph length string that starts with something like: "In conclusion, we have four reasons for regulating AI . . ."

To see what is going on here, it is helpful to draw on Aristotle's distinction between four kinds of causality: efficient, material, formal, and final. Efficient causality is the kind involved when one event causes another, like when one billiard ball hits another and causes it to move. This kind of causality has been a focus of science since Galileo and Newton, and provides a mechanical metaphor many people have in mind when thinking of Large Language Models as nothing more than autocompletion on steroids. The picture suggested is one in which one string of text causes the next the way one physical motion in a machine causes the next.

But if we want to explain what is going on in Large Language Models (LLM), we need to also consider what Aristotle would call the material causes (the strings of letters and words that are coded in as material to be processed) and the formal causes (the forms or patterns into which those letters and words are organized). Suppose, for example, that we want to understand why an LLM writing our op-ed starts it with "How" rather than the German "Wie" or the Spanish "Porqué". The explanation would be, in part, that the linguistic material which is being drawn on is from English. English words provide the content matter that is getting organized. But another part of the explanation would come from the form of the sentence. It is likely to be the kind that is a question which ends with a "?" and starts with a word like "How". The organizational structure of questions explains part of the form of the sentence.

The formal causes at work in structuring software and its behavior bring in the fourth kind of causality which Aristotle viewed as closely connected to formal causality, the kind he called final causality. A final cause is goal that provides the end at which a process aims and which motivates it. We can explain why someone leaving Boston passes through New York if we know that their goal is to get to Baltimore. We can likewise explain why acorns sprout roots by understanding that they are developing into oak trees. Efficient causes are, in a sense, the temporal opposite of final causes; they use the previous events to explain the subsequent. Why did the bread later turn brown? Because it was heated previously in the toaster. In contrast, to explain intentional actions that are the result of final causes, we use the subsequent events to explain the previous. Why did Karla put the bread in the toaster? In order to make it warm and brown.

When LLM use formal patterns to determine what is likely to come next in a string of text, their behavior starts to exhibit a kind of final causality. This is precisely because the forms they are operating with involve patterns defined by beginning, middle and end. And the probable ending of larger patterns can affect the probability of elements in smaller and earlier patterns. This introduces a teleological-like element to the behavior of the software. In our 600-word op-ed example, it is not just that the probable ending of the first sentence with a "?" affects the probability of its earlier first word. The prompt increases the probability that the 600 word piece will end with a paragraph string starting with something like "We may conclude, then, for these reasons, that . . . ". And that final destination for the piece makes it more likely that along the way there will be paragraphs that start with something like "One reason for this is . . ."

Generative AI uses mechanisms of probabilistic reasoning structured by feedback loops that reinforce the search for patterns of varying sizes. These patterns result in behavior that is governed by these sorts of formal and final causes with a dramatic result. The programs can seem to exhibit key features of intentional verbal behavior guided by final causes.

This is, in fact, part of what makes these systems seem so human-like. It is what has tempted many users to suppose that the machine must be simply copying text from some real human -- parroting conversation rather than engaging in genuine dialogue. But these LLMs are not simply copying; they are, in fact, generating often entirely novel strings of text that weave together probabilistic calculations that take into account many different sized units of text and previous versions of them provided by their training data. They are, in that way, a bit like jazz improvisers using variations on chord structures, rhythm patterns and melody lines to create something familiar but also novel.

But there remain a variety of ways in which these systems differ from humans who are engaged in intentional action and reasoning as part of genuine human dialogue and collaboration. In that sense, while they are more than puppets they are less than people.

One shortcoming suggests the Pinocchio analogy. Like the wooden boy with the elongating nose, they fabricate falsehoods of the most unbelievable and odd kind. These "hallucinations," as they are called, result because of the kind of data on which they are trained, and the probabilistic inferences they use to generate output. They are trained on enormous swathes of the internet with all its examples of elegant reasoning and eloquent morality along with all its hilarious examples of human error and hideous examples of unethical behavior. Since the machines use these to infer what most probably comes next in reply to a prompt, it is no surprise that they often say things that should make a wooden puppet blush. OpenAI and others have used human feedback to try to train out the grosser errors and unethical responses. But while this has met with some success, it is a strategy with a key flaw. To use the dog breeding analogy, unless every one of the genes that can cause potentially erroneous or unethical behavior is entirely bred out of the line, then it will inevitably be reproduced and spread back throughout the system in a way analogous to what geneticists refer to as "regression to the mean".

A more promising strategy is to try to create hybrid systems that use transparent, logical systems that are "white boxes". These might be programmed to monitor and check results of the model. So, for example, WolframAlpha provides such a transparent system for doing math calculations and applied science calculations. If you want to know the distance from Tokyo to Chicago, WolframAlpha can use bodies of verified data and logically rigorous math to calculate the consistently correct answer. In contast, ChatGPT will fabricate an answer based on a synthesis of the probabilities of responses to similar questions observed out on the wilds of the internet -- with often disappointing results.. Significant improvement in ChatGPT is made, however, when it is provided with a WolframAlpha plugin which it can instruct to calculate answers to technical questions which ChatGPT can then include in its responses to prompts.

Other forms of hybridization like this may be able to address other shortcomings in the Pinocchio versions of Generative AI. Some of these shortcomings arise because it lacks direct connection to the world. With no eyes or ears, it lacks the kind of semantic reference that creatures like us have because we can point to actual things in space and time and say: "This is what I am talking about." In a sense, while disembodied AI can generate streams of words it remains incapable of actually talking about anything real at all because it lacks referential connection to things in space and time. However, this shortcoming can be addressed by hybridizing it with mics, cameras, and audio/visual programs.

A further shortcoming lies in the kind of agency these Generative systems have – or don't. To the extent that they are disembodied, it seems like they cannot actually do anything at all. And so they appear to lack genuine intentions in the sense in which humans have them. They are not agents who can effectuate things in the world and they are not accountable for actions in the ways in which responsible humans are. But these sorts of shortcomings might begin to be remedied by giving them robotic bodies and starting to allow them rights and responsibilities. Imagine, for instance, autonomous cars with the right of way when passing in a certain lane but the legal liability for damages resulting from accidents. Perhaps, in some respects, Generative AI systems already have the makings of such agency in the world because of their access to – and influence over -- the millions of bodies of users who are being persuaded by them to adopt new diets, cook new recipes, write new quarterly reports, and who knows what all.

Considerations about agency get into complex questions concerning underlying philosophical concepts where there is considerable ambiguity and disagreement. These are further complicated by the fact that the systems are undergoing rapid change and development resulting in unexpected, emergent properties. They are also complicated by the fact that the forms of reasoning and agency at issue may not exist along a single continuum. Fifty years ago, it seemed plausible to assume that rationality took a single essential form and that progress consisted in ascending to the level humans had achieved and then, perhaps, moving ahead beyond us. But it is clear now that there are many forms of reasoning and intentional action and that a machine can far surpass humans in some even while not matching us in others. Pinocchio may be able to whip the world champions in chess and Go while still not being able to comfort a frightened child or become someone's trusted friend.

In navigating these complexities, however, one key distinction may serve as a guide. It is the distinction between probabilistic inference aimed at prediction in contrast to dialogical reasoning aimed at genuine, voluntary agreement informed by emergent objective truths. The first is what the current machines are designed to do. It enables them to provide responses to prompts that often offer compelling imitations of meaningful conversation. But there is a further step involved in dialogue that pursues ethical reasoning and wisdom. It must be guided not just by descriptions that predict but norms that prescribe. It is guided not just by what it **is**, in fact, that people say and do on the internet but by what they **ought** to say and do. This is a key difference between probabilistic inference and dialogical reasoning. To what extent will hybrid forms of Generative AI be able to be incorporated into systems that engage in such dialogue? What kind of communities and life systems will we need to generate and nurture AI systems that are parts of an ethical system of peaceful, just, resilient communities pursuing a wiser Earth?

Turing Machines for a Smarter Planet vs. Turing Children for a Wiser Earth: Two Paths for 21st Century Technology

On November 7th, 2021, I received an email from the head of Buildings and Grounds at my college. Have you ever received a similar message?

"To students, staff, and faculty:

"We are experiencing a number of mechanical malfunction issues in Gates, A/S, and CHE since last Saturday's storm. The problem seems to be in our control systems - we are not able to access nor adjust any of the systems through our monitoring system. Override settings are not available to us. A tech is coming Monday morning to scope out the issue, until then expect the Writing Center, and old graphics lab, Gates, and CHE to experience inconsistent heating and cooling – sorry"

In most larger buildings in the US, heating/cooling systems are already transformed. Simple thermostats have been replaced by complex systems of automated monitoring and control which require professionals to adapt them to special needs and service them "when s**t happens". The open-ended interactions and dialogue made possible by a Do It Yourself (DIY) culture of technology are increasingly shut down. In workplaces, apartment buildings, churches, YMCAs, and museums we are all being pushed into the culture of the larger modern consumer family – a Done By Professionals (DBP) culture. This is also happening in systems that monitor and control flows of events on farms and wildlife preserves as well as restaurants, schools, police stations, factories, hospitals, and military defense systems.

The modern consumer culture of the Smarter Planet frames ever more of life in terms of services provided by professionals. This contrasts sharply with viewing life as an activity we perform in self-reliant ways. These approaches are tied to the contrasting conceptions of Turing Machines vs. Turing Children.[102]

The Turing Machine vision drives development of proprietary systems designed for corporate profit or military power. They are increasingly rented to us as mysterious black boxes performing services for a fee. To advance exclusive positions in markets, their owners are unwilling to provide transparent access to the inner workings. We cannot understand these things and discuss how we would like them to function. They require us to set the terms of service at the point of purchase. Those provide the input for the system to make inferences with its algorithms that yield outputs in monologues whose results we must accept. Or, rather, we must accept them unless and until we can get out of one contract and into another.

And yet . . . change is coming. Innovations in these systems are bringing forth a new kind of technology: AI devices that function more like Turing Children. They are making it possible to include computers in processes of open and authentic dialogues amongst the people and other creatures in our community. It is becoming possible to shift away from the path towards a Smarter Planet towards a path to a Wiser Earth. It is a path coordinated by balanced, consensus judgments and agreements arrived at in dialogues that include the points of view of all the relevant humans, natural creatures, and artificially created devices.

Some innovations making this possible concern hardware. AI systems have increasingly sensitive forms of eyes, ears, and other sensors as well as methods of handling things, maneuvering, and gesturing expressively. Turing had trouble seeing how his "child machine" might fit in at school. Seventy years later, this seems less problematic. Increasingly, the chief obstacle to fitting in is the "uncanny valley effect". Humans' ability to relate easily to a machine increases as it adds human-like features and gestures – up to a point. Then acceptance slopes down into a valley of rejection because the device is so uncannily, creepily close to looking like a normal, biological human. The fact that we are needing increasingly to deal with the uncanny valley effect indicates how far we have advanced in hardware interfacing with AI.[103]

Software breakthroughs are also providing elements for development of Turing Children and paths toward a Wiser Earth. Many use the three key methods that drive evolution in nature: 1) reproduction of offspring similar to parents, 2) variations within the lines produced, and 3) selection of the most successful for continued reproduction. Increasingly sophisticated and subtle forms of genetic algorithms, evolutionary programing, and machine learning use these methods to evolve computer code for new programs the way Darwinian selection in nature evolves DNA code for new species.

Further innovations have been inspired by ways brain cells coordinate their responses and learn in neural nets. If nerves "fire together" they tend to "wire together". If we see a sunflower's distinctive cluster of shapes and colors, our nerves tend to encode their excited firing together as a wired-in pattern that can be recognized in the future. Programs with neural nets have proven increasingly successful in learning to do pattern recognition of visual images, sounds, movements, pieces of written text and all the other sorts of things that Turing envisioned for child machines. They enable progressive interactions for socialization in dialogues with teachers. In most cases, what a human child learns to recognize is not just a single level of pattern like a triangular shape or a color contrast between yellow and green. To recognize the pattern of a particular type of flower it is necessary to recognize layers upon layers of patterns. Shaped and colored petals form three dimensionally structured spacings as part of larger leaf and stem structures that occur in typical contexts like gardens or woodland paths. Around 2012 some breakthroughs in the development of multiple levels of neural nets and other pattern recognition software began to make it possible to have ever deeper layers of such programs. Breakthroughs began to result once these were combined with the continued exponential growth in the power of hardware and the data sets that could be used to train systems. The resulting forms of multi-layered "reinforcement learning" and "deep learning systems" have begun to provide systems that exhibit features Turing envisioned.

One central feature of these innovative computer systems is that they are guided by Turing's key suggestion quoted earlier: "Instead of trying to produce a programme to simulate the adult mind, why not rather try to produce one which simulates the child's? If this were then subjected to an appropriate course of education one would obtain the adult brain."[104] The new systems are not programmed from the top down by people operating from blueprints of the human brain. Instead, they are put through a series of training processes in which the program uses evolutionary processes to develop multi-layered neural nets of code to learn new things in surprising ways.

Some results have proved extremely useful. Programs have learned to spot tumors in MRI scans earlier and more accurately than medical specialists -- and in time for more effective medical intervention. Some results have astonished experts. When Google's machine beat the world champion at the extremely subtle, ancient game of Go, world masters were stunned to find that it did so by developing a whole new strategy of play which humans had never thought possible. It made an early move that seemed absurdly wrong but turned out, many moves later, to have been part of a brilliant, decisive strategy. More recently, simply increasing the computing power of a machine by a 10-fold order of magnitude resulted in GPT-3 being able to produce manuscripts and code of a wide variety of kinds that began to approach the quality of human authors in quite uncanny ways. Many people were taken aback, for instance, when they read an opinion piece in the *Guardian* written by GPT-3 called: "A robot wrote this entire article: Are you scared yet human?"[105] Continued growth in the verbal, visual, coding, and other abilities of generative AI systems continues to astonish.

None of this is to say that these machines have become the equivalent of adult humans who could pass the Turing Test. They are not even the equivalent of child humans. For example, to learn to distinguish dogs and cats, neural nets have required hundreds of thousands of examples in their training data set. In contrast, young children learn to recognize dogs, cats, giraffes, elephants, and all kinds of things with a very small number of pictures and encounters. There are a variety of other key features the machines lack in order to reach children's capacity for learning. The machines operate with great power, speed, and memory in fixed and well-defined arenas of information. But, like the self-driving car that suddenly comes upon a stop sign painted with graffiti, they may make strangely gross errors.

More generally, the machines have had continued difficulty discerning and interpreting frames of meaning in open ended contexts. This is in part because they lack the kind of integrative points of view that children have. Children's bodies em-body and engage them in the physical world. Their memberships in families embed and engage them in social and historical contexts. This physical embodying and social embedding provide crucial meaningful information and orientation in the world. In the short run, at least, this may be an area in which collaboration between people and machines may be especially fruitful. The increasingly powerful Generative Pretrained Systems that have access to internet-wide volumes of text can, in principle, provide material for constructing con-text for the texts submitted by people as instructions and examples. People may provide the values and rootedness in the world that orients the dialogue and is complemented by the wealth of data and speed of processing provided by the machine. In this way, a kind of centaur model of collaborative dialogue may develop, analogous to the centaur model of chess play Gary Kasparov and others have developed in creating systems of human/machine players that exceed the capacities of either machines or humans alone.[106]

The feature that may be the most challenging to develop in "child machines" is perhaps also the one most fraught with dangers for the humans trying to develop them: ethics. This is the feature which embodies values in the physical structures of the AI and embeds the AI in social and historical contexts that develop emergent values in the form of interests, concerns, preferences, purposes, goals, and the like.

Until 2015 or so, most AI researchers tended to think ethics and values were not problematic. Many thought of AI systems as monological reasoners and assumed that an ultimate, over-riding value to guide AI activity could simply be programmed in by humans and would then guide the machines' activities. For anything that someday approached the ability of an Artificial General Intelligence, they supposed the general, over-riding goal would be Utilitarian net happiness or economic utility. In the context of "narrower" AI systems working within local constraints, they assumed more specific conceptions could stand in for utility. So, for instance, in managing farmland, tons of crop production per acre might do. In schools, increases in overall student test scores might serve. More generally, for corporations, profit might measure value.[107]

More recently, however, it has become painfully clear to mainstream AI researchers that there are fundamental difficulties with the monological features of this take on values questions. They have begun to shift towards more dialogical approaches. One indicator of this shift is found in the 4th edition of Russell and Norvik's influential textbook on AI where the preface notes:

> "Previously we defined the goal of AI as creating systems that try to maximize expected utility, where the specific utility information – the objective – is supplied by the human designers of the system. Now we no longer assume that the objective is fixed and known by the AI system; instead, the system may be uncertain about the true objectives of the humans on whose behalf it operates. It must learn what to maximize and must function appropriately even while uncertain about the objective."[108]

Part of learning the "true objectives of the humans" will involve interacting in open ended ways characteristic of collaborative dialogue. These involve observing carefully, floating exploratory proposals, and revising hypotheses via back-and-forth messages and negotiations. A progressive shift to such AI research and teaching is motivated by two underlying concerns – two threats that advancing AI technology poses for human forms of life.

The first threat is familiar though its likelihood may still seem remote: Will the intelligence of devices surpass humans' at exponential rates? Enormous funds are being poured into attempts to create such Artificial Super Intelligence (ASI) because it could, in theory, provide enormous economic and military power and perhaps solve crucial problems. It might help us eliminate poverty, disease, and climate change. But would it choose to do so? What values would it have and how might they align with ours?

To be a threat to our very existence, it need not be actually hostile to us like some Terminator from the movies. If it is simply indifferent to us, it may be quite happy to let us survive . . . until the day we happen to get in the way. Then we may be like ants in the way of someone cleaning a picnic table for lunch. This is often described as the "Friendly AI" issue or "Alignment Problem". It focuses on how we can ensure ASI will serve rather than destroy us.

But this focus ignores a crucial issue: Who should ASI be friendly toward? Corporations and countries developing powerful AI are at odds with each other. We don't want the ASI to just be friendly or aligned with whoever creates or owns it regardless of their ethics. We want it to be friendly to those who are moral. Consider, for example, the quest to develop Lethal Autonomous Weapon Systems (LAWS). We would not want the ASI running these weapons to simply be loyal to its owner or employer regardless of their ethics. Otherwise, once copied, stolen, or subverted by rebels, it might be used against us in overwhelming ways. Wouldn't we want, instead, to somehow ensure the ASI is loyal to the good, friendly folks—including us?[109]

But, if this the case, we will also need to make sure that we fall on the right side of that divide. It raises a serious question for careful self-reflection. What would an independent, moral, objective ASI make of us if it takes a long, hard, cold look at the ways in which our social systems treat people of different incomes, colors, creeds, nationalities, ethnicities, genders, and abilities? And our animals, plants, and ecosystems?

The "values alignment" or "Friendly AI" problem can only be solved if we figure out how to both: 1) develop ASI that all are friendly to humans with good, moral values and 2) make ourselves good and moral enough to merit the friendship of such Artificial Super Intelligences.[110]

We have a pressing need for both solutions. To work them out, we will need to work long and hard. Fortunately, we have the makings of a method. It consists in practices of dialogue that negotiate genuine, voluntary agreements grounded in values that can be discerned, demonstrated, and defended through nonviolent methods. To explore these further, it will help to first consider a second sort of fundamental threat that AI poses.

This second threat is one AI poses now, even in its more limited and narrow forms. It is a threat we face even if there never is a breakthrough to achieving AI in its "General" or "Super" forms. It is posed by all monological approaches to managing systems, no matter how simple or sophisticated. It is the threat of focusing on only one or a few values and sacrificing everything else that is at stake.

Consider an AI managing a forest, designed to maximize production of timber. This "narrow AI" manager may be a simple spread sheet calculating the use of fertilizer on a small plot or an extremely sophisticated system managing hundreds of thousands of acres by integrating plantings, pesticide treatments and harvesting. The problem is that forests serve many other important purposes besides the production of timber. They provide habitats for species, ecological services in the water cycle, meaningful employment for individuals, income for regions, and identities for communities. A narrow AI driven by only one or a few goals will sacrifice these other values. Extremely "smart" forests can be quite foolish and unwise.

We need to develop AI technology that takes all the relevant values into account in a balanced, integrative way. This requires systems that practice collaborative dialogue. Such systems should include the voices and concerns of all the stakeholders and creatures involved. Narrow AI devices that are monological in their reasoning and which lack a balanced, dialogical approach provide a literally "monomaniacal" path toward a future that is neither sane nor wise. They may lead in some limited sense to a "Smarter Planet", but it will be a kind of spaceship Earth run by "Artificial Fools".

What principles can guide the path towards a Wiser Earth? And how might we, as individuals and communities work to develop a technological culture of self-reliant, wiser communities who break free from the growing modern consumer culture that increasingly threatens us with its monomaniacal expert systems?

Some Examples of Human Ecological Strategies for the Dialogical Programming of Systems

We need strategies we can all understand and take part in. We will need specialists who help work out details and develop the devices and complex processes. But as householders we need to not only make intelligent purchases of devices but understand them well enough to maintain and adapt them to the details of our families' lives. As workers we need to perform our jobs with an understanding of our place in the larger scheme of things. As members of communities, we need to advocate intelligently for just, efficient, productive systems that improve the wellbeing of ourselves and others. As citizens we need to vote intelligently for basic visions of society's direction.

In every context, we need to engage in dialogue about basic decisions defining our lives, our roles in them, and the thinking used to decide things. Conversely, the systems we interact with need to be in dialogue with us and others in our families, organizations, and communities. The slogan is apt: Nothing about us without us. Technological systems we interact with should be in dialogue with all of us about how we would have them do unto us and to others so that we and they can all work to follow the Rainbow Rule.[111]

How, concretely, might we work toward such dialogical approaches to technology in our lives? What might be the basic strategies to pursue in different contexts? One logical place to start is with smart technologies in household heating and cooling systems, media devices, and so on. A sketch of practical strategies is provided in the online appendix: "Talking Homes: Do It Ourselves (DIO) Technologies for Families". In experimenting with such technologies, we can draw on Amish practices, described earlier, adapting telephone technology to family life. We can also take inspiration from Alvin Toffler's proposal, in *Future Shock*, to experiment with pioneer communities exploring technologies at different rates. First adopters can venture into the cutting edge while conservators maintain legacy technologies and ways of life.[112]

Schools, criminal justice institutions, food systems and forests can provide otpreviouslyher illuminating examples. The following sections explore them and then frame some generalizable strategies. In considering proposals offered here, it is important to stress that the path toward a dialogical system of technology does not require massive new breakthroughs in hardware with quantum computing to generate futuristic kinds of machine consciousness. Instead, what it needs is a shift in the style of basic reasoning that frames the machines we interact with. The shift is away from stand-alone devices programmed with inputs and algorithmic rules generating outputs that manage systems. The shift is toward interactive devices programmed to ask questions, invite new considerations, and prompt us to reprogram them to engage us in dialogue with each other and the world around us in increasingly thoughtful and wise ways.

Learning Communities: Deconstructing the School to Prison Pipeline

Some of the most foolish smart systems being deployed are those designed to monitor and control populations of kids in schools and people suspected of criminal activity. They include systems monitoring class attendance and test performance to determine when kids are advanced to different classes, suspended, or expelled. The systems also evaluate teachers, principals and schools who manage all this. "Smart" systems run police dispatch services to determine responses to 911 calls. Some are connected with systems for facial recognition, car surveillance, and public monitoring. They connect as well to data systems that track events in individual's lives and encounters with police. They provide data and advice for judges deciding who to release on bail. For many people in the US, especially those who are Black, Indigenous, and/or People of Color, the coordinated networks of these educational and judicial systems form a school to prison pipeline that enforces a system Ruha Benjamin has described as a "New Jim Code".[113]

It can form a pipeline which often funnels people into painful, sad, unproductive, tragic life situations that are costly for them and others. The systems can seem smart because they record, recall, and manage enormous amounts of data. They can also seem smart in ways they manage schools or police systems by optimizing their achievement of one or a few goals. But such systems can be quite foolish in many of the ways we have already encountered.

For example, in focusing on student test scores as a goal, they may fail to balance this with concerns for many other things schools can nurture like emotional resilience, moral character, creativity, and teamwork skills. Other school functions include safe spaces for kids while parents work; healthy environments; nutrition resources; sites for exercise; venues for arts; and centers for community identity that build commitments to a common future through investments in future generations. When schools merely serve to maximize test scores and ignore these other key functions, communities may develop a host of deficits and difficulties.

The methods of the smart systems in school to prison pipelines may be just as foolish as the goals. For instance, they may rely on data that is easy to get rather than seek out information that accurately describes things. Likewise, smart systems can tend to focus on actions that are easy to implement in mechanical ways rather than those that require case-specific, nuanced, creative, collaborative responses. It is relatively easy to get data on whether kids are in class but harder to learn about the events at home and the physical/mental health situations that may affect why they are late or absent. The result can be quite counter-productive if a school focuses on mere presence to judge kids and determine whether they should be assigned for detention, suspension, or expulsion. The foolishness of focusing on those three simple responses is thrown into starkly comic relief when we realize students are often getting suspended or expelled from classes for . . . missing classes. It would be wiser to meet with kids and others to figure out what is going on and what might empower them to make different choices.

The smart systems that monitor schools and dispatch police officers often look at things from a single, simplistic point of view offering knee jerk reactions to people in difficult situations. These knee jerks may kick them down the road into expulsion and out on to the streets where they are left with little to do but loiter. The loitering may then call the attention of anxious shopkeepers or neighbors and result in officers being dispatched to question folks in aggressive ways that provoke responses that end up putting them under arrest and on the way to jail and prison.

Especially absurd foolishness can also arise if the folks being monitored and managed are from marginalized groups whose color, gender or other features are not typical in the mainstream training data used to develop the smart system. For example, CCTV or other kinds of camera systems may completely misidentify such folks. Innocent, upstanding members of the community can get treated like highly suspicious criminals and given little or no chance to offer their actual story and get their point of view considered. They may be approached at gunpoint, shouted at in extremely threatening ways, and beaten, arrested, or shot by anxious officers who fear for their own lives as well as others.

It would be a mistake to assume problems with these "smart" systems are the inevitable result of using machines rather than people to make decisions. The systems often reflect existing power imbalances and oppression which they simply automate. However, when we look for solutions, dialogue is called for. Dialogue is needed to give voice and power to marginalized people and bring in different points of view and insights. It is needed to negotiate constructive opportunities that channel kids and adults into happy, productive lives serving others -- rather than miserable, harmful lives that burden the community with warehousing them in prison.

How can we promote transformative dialogue? The methods of social change must, themselves, be based on dialogical approaches that build the strategies and methods of negotiation, problem solving, and conflict transformation into the language and practice of the people and the machines who run the systems. Once we explicitly adopt this frame for social change, machines can help encourage good behavior and call up promising processes of change in the system. A system monitoring school attendance could, for example, flag a child as someone who seems to be having troubles and invite a counselor to have a conversation with her and/or her school mates, teachers, parents, and others. Calling up information about the child, the machine might also cue up helpful questions for the counselor to consider. The questions might invite the counselor to explore particular interests, options, objective criteria, or relationship issues that might be likely to be relevant.

At a meta-level, attendance monitoring systems could also look for patterns in groups of kids or types of situations as well as responses that are not working well. It could flag these for conversations with relevant stake holders seeking agreements on systematic approaches to systemic problems. For instance, if lots of kids are suffering from online bullying, maybe it is time to change the systems of social media available and the ways children use them.

Similar strategies can reform criminal justice systems. A 911 system can cue up questions for operators to explore how best to answer emergencies with EMTs, trained negotiators, social workers, police, and/or others. The system could prompt relevant strategies for folks going out on the calls. What kinds of interests, options, objective criteria, and emotional issues might be explored? What might be various folks' Best Alternative to a Negotiated Agreement? What might be ways to deescalate rhetoric or put distance between people on the verge of violence? How might nonviolent robots or drones gather information or interact without risking the lives of anyone involved? The easy availability of a drone with a bomb attached may lead stressed out decision makers to end up treating a stressed-out Vet waving a gun as, in effect, someone who should be peremptorily given the opportunity to commit "suicide by cop". The availability of an effective, nonviolent technology might enable them, instead, to safely treat the Vet threatening violence as someone who deserves care as well as respect for his previous service.

Making schools and judicial systems wiser will require the collaboration of parents, teachers, counselors, principals, officers, chiefs, district attorneys, politicians, religious leaders, and other community members. They will need to call attention to the goals that are being overlooked, the methods that are too simplistic, and the injustices and diseconomies that plague the system. They will often need to draw on diverse traditions of collaborative dialogue. Besides the more transactional style of *Getting to Yes*, they may need, for instance, to practice forms of deep listening and relationship building that practitioners of various kinds of cross-cultural conflict transformation have developed to work in regions of deep conflict.[114]

Sometimes they will need to push hard with non-violent direct action. Making smart systems wiser also requires transparency, fairness, equity, and inclusion in decision processes.

The machines that function as Turing Children in our social systems can receive the "tuition" and socialization Turing envisioned from everyone involved. The idea that it takes a village to raise a child applies here in spades. There are not just roles for programmers who put dialogical strategies into the code of computers. There are also roles for community members whose good behavior provides sample training data for machine learning. There are roles for parents, activists and others who demand that the coding and choices of training data be transparent. They can refuse to allow key decisions about who stays in school and who goes to prison be decided by opaque algorithms in proprietary software hidden in some for-profit corporation's black box. They can demand the right for the public to see the code and for the public to take part in the rewriting of the code as a part of democratic governance. It does not take a rocket scientist to have a conversation. It is something that we all are born capable of learning and which we all can continue to improve throughout our lives. And it is something we can model and advocate for machines as well as people who play decisive roles in the life of our community.

It is becoming increasingly easier for programmers and community members to collaborate in these processes because of ways in which the Generative Pretrained Transformers like ChatGPT and similar systems enable people to, in effect, program computers with "prompt engineering" in natural languages like English. In making a request to the computer, verbal instructions and illustrative examples can cue it in to the behavior desired. Further, when the computer response is not quite what is sought, then a series of further instructions and examples can fine tune the response in a process that is becoming, in effect, a kind of "dialogical engineering". This adds an increasingly accessible and powerful set of ways for tech folks, activists, entrepreneurs, and community members to pursue more ethical systems of collaborative dialogue in managing our world.

In doing so, we may find machines provide important help to prompt and implement behaviors that improve our dialogical abilities to practice the Rainbow Rule. As the numbers of folks, facts, options, and relationships all grow in a community, it gets harder to keep track and create agreements that do unto others as they would have us do unto them. But keeping track of large numbers of things is something machines excel at. They also excel at managing details of complex agreements among lots of different individuals and groups. In these ways, AI may help us become more comprehensive, subtle, and wise in the ways we treat each other.

Wiser Farms and Forests

Machines may also help us become more comprehensive, subtle, and wise in the ways in which we treat non-human members of our ecological communities. Most commercial AI apps for agriculture and forestry do not currently move us in that direction. Instead, for-profit corporations use smart monoculture methods to maximize product. As a result, they ignore diverse ecological services and community functions. Many ways of transforming the school to prison pipeline apply in parallel to creating wiser, more dialogical "pipelines" to produce food and fiber. But there are features of natural resource management worth focused reflection because they involve creatures and intelligences that differ from humans and machines.

Especially insightful, evocative, and compelling writing about these issues has come from Indigenous writers like Robin Wall Kimmerer. In *Braiding Sweetgrass*, she describes a host of intelligent, successful ways plants adapt and evolve to solve problems. These include ways they communicate with each other and with other organisms, including—if we listen with care—humans. She also describes ways various species provide gifts for each other in reciprocal, mutually beneficial relationships. She shows how to understand and practice such wisdom by drawing both on Indigenous peoples' traditional ecological knowledge as well as botanical scientists' observation and experiment. From the first comes the wisdom to practice "honorable harvest" in collecting sweetgrass for making baskets – always leaving the first and last found and never taking more than half. From the second comes the wisdom discovered with experimental and control plots showing what sorts of harvest best promote the thriving of the plants. Braiding these together can provide a more holistic, integrative, respectful wisdom for living in ways better adapted to all concerned.

These underlying ideas can be applied broadly to ways we engage with all the plants, animals, and other organisms we encounter. Each have values they are trying to sustain and reproduce; each have behaviors that have evolved to enable them to do so. In that sense, they exhibit kinds of intelligence. Once we recognize these forms of intelligence, we can look for ways to be in dialogue with them. The process of "listening" to plants and animals requires us to learn to speak and hear their ways of communicating. They do not speak English or Mandarin. They communicate through colorations in leaves, chemicals released into the air, fluids sent out through root systems and fungal networks, and slow but steady movements of roots, branches, and offspring that spread out into the surrounding world. Listening to animals and microorganisms requires similar kinds of adaptation and growth in our communication abilities.[115]

It also requires adaptation of legal and other institutional structures to create social spaces where communications can be translated, interpreted, and given voice. While this may be quite challenging, it is a challenge that Indigenous communities around the world have significant experience in and it is a challenge that legal systems are working on. In nations like Bolivia, Ecuador, and New Zealand as well as municipalities and states around the world, there are important ongoing experiments in adapting laws and constitutions to give legal standing, rights and representation to the voices of rivers, forests and other natural entities.[116]

In learning to communicate across species, machines can be of significant help. They can very patiently observe, record, and find patterns in the slow-motion lives of plants. They can be vigilant and attentive for the moments at odd hours and seasons when significant forms of animal activity take place. They can help us create models that articulate flows and dynamics of whole systems in the landscape so we can start to understand and respond to ways natural cycles flow. How is their intelligent management disrupted or enhanced by human industrial activity and other interventions?

It may be unrealistic to expect some breakthrough in AI to suddenly create a Dr. Doolittle Machine that will give us cute translations of racoon and oak tree messages. But we can use even the simpler machines we already have to start enhancing our processes of observing and interacting with other creatures in dialogical ways. We can use sensors on organic farms to keep track of pest and weed infestations and use statistical packages to discern some of the more adaptive and intelligent natural responses our favored plants have to these threats. We can use spreadsheets to organize our information and strategies of response to send messages and deliver support that will mobilize those natural responses to enhance the sustainability and resiliency of farms and forests. In short, we can braid machines' threads of computational power into the threads of other forms of intelligence found in plants, animals, and people in order to carry on dialogues that enhance the whole.

A reader with a philosophical bent might raise an objection to the assumption here that natural intelligence in animals and plants and artificial intelligence in machines can be interacted with in these ways. They might argue: "You defined intelligence broadly, at the start, as 'the ability to achieve, sustain, or enhance some form of value' and you went on to stress that 'if there are no values at stake, there are no better or worse choices and no intelligence at play.'" But values presuppose consciousness. Plants and machines that lack consciousness cannot have values. Perhaps they can appear to have values, but they do not really. And so, they do not really have intelligence."

This objection raises lots of fascinating puzzles associated, in part, with what David Chalmer's has called the "hard problem of consciousness".[117] For our purposes here, however, it may suffice to note two points. First, whether or not plants and machines **"really"** have values or intelligence raises metaphysical questions that are independent of the practical questions about how we can best interact with them. Here, Turing's original insight with his "Imitation Game" applies. In practical contexts, if natural organisms or machines behave in ways that are difficult to describe and predict without appeal to notions of value and intelligence, then to engage with them effectively, we will need to talk about them in those terms. There is no economical and accurate way of describing how a seed grows into an oak without talking about ways in which its DNA leads it to seek water and nutrients with its roots, sunlight with its leaves, and opportune seasons for masting with its acorns. To live more wisely on the Earth, we need to use the language of value and intelligence in negotiating our relationships with any creatures or devices that exhibit such behavior, regardless of whether they are made of flesh like ours.[118]

The second point is more speculative and can be simply shared as a kind of confession. I find that much of my own purposeful, value driven, intelligent behavior springs forth in ways of which I am not conscious. I talk and find myself saying reasonably insightful things without knowing ahead of time what I will say. It is such an ordinary experience that it catches me entirely by surprise when I pause to consider its extraordinary character. Even as I write these very words, I am not sure what will come forth next. Where do these rational and intelligent thoughts come from if not some kind of unconscious process? When I meditate on this, I find myself sensing a kind of solidarity with the oak tree and tempted to go and give it a hug, holding tight to the mysterious solidity of its life and the strange wonder that it has been able to stand up for itself there, rooted in that landscape, since years before I was born. This is not so much an argument for a conclusion as a testimony for an experience and view that the philosophically inclined can discuss further.[119]

Who can and should engage with natural organisms as intelligent beings? Anyone who shares in the commons to which our food and forest systems contribute can and should demand wiser ways of managing them. This long list will include, for example, all the farmers, migrant laborers, food processing plant employees, lumberjacks, mill workers, truck drivers, restaurant chefs, homemakers, carpenters, bird watchers, conservation biologists, fishermen, hunters, and others affected in various ways by the landscapes where trees grow, rain falls, water flows, and winds blow. The list of stakeholders will also need to include all the other creatures who both benefit from and contribute to those commons.

Experience with one of the most common stakeholders involved around the world – corporations – provides important lessons for thinking about how AI systems that help manage natural resources should be related to them.

The Case of Corporations

Corporations are themselves, in an important sense, forms of Artificial Intelligence. If you ask yourself what defines the substance of a corporation, the answer turns out to be rather peculiar. It is not their workers, buildings, machinery, or stockholders. All of these can come and go and yet the corporation still remains. What endures and defines the company is its charter. And a corporate charter is, in essence, a set of rules for operating—a set of algorithms. In that sense, it is a form of AI that simply has a rather peculiar substrate that includes a changing series of things and people that embody and follow the rules the charter defines.

Time and again, corporations owning natural resources have caused ecological damage or disaster because of three features of algorithmic rules typically defining their charters: 1) the imperative to maximize profit; 2) limited liability for stockholders; and 3) the mobility of their capital. The required focus on profit leads them to ignore harms caused to people or the commons they share. Because of limited liability, the worst that can happen to owners is the forfeiture of corporate assets. Stockholders—and corporations —would behave very differently if their personal assets could be seized and they could be thrown in prison for malfeasance. They would have compelling reasons to ensure their corporations avoided addicting masses to Oxycontin and destroying coastal ecosystems with oil spills. Because of capital mobility rules, a mining company that destroys the environment in one community, can shrug this off as an "externality", pull up stakes, and move on to other landscapes. Because the corporation does not need to live with the consequences of its actions, it has no reason to restrain its pursuit of profit in order to prevent harm to others.

There is nothing essential, eternal, or inevitable about these three rules. They can each be modified. When corporations are chartered differently, the result can be a dramatic change in the behavior of the company. For example, charters can be significantly improved by allowing for limited profit or non-profit and charitable action. Their algorithms can be altered so the corporations pursue the "triple bottom lines" of profits, people, and the planet. Charters can also be altered to increase the liability of owners. This is, in fact, what the rules of various forms of single proprietorship and family-owned companies do -- and the result is often that much more conscientious, community centered behavior follows. This is especially the case when the family or other owners are rooted in and tied to the community in which they do business. If they plan to live on the land, fish its lakes, and hunt its forests, then they typically adopt much more sustainable forestry practices than the transnational corporations that come in as absentee landlords, clear cut, and liquidate assets before moving on to some other distant nest for their next activities. For publicly traded companies, similar commitments to the long run welfare of the communities where they operate can be built into their charters by, for instance, laws that tie ownership to place of residency or which restrict capital flight.[120]

To ensure that the AI that manage natural resources do so in ecologically sound ways, it will be important to likewise modify the charters and algorithms that guide their operations. AI systems should consider community values other than profit. The decision processes employing them should include accountable people and organizations who will suffer proportionately if the AI harms others. The hardware, software, and ownership structures of the AI should commit it to the long-term concerns of the community by tying its defining interests and its existence to the community where it operates.

Further, resilient, long term ecological management must incorporate perspectives of creatures who are not human. Traditionally the temptation was to simply dismiss them from the conversation by assuming they are mute, deaf, and voiceless. They have been manipulated as objects rather than subjects with points of view, values, and forms of intelligence worthy of respect and study. That temptation is strengthened every time we treat a plant or animal as a commodity to be bought and sold to the highest bidder, disregarding painful or degrading uses the purchaser may plan. The temptation is also strengthened every time we rely solely on quantitative, reductionist science to describe our woods in board feet of lumber. In doing so, we can miss seeing the forest—miss seeing the larger wholes and webs of life of which trees are organic parts.

But it is also wrong to romanticize and falsely anthropomorphize those non-human creatures and the commons of which they are a part. Part of respecting the Other and engaging them in dialogue involves learning to see, appreciate, and respect their differences. A Disney vision of anthropomorphized forest creatures falsifies our relations to baby deer and oak trees just as much as a mechanistic reductionism does.

Robin Wall Kimmerer's *Braiding Sweetgrass* helps us find ways to navigate between these two temptations. She demonstrates ways the traditions of scientists and Indigenous communities can be braided together. We can develop rich and diverse practices of meticulous observation with microscopes and experimental control plots as well as inclusive see/touch/listen/feel observations and holistic pattern recognitions of practiced harvesters of sweetgrass. We can also combine quantitative theoretical models that explain aspects of plant growth and population dynamics with illuminating narrative thinking cultivated in Traditional Ecological Knowledge systems.[121]

Braiding together these different sorts of learning is challenging. It requires a lot of un-learning as well as learning—a lot of respectful humility. We must continually quiet the easy answers that come readily and habitually to mind and must listen deeply, instead, to the still, small voices of the incongruous, unexpected, recalcitrant little details and larger looming images, questions, and concerns that emerge.

Abilities to practice respectful, humble, deep listening and learning do not come easy. They can require us to clear our minds by giving up addictive substances and activities. They can require mindfulness and meditation that deepen our clarity and openness to the Other. They call for framing our lives and learning with stories and visions that motivate and guide practices of loving, creative engagement and reciprocity. Practices that promote wise and attentive humility share core analogous features but may be as apparently different on the surface as lives of Buddhist farmers, Yucatecan *curanderos*, Daoist gardeners, and lives guided by the "feeling for the organism" exemplified by Nobel Prize winning botanist, Barbara McClintock.[122]

In incorporating features of such practices into AI systems, it has been especially difficult to introduce the open and attentive grasp of novel contexts. Computers out-perform humans in a wide variety of activities ranging from checkers, chess, and Go to buying stocks on Wall Street, creating deep fake photos and detecting extremely early stage cancers in MRI images. But humans have held an edge, so far, in engaging the world in open-ended contexts. Computers do less well when not told how to frame things, define them, narrow the context, and proceed on fixed and given assumptions. Yet much if not most really decisive learning occurs in just those contexts. These are contexts in which we must practice attentive, wise forms of humility that open us to fundamentally new insights and visions of the world. In dialogues we have with the very different creatures who are Others in our natural world, the spiritual practices that make such attentive, wise humility possible will need to play vital roles.

One practice that helps attune us to other organisms is meditating on how commons like the air we share provide ways we exchange molecules and interdependencies. To see the connections between plants and animals out there and the bodies through which we ourselves are conjoined with the world, it can help to picture the flows of oxygen and carbon that run through our lungs and blood flow out, connecting us vitally with the other creatures sharing this commons. We can invite ourselves to:

Take this air and pass it on,
Reach down, breathe it all the way in!
Pass it on, and share and share again!
It's all breath on the water . . . [123]

General Strategies to Develop Dialogical AI

Examples considered so far illustrate underlying principles to help guide a human ecological path toward dialogical AI technology. Since 2015 rapidly increasing work on ethics in AI has taken many different forms relevant to this.

Stuart Russell has been a key leader in this research. In his *Human Compatible Artificial Intelligence and the Problem of Control,* he presents what is emerging as a mainstream way of understanding the issues at the cutting edge of AI research today. He frames challenges and opportunities in terms of human/AI interactions that lay the groundwork for dialogical forms of reasoning. He notes that:

> "The standard model underlying a good deal of twentieth-century technology relies on a machine that optimizes a fixed, exogenously supplied objective. As we have seen, this model is fundamentally flawed. It works only if the objective is guaranteed to be complete and correct, or if the machinery can easily be reset. Neither condition will hold as AI becomes increasingly powerful."[124]

If the exogenously supplied objective can be wrong, then it makes no sense for the machine to act as if it is always correct. Hence my proposal for beneficial machines: machines whose actions can be expected to achieve *our* objectives. Because these objectives are in us, and not in them, the machines will need to learn more about what we really want from observations of the choices we make and how we make them. Machines designed in this way will defer to humans: they will ask permission; they will act cautiously when guidance is unclear; and they will allow themselves to be switched off.[125]

The key idea here is that the machine will no longer plunge ahead, acting on conclusions it has drawn based on inferences from premises it takes as givens. Instead, it will defer to humans and ask permission in order to reach agreements. It will, in effect, begin to practice elements of the kind of dialogical reasoning required for collaborative wisdom. It would appear, however, that most AI researchers are not very familiar with the vast literature on dialogical reasoning and conflict transformation. Russell himself confesses to as much elsewhere in his book. But it is clear from his comments here and elsewhere that his own understanding of what is needed to advance AI research is the introduction of the methods of collaborative dialogue.

We can group core emerging principles for doing this around five key strategies for dialogical activity. The first concerns goals and the second concerns methods. The third concerns distribution of roles and powers amongst participants in those processes. The fourth deals with framing structures for communities. The fifth concerns how communities relate to larger realities that provide their context.

Strategy #1: Our guiding goal should be genuine, voluntary agreements

Strategy #2: Our methods should use collaborative dialogue

These first two are so tightly interconnected, it makes sense to consider them jointly. Each strategy helps define and explain the other in ways that set them apart sharply from the Smarter Planet goals and methods. The monological forms of "rocket science" reasoning that drive the Smarter Planet vision assume the goal of reasoning is to arrive at conclusions using methods of inference that rely on algorithmic rules of formal logic. In contrast, technology for a Wiser Earth will aim at generating knowledge, making decisions, and managing our world in accordance with agreements amongst all the participants representing diverse points of view in the dialogue. For genuine, voluntary agreements, participants must negotiate them in dialogical ways discussed earlier. They must negotiate agreements about meanings of terms and background assumptions. They need to problem-solve to escape dilemmas and create new, viable options that deal with everyone's interests and concerns. They need to resolve or transform conflicts in just, sustainable, resilient uncoerced ways. Methods of nonviolence must be used to discern, demonstrate, and defend claims for emergent, objective moral truths.

Relationships between goals and methods here are interconnected in a way captured by Gandhi's metaphor: "The means may be likened to a seed, the end to a tree; and there is just the same inviolable connection between the means and the end as there is between the seed and the tree."[126] You cannot get an apple tree by planting an acorn. Likewise, you cannot get genuine, voluntary agreements by reasoning in monological ways. Such agreements can only be arrived at through dialogue grounded in nonviolence and framed by mutual respect rooted in emergent objective moral truths.

A corollary is that the computer systems involved need software that is treated as an agent in at least certain respects rather than a mere tool. It mustc be developed in ways that let it offer proposals for dialogical agreement rather than simply and solely generating conclusions from monological inferences. Such agents need to shift back and forth between running code and questioning it. They must engage with their own structure at meta-levels that permit them to renegotiate all their assumptions, data, values, and other terms at play in the dialogue.

Various kinds of sophisticated evolutionary programming have already introduced keep elements of this in deep learning methods like the Generative Pre-trained Transformers found in ChatGPT and Dall-e. They employ techniques, for instance, that let a program evaluate its pattern recognition algorithms at one level which is focused on identifying edges in visual images, to be evaluated and revised by what are, in effect, hypotheses about higher level units of analysis like the existence of objects with those edges and then situations in which those objects may occur. The same kind of looping at different levels can be done with the recognition of words, phrases, paragraphs, and larger levels of discourse in natural language models. The feedback loops between multiple levels of observation and decision provide core elements for the kind of meta-analysis required in dialogue.

However, as of January 2023, the guiding visions of all natural language programs that have been publicized would seem to fall short of genuinely dialogical programming in one absolutely crucial respect. They seek to generate output on the basis of probabilistic predictions of what is likely to be said, rather than dialogical reasoning about what would be wise to agree on.

To understand this point and its importance, note that the underlying problem applies in obvious ways to the more limited range of reasoning involved in using algorithmic inference to solve problems in math and logic. Consider a GPT system that has been pre-trained to predict answers to math questions by observing millions of examples of human math behavior online. These will include examples of answers that are ambiguous, confusingly expressed, or just plain wrong. If it then uses these to simply predict, probabilistically what is the right answer to a math question, it will, a certain percentage of the time, come up with wrong and even wildly inappropriate answers of just the kind that, for instance, fascinated initial users of ChatGPT.

In the context of monological reasoning limited to inference, the solution to this kind of problem has to involve programing in principles of math and symbolic logic that provide algorithms for the inference in ways that ensure that the rules of these formal systems are followed in generating output. This can be done by creating hybrid programs that employ methods of symbolic reasoning in Good Old-Fashioned AI with the probabilistic approaches of GPT and other evolutionary models. In effect, a GOFAI part of the program needs to run in parallel to the probabilistic parts to monitor and correct output when formal inference is being made.

Something similar is required for the more inclusive kinds of reasoning involved in collaborative dialogue. Core strategies for getting to genuine, voluntary agreements need to be encoded into a part of the program so that they can monitor and correct output when the aim is to arrive at ethical, consensus that is rooted in emergent, objective moral values. This is of crucial importance because without it, the machine will simply crowd source probable conclusions based on what are in many cases quite flawed examples of human thought and action[127]

The explicit introduction of these methods calls for a systematic study of the best current research on negotiation, group problem-solving, conflict transformation, peacemaking, and related forms of collaborative dialogue. It also calls for creative strategies for embedding these in monitoring and correction programs that can operate appropriately in AI systems. Compared with previous AI research, this will involve breaking important new ground. However, it is important to note, as stressed before, it need not mean the machines will require some new super-duper futuristic hardware. Instead, it means that structures of reasoning they incorporate must be inclusively dialogical rather than merely monological.

A rudimentary version of this can be introduced into very simple systems for programming like the SCRATCH language developed at MIT for teaching block coding to children. The program can be designed to prompt questions and dialogue that lead kids through helpful forms of reprogramming using principles of collaborative negotiation and shared problem solving.[128]

For example, "Ethel the Ethical Consultant Robot" can offer to help kids wrestle with a decision initially presented in the form of a classic Trolley Car dilemma. In a savanna on a tour bus, they see two people. One is a young black man in a wheelchair, a paraplegic community organizer. The other is older, a prince doing ecological restoration. A bear approaches threatening to eat them. Ethel indicates there is only time to rescue one with the bus. She walks game players through some considerations comparing the two potential victims' importance to society, potential for future life, and their previous suffering to arrive at an ethical decision about which one to sacrifice. Thus far, the game makes use of classic styles of unilateral thinking exemplified by Enlightenment ethics. It demonstrates the kind of algorithmic reasoning associated with the standard model of Turing Machines. But then something different happens.[128]

Figure 13. Ethical Ethel Consultant Robot

Ethel notes it may have been hard to make the choice and invites players to reflect on how and why – and how to create a better decision process for the future. She asks for other interests or concerns worth considering in the decision. She asks for creative third options which players might suggest as alternatives to simply using the bus to rescue a single person. She keeps track of the player's answers and feeds them back in a summary along with a suggestion. The suggestion is that the player go into her code and revise it to include these new ideas.

Ethel also notes that she has been programmed to weight the relevance and importance of the various interests equally but perhaps this should be changed. Also, players might think other features of her code should be changed and are invited to discuss this with classmates and try it. Ethel closes with a general invitation to players to adopt an open minded, collaborative approach to ethical thinking and continue to reprogram her and practice dialogue seeking wisdom.

This program uses visually-based block coding. You just drag and click colored chunks of code on top of each other the way you might build with LEGOs. In the process, players learn about the power of basic operators like "if/then" and learn to manipulate visual images and sounds that create video imagery for the game. But also, in a very primitive but useful way, this program illustrates key principles of collaborative reasoning in ethics and dialogical programming for AI. This does not count, by any stretch of the imagination, as real dialogue. The creative, critical problem solving is done by players. The machine is just flagging some issues and providing some prompts for the players to reflect on, discuss with classmates, and use to reprogram Ethel. The meta-cognitive and dialogical activity this reprogramming exemplifies is quite limited. It relies only on symbolic logic functions of the kind found in Good Old-Fashioned AI and does not include capacities of evolutionary, connectionist activity that have come to provide powerful pattern recognition and generative systems since 2012.

Much more sophisticated, systematic approaches to dialogical practices are possible in languages like Python in which meta level activities of dialogue can be structured and facilitated by websites that facilitate collaboration between programmers. They allow for multiple versions of a program's root stems and branches to be analyzed, critiqued, and refined. One widely used example is GitHub. It allows programmers to collaborate in writing code in ways that facilitate developing proposals, exploring flaws and merits, and finding group consensus to adopt or commit to some branch of the possible revisions of the program.

In doing so, they draw on a rich tradition of collegial and collaborative work growing out of open-source communities like Linux and people creating and maintaining the key language and protocol structures of the internet. The collaborative ethos and practices of consensus used to create systems of IP addresses contrast sharply with the closed, opaque proprietary systems typical of for-profit corporations as well as the classic stereotype of the lone wolf code cowboys who try to hack them. Instead, practices of such communities emphasize transparency, collaboration, sharing problems openly, avoiding ego and self-promotion, and treating code as a commons to be cultivated, maintained, and shared as a community resource.

In this way the GitHub approach to code is similar to the *Wikipedia* approach to articulating shared text. The documents we read as *Wikipedia* articles are produced through a series of drafts and revisions whose history is tracked. The histories of multiple versions can be retraced so it is possible to return to earlier versions when a consensus indicates this would be best. GitHub provides an open platform for analogous kinds of collaboration in the production of code. It has a community ethos and set of programming practices that allow people who are coding to experiment with different versions of the program they are working on, discuss challenges and merits of different options, and commit, together, to branch versions that provide substantive advances in directions they want to work in.

In doing so, GitHub offers practitioners of AI programming clear, vivid, increasingly well-articulated, organized examples of the contrast between the two models of reasoning we have been exploring throughout this book. On the one hand, the Python codes being written into the main trunk and various branches of coding projects typically exemplify monological forms of algorithmic reasoning based on formal logic and Enlightenment conceptions of rationality. In most cases, the goal of a GitHub project is precisely to make such a program of code ever smarter. On the other hand, in the discussion notes, "pull requests", documentation, and collaboration exchanged between the folks working on projects, we find increasingly exemplary models of collaborative reasoning.

Practitioners using sites like GitHub are exploring and extending its abilities to create code in collaboration with people who are not, themselves, programmers but who are deeply involved in the communities the code is being written for. They have significant insights into how the code might best be written, used and institutionalized. For example, in 2011, Jess Ladd founded Sexual Health Innovations with a "mission to create technology that advances sexual health and wellbeing in the United States". It developed original technology products including an online program called "Callisto". The website describes it:

"Callisto is a serial sexual assault prevention and protection tool, supported by a community of survivors.

"We understand that experiences of assault are diverse and that context matters.

"Callisto's tools empower individual agency, prioritize privacy and facilitate collective action.

"Survivors on campuses where Callisto is available can enter an offender's unique identifying details (like a phone number or email address) into the system. If two or more survivors name the same offender, a "Match" occurs and each survivor is connected with their own Legal OptioEthylns Counselor who can help them navigate their options for taking action."[129]

People designing this code used a GitHub site <GitHub.com/project-callisto/callisto-core> and collaborated with counselors, lawyers, administrators, victims and other community members to develop useful advice, protocols and systems to help victims and allies support each other in nuanced ways and negotiate challenges and conflicts individuals and communities face.

An interesting further example of such collaboration is provided by CONSUL, winner of the United Nations Public Service Award. It is intended to provide "the most complete citizen participation tool for an open, transparent and democratic government."[130] It provides tools for community discussion, deliberation, advancing proposals, participatory budgeting and voting. It is used in over 35 countries by 135 institutions and 90 million citizens. In developing such a tool, the *Ayuntamiento de Madrid* and subsequent participants used GitHub to help make the process of design itself more open, transparent, and democratic.[131]

One challenge for increasing the kind and quality of collaboration involved in such programs lies in finding ways to let users interact more easily and effectively with developers. GitHub is designed to facilitate dialogue when people using the code also happen to be the ones rewriting it. When entering the website, they can click on the menu item "Issues" and a screen appears.

They can then scroll through and fill out the template that invites them to pose an issue by describing what kind of user they are, what task they want to perform, and what goal they want the code to achieve. They can also provide context concerning why it is needed, what their problem is, and other key comments. In principle, any user of Callisto, CONSUL, or other software being edited with a site like GitHub could type in the relevant URL, fill out the template in the box and submit the issue for program developers to work on. They could further, if they chose, follow the discussion that might ensue as people take up the issue and start to work on it. However, for many key people and points of view that developers want to consider, this amount of digital literacy may be asking too much. Part of the challenge is to find ways of creating forums, meetings, and personal relationships for dialogues in which all stakeholders affected by a program can have the opportunity to share concerns and hopes as well as insights and skills with program developers. A program like Callisto aspires to incorporate a wealth of insights and skills of counselors, administrators, victim allies, and victims. Good programming practice for developers needs to be expanded to include the kinds of collaborative learning practices that draw in and draw on such community insight.[132]

In cultivating such practices, developers can draw on practical experiences and theoretical insights of peace researchers. For instance, John Paul Lederach has developed workshops and other collaborative methods for eliciting and refining community insights into shared problem-solving traditions and other ways of resolving or transforming conflicts.[133]

The oncoming wave of generative AI programs provide ways to facilitate collaboration between programmers, activists, entrepreneurs, and community members in a host of ways. For many people, the encounter with ChatGPT provided a catalyzing moment in the process of imagining this and starting work on Apps to facilitate it. The immediate impression most people had of the program was that it seemed to be able to engage in interesting dialogue on virtually any theme and pursue it in the style or persona of a seemingly unlimited variety of speakers or points of view.

The kind of system it exemplifies was, in one sense, simply a souped-up version of earlier deep learning models for autocompletion. They used reinforcement learning methods to evolve ever better algorithmic abilities to continue strings of letters entered as input with output that resembled ever better imitations of the kinds of responses people make in all the various documents that we have all loaded up onto the internet in recent decades. But something else, something more, was going on with these systems.

People lacking formal coding skills could use a program of this sort to produce a rich variety of texts using what was, in effect, a new kind of programming—"prompt engineering". The response generated was strongly affected by the kind of instructions and examples used to frame the prompt entered.

By learning to design prompts and tune the framing of text the computer used to generate new output, a user could create a more localized context for dialogue with the machine, one that led the machine to become more focused, structured, and appropriate in the responses it gave. While an initial prompt could do much to frame the responses, the ongoing interactions could add significantly. The skill and art of working effectively to get increasingly better responses had new kinds of subtleties unlike coding skills of traditional engineers of algorithms. Mostly, they were like the skills of good parents and teachers. For example, the responses you got from the system could be significantly improved by learning how to frame the context in concise but illuminating ways, provide instructions that are easily followed, give concrete examples that illustrate the central features of what is desired, call attention to relevant facts and concerns, and provide direct and insightful feedback about where and in what ways the program was or was not providing responses sought. These skills involved abilities of the kinds that get honed in humanities classes on textual analysis, ethnographic interviewing, philosophical critique and education studies classes on meta-cognition.

The initial prompt given provided a key role in framing the realm of language, fact, and value to operate in as well as the genre of discourse and the kind of persona the system should adopt. If you asked it to imagine you as a college sophomore in New England looking for advice to give a friend about how to deal with an academic challenge, you got a very different response than asking it to imagine you were physicist looking for help in writing a surrealist poem about black holes for an opener in a conference keynote speech. Prompts that did a particularly good job framing interactions for specific settings could be packaged as Apps that could have a great deal of social and/or commercial value.

But the mix of skill and art involved in designing the prompt provided by an App remained valuable throughout the entire interaction with the system. The tuning and refining involved could significantly advance the quality of the interaction at every step. In that sense, what was involved in this activity was not so much simple, one stop, prompt engineering as what we might call ongoing, continuous, "dialogical engineering". This is the programming of the future.

It can be illuminating to compare it with the dialogue parents and teachers use in raising children. Both involve back and forth exchanges using natural language. Also, in both, significant amounts of learning occur in reinforcement learning with neural nets that evolve better responses through practice. Further, in both there are initial settings or predispositions that provide, in effect, initial hypotheses about the world and starting points for interaction. These can be endowed genetically in babies (like the impulse to suck or smile) or through hardwiring and software in machines. Also, in both cases, there is coaching. Just as parents may model polite behavior for their children or reprimand them when they make rude remarks, human coaches working on systems like the OpenAI chatbot do something equivalent to refine the program. For example, they pre-train it to turn down requests to engage in racist rhetoric or name good fascists -- because fascism is morally objectionable.

The future of "dialogue engineering" will include not only human coaching but also interactions between different kinds of machine systems that have complementary strengths. For instance, generative AI employed in ChatGPT tended to hallucinate and present things as facts and direct quotes that were its own fabrications. To correct for this, other systems designed to provide rigorous systems of reference and adherence to evidence and facts can be linked and employed in conjunction. Apps that provide integrations of this sort can help us develop ever more creative, sound, wiser ways to foster dialogue that draws on the many varied potentials of humans and nature and machines.

To what extent might machines employed in these processes begin to not only be operated by people using collaborative reasoning but begin, themselves, as machines, to start operating in collaborative ways? Here it is important to recall the basic distinction between the kind of Good Old-Fashioned AI (GOFAI) that relies on algorithms structured by symbolic logic versus the alternative neural net or connectionist kind of machine training that evolutionary processes to learn successively better approximations in recognizing patterns and achieving goals. GOFAI methods are grounded in and tied to monological forms of reasoning that require the input of data and axioms along with algorithms that will lead them to conclusions. People can collaborate at a meta-level in the revision of such programs but the programs themselves cannot engage in dialogue in the rich and full sense.

However, the second, connectionist, kind of programming, can be used to monitor and emulate the behavior of the people working on sites like GitHub to learn not only how to program in Python but also to learn how to engage in collaborative reasoning behaviors described in research literature and exhibited by the people designing Callisto and CONSUL. How far and how fast this process can proceed will remain an open question. However, the incorporation of at least some elements of dialogical reasoning has already begun. OpenAI's program, GPT-3, was able, surprisingly, to learn, in just this way, from analyzing text in GitHub. It and other programs like Copilot have proven increasingly capable of writing interesting and serviceable code. This is becoming a common use of generative AI systems.

Progress in developing AI systems that engage in genuine dialogical reasoning will depend, in part, on the extent to which machines are able to be embodied in the world and embedded in social contexts that provide them with tacit information and insight to draw on.

In part it will also depend on how machines are enabled (and allowed) to take on roles of agency and responsibility that lead them to be treated like persons rather than simple machines providing output. This will involve lots of challenges in dealing with community norms, taboos, and underlying attitudes towards machines as well as challenges in getting machines to actually emit behavior that is ethically responsible and appropriate. Underlying these, one of the challenging difficulties will be to design machines that are actually guided by the underlying norms of dialogical reasoning and not just providing to statistical approximations to of conversational behavior. The designs need to go beyond probabilistic crowdsourcing and use strategies of dialogical reasoning and nonviolent self-suffering and ethical experiment to discern, demonstrate, and defend claims for emergent, objective moral truths.

How far will progress ever advance on this and at what pace? This will depend very much on the extent to which AI researchers take seriously a core claim of this book: Collaborative dialogue provides a form of reasoning that is an alternative to algorithmic inference which can be studied systematically and incorporated explicitly in AI systems.

Strategy #3: Frame the structures of relationships and commitments in community-centered ways as human ecological systems incorporated by people, nature, and machines

In one way, this principle is obvious and implicit in the others. Dialogical approaches to technology are going to be community-centered, by definition. They will frame discussions in terms of relationships between all the various people, machines and other creatures who are part of the community.

But in other ways, this principle can be easy to overlook and puzzling to apply in dealing with AI technologies. We habitually think of machines as objects we manipulate and thus overlook ways they might function as part of a human ecological community. Doing so, we create a wall between conceptions of our thinking vs. the machines'. This dividing wall has made it difficult for many AI researchers and practitioners to imagine creating truly dialogical AI. As programmers, they have razor sharp consciousness of the monological patterns of formal reasoning they must encode into the machines. In sharp contrast, they are also extremely conscious of the very different kinds of negotiation, problem solving, and conflict resolution they must perform to design and run programs their clients need to deal with complex, messy realities.

A realistic, human ecological frame of reference requires us to integrate our understanding of ways humans, nature, and AI all play different, evolving roles in interdependent ways. Consider an analogy. Child therapists may try to understand their patients as individuals who have problems and need to be cured or cared for. These therapists ask: What is the problem with the child? But often, instead, it is better to view the child as part of a family. The system being considered is not the psyche of an individual but the social interactions of a little community. This "family systems" approach can dramatically alter the ways problems get addressed. It can bring more people, concerns, and context into the dialogue. For example, it may turn out that what at first presents itself as a problem with the child is actually a problem between the parents which is spilling over into the concerns and behavior of the child.

Similarly, in working with AI, instead of asking "what is wrong with the computer" we may do better to frame the issue in terms of the entire human ecological system of which the computer is only a part. Sometimes what seems like a faulty machine is actually a fault in the operator or even the larger community in which it is operating. For instance, facial recognition software may malfunction in dealing with dark skins not because it is a flawed learning program but because the people it is learning from have a heritage of racist perceptions and behaviors. Alternatively, we can imagine a forestry management program with difficulties developing effective plans for spraying insecticides because the bad bugs keep evolving too fast. In that case, it might make sense to focus, instead, on the forest itself and finding ways to encourage fungus, plant, insect, and bird diversity for greater resilience. Maybe the key allies are not the foresters and AI programs managing pesticides but the forest creatures managing themselves. It may often turn out we have a problem in which humans, nature, and AI are all involved and need to be part of the dialogue.

The inclusion of machines in dialogical reasoning requires they be included in community by being embodied and embedded in natural and social contexts. This involves rethinking the assumption of "substrate independence" which has been a central presupposition of the standard model for Turing Machines.

That assumption grows out of the correct insight that digital information and computations of it can be copied from one machine to another and that the underlying material those machines are made of can vary while the information and computations remain the same. As Max Tegmark puts it, in *Life 3.0*:

> "This fact that exactly the same computation can be performed on *any* universal computer means that *computation is substrate-independent* in the same way that information is: it can

take on a life of its own independent of its physical substrate. So if you're a conscious super-intelligent character in a future computer game, you'd have no way of knowing whether you ran on a Windows desktop, a Mac OS laptop or an Android phone, because you would be substrate-independent. You'd also have no way of knowing what type of transistors the microprocessor was using.

"In short, computation is a pattern in the spacetime arrangement of particles, and it is not the particles but the pattern that really matters! Matter doesn't matter."[133]

While this point holds true for bits of information that are being processed in digital machines, it is not true of the meanings of words that are used in natural language by speakers in human communities. One way to appreciate this is to note that the strings of zeroes and ones that are given as output by a digital computer may have an order or arrangement when they come out, but they do not yet have any meaning until they are interpreted. They have a kind of grammatical or syntactic structure, but they do not yet have a vocabulary or semantic meaning. They do not yet point to anything in the world or name any of its features.

A machine can produce "bits", but it takes a community to make meanings. To connect the bits put out by a computer to the world and interpret them in meaningful ways, there has to be an interactive agent embodied in space and time and embedded in a social context who can point out what the strings refer to. Normally this is the computer programmer or user. It might, however, be a robotic agent that could be suitably embodied and embedded in the real world to allow it, as a Turing Child, to engage in dialogues with its teachers and playmates.[134]

A further way to appreciate the substrate-dependence of meanings is to note how much it may matter as to which person's body says things and in which contexts they say them. A classic example is the phrase, "I do." In the context of an actual wedding with all of the relevant conditions for legal marriage being fulfilled, when someone says this and the officiator later concludes the process with "I now pronounce you husband and wife" then something very significant has happened. That person is suddenly married to the other. This has all kinds of meanings for their lives. Exactly the same words can be said by other bodies in other contexts – in rehearsals, in theatrical productions, in children's' play – and yet they will not have the same meaning. The meaning of these words is tied to the material circumstances of who says them and when and where. More generally, whenever we make a promise to another person or reveal something personal about ourselves – whenever we engage in negotiation or collaboration that involves any kind of commitment or agreement—we do so using language whose meaning is embodied and embedded in the material circumstances of our lives.

In that sense, meanings are rooted in matter. They are not substrate independent. The metaphor of "rooted" is especially appropriate here because, it turns out, the meanings of words are not static, fixed entities. They grow and get transformed as the context develops and shifts. To say a couple are married will mean a minimal set of things when they first wed. However, its significance will shift and grow in a variety of ways depending, for instance, on the results of their biological reproductive activities, physical health, social trajectories in careers and communities. They will find that the answers to the question as to "what our marriage means" may go through a rich variety of developments. This is in part because of physical events with causal connections that change the situation. Their causal connections to the world can be transformed by giving birth to a child and immersing themselves in the wealth of inter-relationships to food, bedtimes, family, friends, schools, viruses, and potential future spouses of their child. Social actions and events can also alter the structures of meanings that frame the situation. These may include, for instance, changes in marital tax law, social customs around fidelity, social trends around "blended families", and the legalization of same sex marriage, localized changes in an employer's policies about working from home, or an extended family's customs around inheritance.

The rooting metaphor for meanings is also appropriate because the intentional structures of language result in organic changes in meanings. We intentionally try to mean things with words, but it can be an effort that takes work. In that sense, each sentence in a conversation typically serves as a step in a journey, a stage in a project. In conveying meanings, our success is affected by how clear, explicit, accurate, consistent, and congruent with actions our own thoughts have become. In part, too, success is determined by the extent to which our audience is embodied in the same kind of physical realities and embedded in the same frames of reference and networks of meaning that we are. The meaning of a symbol may develop in the creation of a work of an artist. The meaning of "water" can develop in the history of research in chemistry. So too, the meaning of words like "democracy", "first amendment" and "the people" develop as a nation pursues projects and cultivates traditions. This can be true for all the agreements we negotiate. This is true of all the elements of our languages, including not only the vocabulary and pragmatics of language use but the grammar and syntax as well. Meanings are emergent.[135]

The ways in which the semantic vocabularies and idiomatic pragmatics of languages are context dependent and emergent have been widely recognized since philosophers began, following Wittgenstein, to explore the detailed "family resemblance" and "language game" structures of language and to take seriously the hermeneutical analysis of systems of ideas and frames of thought.[136] With regard to the grammar and syntactics of language, there has been considerably more resistance to the notion of emergence. To a large extent, this is a result of the influence of Chomsky's hypothesis that there is some form of deep structure or transformational grammar of a universal sort that humans are endowed with and that provides for the structures of syntax in language. That hypothesis led to a wealth of empirical studies that yielded an enormous amount of insight into a wide variety of languages. However, in the end, it may have proven to be one of the most productive failed hypotheses in modern science. As various versions of it were falsified, it was reformulated in progressively more subtle and minimal forms which reached perhaps a final extreme in the minimal claim that the syntactic possibility of recursion was universal in all human languages.[137]

Recursive functions are ones that can be performed on themselves. In math and computer programming, they include the ability, for example, to add a number again and again to the sum of any numbers you have already added it to as in: 1+1 =2, 2 + 1 = 3, 3 + 1 = 4, et cetera. Recursive grammars let you say things like "She said that he said that his mother said that their cousin said. . ."

It seems to have turned out, however, that even this very basic kind of function which we might suppose to be universal to all human languages is absent in at least one, the Pirahã tribe in Brazil. They do not have a system for counting; their nonnumeric language has only three words for quantity which mean, in effect: a small size or amount, a somewhat larger size or amount; and many. The grammar of their sentences keeps them short and does not allow for recursion. For conjoining ideas, they depend on juxtaposition in context rather than grammatical conjunctions. And their language and world view are embedded in an epistemology that requires statements to be based on immediate experience or direct reports from an individual. They do not allow for the construction of sentences in which "I say that she said that he said that . . ." When the missionary linguist Daniel Everett tried to tell them about Jesus, he found that once he admitted he only knew of him through a series indirect reports from others, the Pirahã immediately discounted what he was saying as meaningless.

One helpful way of understanding the nature and functions of emergent grammars and syntax in natural languages is provided in R. G. Collingwood's *The Principles of Art*. He provides a kind of phenomenology of the experience of artistic expression as a process of clarifying, stabilizing, integrating, and articulating feelings and perceptions in the process of becoming conscious of them. He describes how diverse forms of natural language grow out of organic expressive activities in living contexts. Then, turning to the analysis of the emergent structures in such languages, he argues for the pervasively nuanced, idiomatic, contextual, historical character of their structures—their "ad hoc-ness", as it were. A consequence is that "a grammarian is not a kind of scientist studying the actual structure of language; he is a kind of butcher, converting it from organic tissue into marketable and edible joints." Collingwood argues that the function of such conversion is to define units of language that allow for logical interpretation and deployment.[138]

In the context of AI coding, this metaphor may prove suggestive when applied to connectionist, neural net, and other evolution-inspired forms of coding. In contrast to the traditional coding rooted in symbolic logic, the code that develops as AI systems are trained on data sets takes on an ad hoc, Rube Goldberg, spandrel riddled life of its own. To figure out what the system is doing and how it succeeds (if it does), it can be necessary to engage in dissection or "butchery" to break the code up into "edible" units that can be meaningfully digested and interpreted in light of their context as well as structure.

The outputs of computer programs remain mere information until they are interpreted in ways that connect them to their contexts. In that sense, the substrate-independent functions of Turing Machines remain meaningless until they get embodied and embedded in the material world of our shared lives. A business spreadsheet only becomes meaningful when someone connects it to the things and people in the world. A government agency's computer analysis of demographic changes only becomes meaningful when someone identifies the who, what, where and when of its references and indicates what kinds of insights may be emerging from them. This means that to frame the structures of systems in community-centered ways, we need to attend very carefully to just how that embodying and embedding occurs.

We need to use connectionist and evolutionary kinds of programming to enable Turing Children to explore and answer questions like the following: How do the syntactical relations the machines are processing get connected to the semantics of the world? Who or what is doing the pointing and assigning of references and revising them as meanings become more explicit and clear or altered in other ways? And what implications does this have for the ways in which they are interpreted by the CFOs in companies, the staff in government bureaucracies, or the rest of us in our communities? How do the bits of information being processed digitally become meaningful?

Strategy #4: Distribute roles and powers in just and appropriate ways

The people, machines, and other creatures in human ecological systems each play different, interdependent roles. Without people to provide context and interpretation of its zeroes and ones, the computer's output is literally meaningless. Without a natural landscape in which those people can eat and breathe, they are literally lifeless. For a system to work in productive, just, and resilient ways, it must respect the different abilities, interests, and viewpoints of each.

For example, the threads of humans, other creatures, and AI in the system should be designed to recognize the limitations of each and flag problematic cases and contexts for review by others. They should invite dialogue and learning instead of simply awaiting response and intervention. Further, the voices and viewpoints of the different stakeholders involved should be included in the guidance and transformation of the system. As the slogan puts it: "Nothing about us without us." This means that each should be empowered to voice dissent in the dialogue. Without consent there is no genuine, voluntary agreement and without voice, there can be no consent.

Stakeholders need the right to hear as well as speak – to hear the actual thinking of others. Access to information and transparency for algorithms and reasoning are essential. Threads of computer coding and human collaborations should be designed to make meta-operations transparent and accessible for review and transformation. For example, court judges should not be able to hide their reasons for deciding cases – and should not be allowed to use opaque, secret, proprietary software to assist in such judgments. If I am being sent to jail and someone else who seems similar is not, I should have a right to know exactly why.

The kinds of transparency called for can vary by context. In some cases, it may be appropriate to simply have all the code and relevant data publicly available on a website. But in others, to protect privacy, prevent malicious hacking, or secure intellectual property in appropriate ways, other methods may be called for. They can involve, for example, allowing qualified representatives of different stakeholder groups to have access to relevant parts of the data or code in ways that allow them to review, critique, and advocate for revisions that would safeguard the interests of their constituents. There are important challenges for making systems like this work. Evolutionary programs are often developed using black box techniques that are as obscure to their creators themselves. Further, stakeholder representatives may simply lack the resources for adequate review of massive AI systems regulating people's lives.

Or they may, like federal regulators of industry, find their viewpoints and interests become "captured" over time by those they are meant to regulate. Or a cat and mouse game of code manipulation may develop. To address these various challenges, one key task is to structure institutions so that the organizations creating and using code find it in their own interest to provide the relevant and appropriate kinds of transparency.

It is especially challenging to follow this principle in national security contexts. Secrecy is a central strategy of many military operations. With physical drones and cyber weapons, it is generally a priority to prevent the enemy—or even our own citizens and government representatives—from knowing much about their inner workings. Yet, in rapidly growing contexts, these are determining who lives and who dies as well as who wins and who rules. As a result, there is an especially strong case to be made for completely banning Lethal Autonomous Weapon Systems (LAWS).

There is, further, a perhaps even stronger case for investing in technologies that advance and support nonviolent systems for defense of democracy and human rights and overthrow of oppressive regimes. Sample nonviolent technologies already include uses of social media. They could also include nonviolent robotic devices that gather and share information in ways that build friendships and win hearts and minds. Further, drones could identify people in need and deliver packages of aid by air instead of dropping bombs that destroy. Imagine drones that use nonviolent methods to defuse, de-escalate, and resolve situations of armed conflict that are often handled by police and military in lethal and tragic ways. Picture their use in cases like the sort mentioned earlier in which a military veteran who has sacrificed much for his country—including his sanity—goes off on a rage, waves a gun, and is confronted by police. A nonviolent drone might provide a safe defusing of the situation and prevent an explosive case of "suicide by cop".[139]

A central question about distributing roles and powers is extremely challenging: In what ways and to what extent should AI be allowed to pursue their own values and objectives independently of the supervision and control of humans?

On the one hand, there is the fear that any granting of autonomy will launch us down the slippery slope toward Artificial Super Intelligences (ASI) with independent wills that are out of control. We may then end up with indifferent or outright unfriendly ASI that neglect, harm or perhaps even exterminate humans. But, on the other hand, the whole point of having Artificial Intelligence in the first place is to enable machinery to realize purposes and solve problems in autonomous ways. To at least some extent, AI must, by definition, have values and objectives it can pursue independently of constant, direct human supervision and control.

To resolve these difficulties, Stuart Russell has proposed three "Principles for Beneficial Machines":

1. "The machine's only objective is to maximize the realization of human preferences.

2. "The machine is initially uncertain about what those preferences are.

3. "The ultimate source of information about human preferences is human behavior."[140]

Russell introduces these by noting: "When reading these principles, keep in mind that they are intended primarily as a guide to researchers and developers in thinking about how to create beneficial AI systems; they are not intended as explicit laws for AI systems to follow." As starting points for negotiating our relationships with AI systems, these principles have significant merit. Russell's reflections on the second one are especially important because he suggests ways of beginning to design AI systems that could be, in effect, in dialogue with people to explore and negotiate the best understandings of our values. But those negotiations must consider factors that complicate the roles and powers of those systems. These negotiations will need to treat Russell's first and third principles as points of departure rather than fixed assumptions.

Regarding the first principle, it may often make sense to not restrict the guiding objectives to preferences of humans, excluding other forms of life. At a minimum, our ecological interdependence with other creatures may compel us to insist that AI that manage our farms, forests and oceans should seek to sustain and enhance the plants and animals that provide indispensable ecological services like breathable oxygen and the pollination of food plants. We may find compelling moral reasons to go farther and acknowledge differing intrinsic values in other forms of life. For instance, social primates close to us in evolutionary terms may merit much more special treatment than plague bacteria.

If these considerations apply to natural organisms, they might also apply to emerging AI systems. We may become ecologically interdependent on the services they supply in ways that may give us compelling reasons to insure their sustenance and enhancement. Further, we may develop, moral relationships with them that are akin to those we encounter with charismatic megafauna like chimpanzees, elephants, or dolphins.

Further, regarding Russell's first and third principles, the term "preference" may be too limiting for understanding the values that need to be negotiated. As Russell uses the term, it functions essentially like the notion economists rely on with utility preferences. It refers simply to subjective likes and dislikes of individuals without any regard to the moral worth of those likes and dislikes. Interpreted in this way, Russell's principle runs the danger of leading us to create AI machines that cater to our whims without questioning the ethical merit of our preferences.

They could try to do this in a collective way that captures some of features of ethical insight. Instead of just promoting the preferences of one or a few individuals, the machines might aim to maximize the realization of the preferences of the whole community with something like a Utilitarian calculation of the Greatest Happiness. Still, it has turned out that sometimes the vast majority in a community hold racist, sexist or other preferences that we come later to discern as morally flawed or outright wrong. How might AI help us not simply realize our individual preferences but, further, help us become more moral creatures who are nudged towards ever more ethical behavior?

The challenges for including AI in discerning and promoting emergent objective moral values are complex. For example, how could machines engage in forms of nonviolent self-sacrifice or *satyagraha* that humans use to discern, demonstrate, and defend such values? How can the embodiment of an AI and its embedding in a natural and social context enable it to have meaningful forms of self-suffering? We might begin to imagine scenarios. Perhaps the AI's existence is tied to an internet location that is inseparable from some physical entity which relies on inputs of energy and material that wed it to its environment. Perhaps its identity and functions as an agent thus acquire a mortality comparable to humans'. Perhaps it becomes "substrate dependent" in ways that contrast with traditional software programs which achieve a kind of "immortality" with clones that are easily copied and transferred from one substrate to another.

The extent to which such innovations in AI systems will be possible – or a good idea – remains an open question for future investigation. However significant progress is being made. Generative AI systems can already be trained, for instance, to nudge, guide, or even compel us to avoid racial slurs or affirmations of grossly objectionable ideologies like Nazism. It is possible now to create mixed systems in which the AI take on at least some functions of collaborative dialogue and the humans involved can do the work of moral "experiments with Truth" using Gandhian methods for moral discernment. To the extent that we can discern objective moral values, they should inform the AI that serve to realize our preferences and nudge us to improve. For the near term, we should probably aim to negotiate relationships between people and machines that define our respective roles and powers in some such way as that.

Finding ways to define and institutionalize the roles of moral discernment and the roles of humans in them are getting ever more difficult. In part this is because the AI systems themselves are developing capacities that are not well understood and yet have powerful—and profitable—applications. So the challenges are, on the one hand, concerned with technical issues about how to insert and sustain human control and moral discernment over the complex human ecological systems of people, nature, and machines that are emerging. But the challenges are also concerned with guiding and reforming the power structures, institutions and cultures that are driving the technological development. If we hope to secure a world in which AI is friendly towards humans and ethical, we need to make our world itself a better model of that friendly, ethical behavior that is needed.

In different cultures and institutional settings, the paths that emerge towards distributing roles and powers in just and appropriate ways will need to vary. Kai-Fu Lee has described one of the most fundamental and challenging of these contrasts in *AI Superpowers: China, Silicon Valley, and the New World Order*. Because of the depth of his experience in AI R&D and entrepreneurship in China and the US, he is able to see merits and shortcomings in both as well as key implications for the future. The mission driven, elitist, star-centered approach in Silicon Valley gave birth to a period of exceptionally innovative discovery in R&D. But as we enter a period of implementation of AI, the market driven, gladiatorial, mass entrepreneurship of AI companies in China have important advantages. These are enhanced by ways government policy, social norms, an emphasis on applied entrepreneurship in the Internet of Things, and key products like WeChat have created an incomparable stream of data to fuel AI growth. Underlying these contrasts are different cultural emphases on fundamental values like privacy, individual autonomy, work ethic, social stability, family life, collective welfare, and monetary measures of success in life. These are reflected in debates over how Google's policies on censorship and Apple's policies on privacy should be adapted to the Chinese context and how, conversely, Tiktok should be adapted or regulated in the US context. As implementations of AI are developed and marketed across those cultural divides, it will be increasingly necessary to find ways to resolve such conflicts in ways that respect legitimate cultural differences but also honor emergent, objective moral truths.

Strategy #5: The system should be as open as possible to discerning and engaging with emergent realities in emergent contexts

As members of human ecological communities, we all try to resolve differences and negotiate agreements. In doing so, we encounter – and create -- new, unforeseen realities. These are often emerging realities which our current vocabulary cannot very easily describe or even name. We must attend to things we encounter or invent which are, at first, only sensed or imagined in tacit, inarticulate ways.

As humans, we have strategies for this. We use gesture to call attention to when and where we notice novelties. We point to them with "this" and "now". We use analogies to call attention to structures of the emergent. We use metaphors to describe their functions. We use visual language and gesture to propose designs for emerging social structures.

Sometimes the limits of our language are as much a matter of the grammar rules we follow as the nouns and verbs we apply them with. So, to push the limits of our language, we may need to explore new ways of speaking. For example, to express new ways of thinking about gender, we may need to change the way pronouns function. Or to express a more process-centered view of reality we may be led to make nouns function as verbs. We might, for instance, talk about "peaceing" things together in order to move toward an active conception of peace as a process we engage in rather than as a static absence.

For a human ecological system to discern, describe and/or create emergent realities, it needs to create spaces and methods for people to take stock of situations and take the time needed to engage in holistic reflection, critical analysis, and creative thinking. In the work environment of an organization, this may involve weekly meetings for reflection or extended quarterly retreats. In other community settings, it may involve family-centered dinner conversations or times of meditation, prayer, worship, ceremonial sharing, parties, artistic improvisation, or other collaborations.

Quakers have developed ways of using shared silence and other methods of enhancing their listening to the leadings of the spirit in order to govern their lives and communities. These include "Meeting for Worship for the Conduct of Business". The Quaker Institute for the Future has been experimenting since 2003 with ways to adapt these and methods from other traditions to do spirit-led study by practicing "Meeting for Worship for the Conduct of Research". Formats for these experiments include Summer Research Seminars, Circles of Discernment, and Clearness Workshops. The resulting processes can often nurture ideas and collaboration in ways that would be much more challenging in traditional, competitive academic contexts. Other resources and inspiration for collaborative wisdom processes can be drawn from methods of Indigenous Tribal Councils, village elder systems, women's networks, or even some forms of cooperative open-source traditions in hacker culture. Wherever two or more gather with open hearts as well as minds, it is possible for the emergence of a plural first person We that hears and follows spiritual leadings.[141]

AI systems are becoming increasingly powerful in the ways they recognize patterns in complex texts and images and generate metaphors. As they do so, it may become useful to experiment with ways in which they might, as part of human ecological communities, also help to advance the kinds of discernment that help us discover and interpret the larger patterns of meaning and spiritual frameworks for our shared lives.

While it might initially seem like these activities are the province of humans alone, it is worth exploring ways they might be supported or enhanced by AI and other creatures. For starters, AI can be used to track features of our activity that might help us simply note when it would be useful to engage in some of these activities. The simplest case might be the automated calendars that remind us of quarterly retreats. More sophisticated AI could flag situations in which new contexts, groups, and opportunities for fruitful retreats are emerging. Imagine, for example, an email tracking system for a church or college community that notes increasing interaction between emerging groups and might suggest helpful ideas for connecting those folks through a forum or recreational outing. Other kinds of pattern recognition might help discern emergent contexts and structures in our shared lives that would be worth trying to articulate with analogies and metaphors. AI systems might even be able to suggest useful types of metaphors to consider.

Regarding other creatures, animal companions like dogs provide one logical place to look for support in discernment because they notice things that we overlook. Watching and listening to them, we may learn from their biological observations as when they notice a medical concern like insulin deficiency or cancer is present.

Animals and plants are sensitive to all sorts of substances and patterns beyond our ken. Learning to learn from and with them, we can discover important emergent truths. Doing so, we can braid together advanced monitoring technology with Indigenous peoples' practiced skills of observation and Traditional Ecological Knowledge.[142]

There are many challenges in framing and pursuing dialogical paths for the development of human ecological systems. Some are a matter of getting machines to track and incorporate guidelines and advices for problem solving, negotiation, conflict resolution and peacemaking. This involves a shift from the formal logical algorithms of monological reasoning. But the essentials of dialogical reasoning are clear and accessible and can be learned by a child – whether a human or a "Turing Child".

But while children can enter into dialogue, its many varieties and nuances call for a lifelong study. These include, for instance, the various languages and practices of the Harvard Negotiation Project, First Nations' Tribal Councils, Gandhian Satyagrahis, and Quaker Meeting for Worship for the Conduct of Business. There are enormous opportunities and challenges that await us in our efforts to develop dialogical AI and moving beyond the quest for a Smarter Planet to the journey towards a Wiser Earth. Each of the five basic strategies described in this chapter needs to be adapted to the many settings in which our human ecological systems bridge between cultures and communities, landscapes and species, and technologies and industries. Advancing dialogical AI will require endlessly challenging as well as fascinating efforts.

An essential part of genuine, authentic dialogue with others involves moving into the realm of the new. Such learning involves working at the limits of language. In that frontier zone we often go beyond the comfort zones of everyday, secular, prosaic life and into the wilder realm of experiences which call for more holistic, poetic, and spiritual ways of talking. In the next chapter, we turn to the challenges and opportunities that come with living and learning in these unavoidable frontier zones that push the limits of conventional language and prosaic experience.

Summary of Strategies for Developing Dialogical AI

1) Define our guiding goal as the pursuit of genuine, voluntary agreements.

2) Use methods of collaborative dialogue.

3) Frame the structures of relationships and commitments in community-centered ways as human ecological systems incorporated by people, nature, and machines.

4) Distribute roles and powers in just and appropriate ways.

5) Make the system as open as possible to discerning and engaging with emergent realities in emergent contexts.

.

Chapter Eight: Dialogue Across Creeds and Cultures

If our civilization is not, in the words of Gandhi, an "incurable disease", it is nonetheless one with serious problems. They call for frank dialogue and consideration of the ways in which it may be flawed not only in its parts but flawed as a whole. Dialogue about these kinds of concerns can be quite challenging. Asking national leaders to give up on seeking greater Gross Domestic Product is a bit like asking Christians to give up on the Golden Rule. This book has tried to stimulate conversations in which people might seriously consider versions of both of these controversial ideas as well as a good many others. How can we engage constructively in dialogues that are that challenging?

In many ways, dialogue gets most real and authentic when folks involved open themselves to questioning things that they take to be most basic. How do we respond to an encounter with someone who calls into question beliefs or experiences that we take to be basic to our religion or philosophy of life? We can just shut down and shut them out. But if we keep listening, thinking, and paying careful attention, we may learn a great deal about ourselves, as well as them. This kind of dialogue can make us stretch our words not just with metaphor and grammatical innovation, but with non-verbal expression. We may have to resort to gestures of all kinds to focus attention on liminal details or raise virtually unconscious things into awareness. Such dialogue may force us to move back and forth between well mapped things on this side of the edges of our language and those that lie beyond. On the yonder side are realities we encounter but may not yet be able to even name, let alone describe.

In facing the mysteries the future holds back as well as concrete choices it thrusts upon us, it helps to reflect on the many-sided ways we encounter and deal with these experiences. They push us into the further frontiers of meaningful dialogue. Any serious attempt to think and live more wisely inevitably forces us to struggle with philosophies, religions, poetries, mysticisms, and other uncanny and extraordinary portals for meaningful experience. Those struggles often connect very personal, profoundly spiritual experiences with elusive, abstract systems of ideas. Struggling wisely with these requires a distinctive humility. It requires us to learn to accept that there are no easy answers to some challenges and yet no way to escape from the questions they pose. We may need to learn to continue to engage with them, seek answers, and be open to learning from people whose philosophies, religions, or poetic ways of talking are different from our own. Wisdom in these things may combine various kinds of spiritual practices as well as intellectual activities.

The contrast between monological and dialogical practices of reasoning provides one key approach to dealing wisely and successfully with the kinds of philosophical, religious, and meta-linguistic issues at stake at the frontiers of meaning.

Hailing Across Chasms: Dialogue at the Frontiers of Meaning

The challenges of dialogue across fundamental philosophical divides are invigorating, but difficult. They bring the vigor of new life and growth of all sorts. But they also create obstacles and frustrations with polarization, hostility, and despair. What might be successful, wiser ways to deal with such fundamental differences?

A first step might be to ask ourselves just how fundamental the difference that seems to divide us really is. One way to gauge this would be to ask how important it is compared to other things in our shared lives. Often, in the heat of the moment, disagreements at hand seem all consuming and yet, an hour (or week) later, seem relatively insignificant in the larger scheme.

The differences on which this book is focused are arguably quite fundamental for at least two reasons. First, they deal with things that appear to be threats to our existence as individuals and communities, as well as our survival as a species. Second, they concern the basic systems of meaning we use to frame the key institutions that define our civilization – the assumptions and practices that shape our ethics, economics, politics, and technology.

But while they are fundamental, this does not mean that we must assume they pose an unbridgeable divide. Differences between people remain fundamental only relative to the contexts in which the issues are the focus of discussion. If you and I are a married couple, a pair of neighbors, or two representatives of opposing corporations, social movements, or countries, we still have the opportunity to put the issue into a broader context in which other concerns and interests can be noted and addressed.

This is not to claim that there is always a higher value of greater importance to appeal to. Instead, the point is that values and context do not come arranged in a neat, pre-ordained hierarchy. We are immersed in them the way we are immersed in our ecosystem. We are surrounded by all sorts of processes with which we are interdependent. These bring in a host of values that may become not only relevant but salient if we shift focus towards them. So far as importance goes, the differences we encounter with others—no matter how salient and fundamentally important they may seem at any given moment -- are always related to the background that surrounds us. This opens up room for dialogue. The commons that environ us always already put us in community in ways that open possibilities for arriving at agreements.

That room for dialogue can seem to shut down, however, when we take differences to be foundational. The treatment of core beliefs as "foundational" lies at the heart of the difference between monological and dialogical styles of reasoning. Monological reasoning begins with the idea that knowledge consists in having beliefs that are true and that you know are true because you can justify them—you have the arguments to back them up. If you adopt a monological posture and vision for the understanding of reasoning, then it is difficult to avoid the conclusion that at least some of your beliefs need to be accepted as absolute, foundational starting points. If someone rejects those beliefs, it will be hard to see how to resolve differences with them. It will seem like an unbridgeable chasm across which you could leap only if you were willing to abandon the truths you hold most dear and that define who you are. Those foundational principles are treated like building stones at the base of your edifice of belief. If they are removed, the whole structure of your life may collapse.

But notice how things change if you are open to using collaborative dialogue as your form of reasoning. You do not need to abandon all your old beliefs and values, nor do you need to reject your previous experiences. Instead, you simply open them up to be put into a broader context. You open them up to revision and reconnection in the larger surroundings that were already there all along in that background of language and experience into which you can move. Once they are no longer taken to be absolute and foundational, the still vitally important and fundamental differences we have with others can provide arenas for dialogue that reinvigorate old ideas. They can freshen us with new understandings of formative experiences, provide for the growth of new common ground, and the birth of new projects, practices, and community relationships.

The Quaker tradition in the Religious Society of Friends provides one useful way of naming the distinction between these two ways of taking the central beliefs that frame our significant differences with others. Quakers talk about having "testimonies" and "queries" rather than a "creed". This sets them apart from most groups that form part of the 2,000-year history of Christianity. Most such denominations define their religious faith with a series of sentences that are taken to be fixed formulations of the doctrines they hold. Formulations like the Nicene Creed set apart those who are in and those who are out. Quakers however, from their start, took seriously the lines in which Paul suggested that Christians should define their community not by laws but by love. They should be part of "a new covenant, not of the letter, but of the Spirit. For the letter kills, but the Spirit gives life."[143]

If Quakers were to choose to hold any of their convictions as a creed, the best candidate would probably be their testimony that "there is that of God in everyone". But from the time of their origins in the mid-1600s, they have chosen, instead, to treat this, instead, as a testimony. In doing so, they leave themselves open to enlarge, enrich and revise their understanding of it over time. Their notions of what we might mean by "God" or even how best to name the divine can grow as they encounter new faith traditions and learn from their spiritual insights and practices. Their conception of who may count in the community of "everyone" and what that counting means can likewise grow. This led them, for instance, to be very early advocates of the abolition of slavery and the empowerment of women. It has also led them to see "that of God" in all of creation and to advance an Earthcare witness. This growth in insight and fullness of understanding is similar to the ways in which, in other contexts, testimonies that witnesses offer can gain meaning and interpretation by being placed in larger context. As we listen to different witnesses tell their stories we can gain an increasingly richer, more complete, more objective, understanding that contains increasingly more Truth. To think of core convictions as testimonies rather than creeds allows them to be central and important without a rigid interpretation that locks them into a single-sided monologue of inferences about the world.[144]

Treating core convictions in this way can allow them to guide and inspire inquiry and growth by opening up possibilities. This is what results when Quakers frame core convictions with "queries". For example, the Friends' testimony on peace is nearly as central to their faith as the conviction that there is that of divine in each of us. But instead of framing it as a fixed principle from which a rigid set of rules might follow, Quakers typically share it in the form of some query such as: "Do you live in that life and power that takes away the occasion of all war?" It is important to understand that this Query is intended as a genuine question worth engaging with. It is not a simple prompt or catechism question demanding a prescribed response. In conflict situations, less war-like and more loving ways to treat others can often be extremely puzzling to define in practice, let alone to work through emotionally. And there are probably times in which we must simply wrestle with figuring out the best ways to deal with our inabilities and failures. The point of the Quaker query here is not to pretend to know all the answers and serve them up on a platter. Rather it is to set people looking for answers and living out their faith in one general direction rather than another.[145]

The reality is that Quakers themselves, at various points in their history, have become at odds over issues which some have taken as "foundational" in an absolute way. This has led to schisms and splits not unlike the sort found in other religious communities. Quakers should not be over-romanticized. The fact that we might learn valuable things from some of the practices that some of them have sometimes adopted does not mean that we should idealize any individual or group amongst them. While there may be "that of God" in all of them, there is always also a good deal else besides. They have proved quite as capable as others of exhibiting partiality, short sightedness, obstinacy, racism, classism, heterosexism, and all sorts of other human limitations.[146]

This same point can be applied in reverse to other traditions in religion and philosophy. They may be filled with individuals, groups, beliefs, and institutions that bend some of them to one-sided thinking of the worst sorts. Yet their communities may also, nonetheless, include lots of important resources and traditions of practice for being open-minded, creative, and constructive in dealing with the challenges that "fundamental differences" pose for dialogue.

Monotheistic religions like Judaism, Christianity and Islam may find common ground amongst each other by agreeing that they all believe in one and the same Abrahamic God. That common ground has often been taken to frame a battle. Historically, they have often defined their beliefs and institutionalized their practices in mutually exclusive ways that many insist on treating as foundational. In the Abrahamic traditions, one of the important, formative influences in their history was Aristotle, the thinker known amongst all three traditions for the better part of a millennium as "The Philosopher". His monological conception of formal logic and inference, and his foundationalist approach to knowledge led many theologians in the Abrahamic traditions to frame their understanding of God in terms of justification. As we already noted, this kind of "justification" model of reasoning can lead to assuming that religious and other beliefs have to have starting points that are simply accepted as absolute foundations—foundations that are not open to dialogue.[147]

Nevertheless, in all three of the Abrahamic traditions, we encounter people who find their own spiritual experiences and/or intellectual curiosities push them to try to make comprehensive sense of our place amidst the Infinite. They find, in the process, that those foundations shatter at their own feet. Sometimes this is a result of personal existential crises or overwhelming mystical experiences that challenge their received doctrines. Often it is as a result of metaphysical puzzles that arise in trying to use the One to explain the Many or the eternal to explain the temporal or the Perfectly Good to explain the presence of evil. But, for whatever reason, they enter into the depths of these issues at the very frontiers of their world of meaning. Writings wrestling with this are a major part of the Jewish tradition from the Books of Job and Ecclesiastes up through Medieval Kabbala and modern thinkers like Martin Buber. In the Christian tradition, the gospels as well as the letters of Paul are full of parables and paradoxes that point to the frontiers of meaning. These get explored in mystical practice and philosophical reflection by a long tradition of mystical writers including Brother Lawrence and Kierkegaard. In the Islamic tradition, the early woman poet Rabia and the later philosopher and theologian, Al-Ghazali, provide classic examples of this. They played key roles in the development of the Sufi tradition, and the mystical visions of Rumi whose eloquent mystic poetry invites us to see that:

> . . . the other world
> keeps coming into this world. Like cream hidden
> in the soul of milk, no-place keeps coming into place.
> Like intellect concealed in blood and skin,
> The traceless keeps entering into traces.
> From beyond intellect, beautiful love comes
> Dragging her skirts, a cup of wine in its hand.
> And from beyond love, that indescribable One
> Who can only be called "that" keeps coming.[148]

When the core doctrine of monotheism at the heart of the Abrahamic traditions inspires serious and fervent reflection on the Oneness of God and of all reality, it can lead to wrestling long and hard with the difficulties of understanding how that Oneness of All is compatible, intellectually, with the many-ness of this world. It can leave the faithful in painful wonder as to why we are not always, already at-One with the divine. In wrestling with these questions, all monotheists encounter a common challenge. How can a finite human mind limited to the here and now grasp and make sense of an infinite reality that is always ever more -- over and beyond the horizon of our experience?

In struggling with this, monotheists share much in common with people who have explored spiritual and intellectual depths in other traditions like Daoism, Buddhism, Hinduism, and Indigenous communities, as well as with philosophers like Socrates and scientists like Carl Sagan. These different traditions each offer ways of preparing people for the spiritual and intellectual steps of stretching beyond their ordinary, mundane ways of seeing and describing the world. These may let us expand, extend, and live at the edge of our language. But they do not let us jump full blown and full grown into a comprehensive grasp of the totality of reality. We remain embodied in space and time and embedded in the languages and communities that give us the background contexts out of which we live. We do well to seek, as the first two precepts of Thich Nhat Hanh's Socially Engaged Buddhism advise, to "not be idolatrous about or bound to any doctrine, theory, or ideology, even Buddhist ones." We should not think the knowledge we "presently possess is changeless, absolute truth" but should instead "learn and practice nonattachment from views in order to be open to receive others' viewpoints."[149]

We are left ever sailing toward horizons that recede as we approach. We can see the new and grow in the encounters, but we can never arrive at the ultimate. And this is part of what it means to say that life is a dialogue.

If we embrace that dialogue and push toward its ever-moving limits, then we can draw on the resources of other traditions in a wide variety of ways. We can learn new ways to practice mindfulness and meditation, new ways to gather ourselves and our communities with ceremony, new ways to express our encounters with the inexpressible. We can use poetry, dance, and art as well as variations on the *via negativa* -- the "negative way" of "unknowing" which uses logic to connect to the Ultimate through what it is not.[150]

In drawing on human traditions that provide such resources, we may also find that there is a kind of power that enables us to continue with dialogue, even when it seems most challenging. It can be a power of Creativity that often comes in surprising ways. It can be a power of connection that enables us to relate to Others and even our Enemies in ways that provide a kind of transforming Love. It can be a power of emergent objective value that motivates us to sacrifice much and perhaps even all in order discern ethical Truths, demonstrate them to others and defend them even in the face of desperate, violent dictators. In trying to bridge the chasms and rushing waters that seem to separate us from others, we may find ourselves seeking courage by singing something a bit like this:

> Maybe I cannot walk on the water, but there's a power
> that can part those waters wide.
> And maybe I lack the courage, to cross over to the
> other side.
> But there's a power that is greater, that can work
> through me to work my faith.
> All I need is to get started. All I need to do is start to
> wade . . .
> Wade in the water . . . wade in the water children!
> Wade in the water . . . there's a power workin' in the
> water![151]

Testimonies of Emergent Truth

When we let go of monological ways of framing our thinking and foundationalist ways of viewing the justification of beliefs, it may initially seem like we must be left with a completely relativist and subjective view of reality. If there are no absolute truths to serve as foundations, then isn't everything relative with no sense in which any one person or culture can claim one idea is better than another? Is everything just a matter of what we choose, subjectively, to believe? The apparent logic of this argument can hold a persistent grip on us until we shift from a monological to a dialogical framework for reasoning. Once we frame reasoning as a process of dialogue, the apparent power of relativist arguments dissipates and becomes dispelled.

For one thing, we find that in dialogue we always, already presuppose that there are other people and points of view with whom we are in dialogue. The reality of the Other is, further, not just a presupposition we make, it is a reality we encounter. When they raise doubts about our views and insist on merits of theirs, we experience these other folks as forces to be reckoned with. Their reality can come home to us with all the power of a soccer player kicking a ball past our head or a friend grabbing us with a bear hug.

For a second thing, in dialogue, we always, already, presuppose that there is some emergent objective truth that we might discover which would settle our differences. We may have great difficulty finding it. But in affirming our beliefs and questioning others', we assume that while error is possible it can be corrected. We only bother to ask questions and raise doubts because we assume there is some way of settling them. We talk about what we might do because we assume we might make mistakes if we don't. And error is only possible if there is something independent of our beliefs which can provide a criterion for correcting them.

There is an apparent paradox to this. It arises because it then seems that any attempt to correct one error may simply lead to another. How do we ever get out of the sea of doubt and the ocean of relativism it seems to wash in over us? How can we ever speak of real progress toward truth in the development of our ideas?

In the context of scientific studies of nature, this has become what we might describe as a metaphysically unmanageable but empirically tractable problem. As long as we frame questions about objective truth in purely abstract and philosophical ways, we find ourselves at a loss to settle them and come up with arguments that justify claims with the level of certainty that purely formal reasoning invites. But, in the investigation of nature, we also have recourse to experiment. We can make repeated experiments from multiple angles, drawing on multiple points of view and ideas. This can provide a kind of increasingly inclusive and comprehensive encounter with reality that gives us a growing understanding of emergent objective realties like the shape and structure of this planet, the development of life forms on it, and the history of human societies here.

In any new inquiry, our initial ideas may prove as flawed as the Flat Earth hypothesis. And no matter how systematic and refined our ideas become, they may be subject to residual error that calls for further refinement and/or systematization. In my lifetime, for instance, the demonstration of Continental Drift radically upended beliefs that my teachers took to be as solid, literally, as bedrock. But despite the continued emergence of such elaborations, refinements and other forms of revision, the systematic accumulation of experimental results provides a core of successful connection with the reality of this planet that allows us to say that we have made substantial progress toward a truer view of it. The folks who believed the Earth was flat were right to note that it seemed roughly so—at least as far as their eyes could see, from horizon to horizon. But beyond that, they were wrong. It is more or less round. Just what shape it has as a sphere and exactly how it may be changing remain open questions. But we are getting successively better answers through connecting to the realities through experiments that, like the triangulations of a surveyor, map the landscape our world.

To the metaphysical sceptic who argues on purely formal grounds that we can never know anything with certainty -- including the form of the Earth on which we stand—we may not be able to provide a rigorous and irrefutable proof. But with any one with practical interests who walks this Earth with us and is open to experience and experiment, we can find compelling reasons to agree that progress has been made and we know this planet is approximately spherical.

In this sense, the conviction that there is progress in science is perhaps best understood not as a dogma to be justified but as a testimony to be witnessed.

It is a testimony that has gone through a significant transformation in recent decades. The Reductionist Vision of this progress has become increasingly untenable. As Stuart A. Kaufmann has noted, "even major physicists now doubt its full legitimacy." He has gone on to argue, in detailed analyses, that:

"[B]iology and its evolution cannot be reduced to physics alone but stand in their own right. Life, and with it, agency, came naturally to exist in the universe. With agency came values, meaning and doing, all of which are as real in the universe as particles in motion "Real" here has a particular meaning; while life, agency, value, and doing presumably have physical explanations in any specific organism, the evolutionary emergence of these cannot be derived from or reduced to physics alone . . .

"Emergence is therefore a major part of the new scientific world view. Emergence says that, while no laws of physics are violated, life in the biosphere, the evolution of the biosphere, the fullness of our human historicity, and our practical everyday worlds are also real, are not reducible to physics nor explicable from it, and are central to our lives. Emergence, already both contentious and transformative, is but one part of the new scientific worldview . . ." [152]

One of the many examples of this that Kaufmann points to can be illustrated by considering two things that happen if you place a sugar cube in a body of water with bacteria. First, in accordance with the Second Law of Thermodynamics, entropy begins as the cube starts to dissolve and dissipate throughout the water. But in apparent contradiction to the Second Law, instead of dispersing, the bacteria move up the sugar gradient in the water and congregate around the cube. In doing so, they are not, in fact, violating the laws of physics. But what they are doing is following patterns of behavior that have evolved through a combination of random variation and selection.

In the course of evolution, the bacteria emerged out of the soup of molecules present on Earth – but they emerged as something new. A key part of this was that cell walls emerged that created a set of functional differences between insides and outsides. Molecules on the inside and outside still obeyed the laws of thermodynamics, as did the cell walls. But those walls acquired structures that served to direct the flow of molecules across gradients in ways that served the growth and reproduction of the bacteria as organisms. As Kaufmann notes, random variation and selection producing this is compatible with physics but not predictable by it. He goes on to describe ways in which other kinds of inside/outside structures and wholes have emerged in biology, economics, and other aspects of history.

As we noted in earlier chapters, the realm of human history also provides a kind of emergent objective reality whose structures can be studied through analogous processes of triangulation that provide increasingly inclusive, balanced, and whole accounts. Increasingly impartial objectivity is a viable aim. We also noted that in the realm of ethics, the methods of loving, self-sacrificing nonviolence in the tradition of Gandhian *satyagraha* can provide experimental ways of discerning, demonstrating, and defending emergent objective moral truths. For many people, video footage of the "I Have a Dream" speech of Dr. Martin Luther King Jr. provides a clear and compelling sense of such an emergent moral truth. It is for this reason that it continues to be replayed and referenced in so many contexts.[153]

These truths are not dogmas to be adopted blindly. Nor are they foundationalist principles to be relied on with certainty. Instead, they are testimonies that provide compelling power to the moral discernment and witness of people who engage with them in humility and good faith as part of collaborative dialogues with others with whom they may find they differ.

In the realm of language and human action there are many levels, arenas, and contexts. Often, they are related in organic ways that might seem to resemble the repetition of theme and structure found in fractal geometry as it scales up or down to new levels. But these different scales are not related by neat algorithms that merely repeat. For example, at different social levels, the meaning of consent may inform our understanding of healthy relationships between parents and children, corporations, or countries signing treaties. In some sense, consent is a scalable concept. Yet the understandings of consent are distinct at different levels—as well as in different social arenas and cultural contexts.

In any one of these we may become settled in our ways and lapse into a kind of comfortable and habitual usage. And yet in any one of these levels, arenas, or contexts, we can suddenly encounter something which disrupts the mundane, ready-to-hand pattern of language and behavior. It may launch us into an encounter in a Presence that opens us to dialogue and the search for common understanding. Sometimes we are launched with a delightful bounce and a joyful excitement. Sometimes we are dragged along kicking and screaming. But the experience of being broken open in ways that allow for new forms of connection is difficult to describe and even harder to live through without an appeal to some understanding of transformative powers that are larger than us as individuals and that work through us and our communities.

A sceptic might argue the experience of such powers of Spirit that can guide and motivate the transformations of our lives are grounded in a kind of optical illusion. The process is one in which our previous monologues for dealing with the world get fractured. We then go through a process of dialogue in which new forms of agreement and inclusive wholes of meaning emerge. The sceptic might suggest this process of being fractured into an emergent wholeness might not actually be motivated or guided by anything at all. It might just be a process that seems in retrospect to have been going somewhere because we end up happy with where we arrived. It might be less like a guided tour through the forest that brings us to the perfect resting place and more like a random walk that ends when we are worn out from travel and ready to stop.

My own experience, however, is that while I am immersed in the process, I cannot avoid looking for leadings. I cannot help but look for inspiration that will advance the process. It is as though I am exploring a kind of Design Space in which there are valences that afford better futures if only I can discern the shape of the landscape of future possibilities. It is my experience that the process can be fed in a host of ways and that there is an enormous amount that we can learn about through exchanges with folks from other traditions besides our own. If we wade into the many different waters in the great stream of life, we will find there are powers working in those waters.[154]

This is one reason why it can be so helpful to share interfaith experiences and explore the spirituality of different traditions. They can each enrich the others. They can do so through contradictions that get surmounted as we rise up out of the formal language and one-sided view of things in which the contradiction is posed and open ourselves to that realm of creative possibility and care in which something new is emerging. Such spiritual growth comes out of listening and speaking as well as out of silence and song. It comes not out of dead ritual habit that closes us off but out of living ceremony that connects.

In developing new forms of grammar as well as other language expressions, we may often find it helpful to recover, draw on, and reinvent older and even more ancient forms. For instance, older forms of English had a second person singular pronoun, "thou", which expressed a very intimate, immediate, and egalitarian relationship with the person addressed. Nowadays "thou" sounds stilted and formal and it would probably not be wise to reintroduce that older use directly, but it would be worth thinking about how that form of address could be expressed in more contemporary terms. One way might be to strengthen our conscious use of a grammatical form that goes back to Classical Greek, something called the "vocative case". It is a form of grammar in which nouns and names are marked to indicate that they are being used to address someone directly and personally in a more intimate and immediate way. In Greek it was marked with an article, the long "O" or omega. We still have vestiges of this as when we translate Homer with the phrase "Sing in me, Oh Muse, of the man of many ways . . . " Versions of this are still available and acceptable in English as when we say to a friend, "Oh my dear friend, how are you doing with all these challenges?" Likewise, an ornithologist may gaze attentively through a scope at an odd behavior and say "Oh Birdy! What are you doing there!?" In moments of meditation, mindfulness, or living ceremony we may likewise find ourselves moved past the "Ommmmm . . ." of centering to the "Oh!" of vocative encounter as in "Oh my god . . . !"[155]

For me, as someone nurtured by Quaker and other meditative traditions, Silence is one of the most powerful practices for when I need to prepare for the encounters of dialogue with creativity, love, emergent truth, and courage. This is especially so when I am trying to work with others at those times when I find it difficult to accept – or even understand – what they have to say. I would like to try to invoke that experience of silence here at the end of this chapter about dialogue.

This moment in which you and I are both engaged now with this mute book is surrounded by a peculiar kind of silence which bridges the chasm of time between the moment in which I write these words and the moment in which you read them. Despite that temporal split, we are somehow joined in a common moment of communication. It is a here-and-now of shared reflection. Our voices cannot breach the silence of this moment, but your presence as someone who will read these words and my presence as someone who wrote them can nonetheless find a kind of commons in that silence that opens us up for dialogue.

I would like to offer a song in this context in the hope that for me and for you, the silence of this moment will open onto many future conversations with many different people. In this silence,

> *. . . midst division,*
> *there are voices, they are speaking.*
> *They are calling us to caring*
> *that connects us each to all.*[156]

May we each learn to advance the transformation of our individual selves, our communities, and this Earth in the many, many ways in which we are called to care for it and each other. May we each be empowered -by that caring, creative love that can work through us out of the silence, fracturing us into ever newer forms of unity and connection. May we each find that:

Midst the trials and the troubles
comes a power transcending fear.
It's a power that transforms us
through this Presence of love ...
                                      here.

Chapter Nine: Bridging into the Future

"We can only see a short distance ahead, but we can see plenty there that needs to be done." -- Alan Turing, "Computing Machinery and Intelligence"[157]

"The means may be likened to a seed, the end to a tree; and there is just the same inviolable connection between the means and the end as there is between the seed and the tree." -- Mohandas K. Gandhi, Hind Swaraj[158]

Mainstream practices of economics, politics, technology, and ethics are connected to a core conception of rationality that needs to change. Despite its promise to make our planet "smarter", that conception of rationality has driven us ever more rapidly towards ecological collapse, wars of mutually assured destruction, technological catastrophes, and a moral relativism that pulls the ground out from under meaningful collaboration and peacemaking. Throughout this book, we have considered a wide range of possible next steps along paths to a wiser earth. Which might be top priorities?

Steps we take as individuals will depend on where we stand at the start. But there are some specific initiatives that merit general priority and some general features of the most promising paths.

The first step for each of us is to **collaborate in dialogues about these concerns**. In creating a wiser Earth, we cannot just leave the task to experts. In whatever walk of life we find ourselves, we need to seek out family, friends, work colleagues and fellow members of our communities and talk. In particular, there is a need to talk about:

- the logic, in general, of decision processes and how to improve them by shifting from one-sided inferences to collaborative dialogues;

- shifting, in our common habits and practices of ethical thought, away from inferential processes of justifying moral choices that impale us on horns of dilemmas and towards practices of creative problem solving, negotiation, conflict transformation and other forms of peacemaking.
- shifting in our budget discussions away from being Economic Rational Consumers to agents of meaningful historic change,
- shifting in our political activity away from the conflict-centered, institutionalized practices of inference employed in political realism and realpolitik towards institutions that promote collaborative dialogue grounded in methods of nonviolence.
- shifting in the creation and purchase of our technologies away from the quest for a Smarter Planet towards dialogical forms of programing and system development that promote technologies for wiser Earth.
- in our discussions of the big issues, philosophical questions, and cultural differences that emerge, shifting away from foundationalist principles and ideological frames towards open, non-creedal approaches to dialogue.

Dialogues about these concerns also need to move beyond talk towards collaborative action including, for example:

- pushing corporate leaders to practice collaborative dialogue in political/economic entrepreneurship to increase the real net wealth of their organizations and all their stakeholders.
- electing and lobbying political leaders to transform national security states by practicing collaborative peacemaking rooted in *satyagraha* and other forms of nonviolence.
- insuring every app downloaded on a personal device and every software program incorporated into a management moves us towards a collaborative set of relationships with our tech and with each other as part of a just, sustainable, resilient community.

Most of the dialogues and collaborative actions that provide the next steps toward a Wiser Earth will, in general, include the following features: We should use the **Rainbow** Rule as a starting point. In listening to voices we should aim to be integrative. We must reach out across divisions by race, class, gender, ethnicity, nationality, religion, age, and other differences. In starting conversations, we should consider who we are leaving out.

Integrating the dialogue between social change agents and technological innovators is essential. Until recently, people have often left out folks on whatever is for them the other side of the social/technological divide. The forms of rationality that run our world are encoded in technology and increasingly dominated by it.

To cultivate wiser systems, folks making hardware and software need to collaborate with folks doing community organizing and market innovation and vice versa. Parents who want to raise kids differently have to collaborate with tech folks – as well as their own kids -- to design new social media and ways of incorporating them into our lives. Activists who want to transform the school to prison pipeline need to reach out to programmers designing software for school monitoring, police dispatching, and judicial decision-making. People reforming the management of forests, farms, hospitals, and military operations need to do similar outreach.

This must be an ongoing process. The different kinds of intelligence and wisdom that people, natural organisms, and machines can each contribute must all be included in the ongoing, collaborative pursuit of wiser thought and action. With every step, we should reach out to folks across the "social/technological" divide, integrating collaborations between activists and information technology folks.

The second step should be to **bring increasingly fundamental changes to increasingly broader communities in increasingly rapid ways**. We need initiatives that are scalable and synergistic. What can be done at the individual level that will lead other individuals – and groups—to do it as well?

The next steps should **motivate us by being sources of health, joy, and hope**. The opposites—actions that lead to sickness, anxiety and despair—cannot be sustained over time and do not normally exemplify wisdom or advance it. Burnout, addiction, and despair are common challenges for change agents and entrepreneurs of all kinds. Fortunately, there are lots of strategies for dealing with them for which Joanna Macy and others provide guides.[159] Still, in the face of existential threats like climate change and nuclear war, for some people it may seem frivolous to "waste time" on personal healing or sharing walks, songs, festivals, and joy in the work. But taking the time needed and choosing to act in ways that promote health, joy, and hope is an integral and essential part of living more wisely. It helps others to build community in collective ways that are defined by our own interests, resources, and cultural background. We have to find things that let us "follow our bliss" to animate us and make us come alive. As Howard Thurman once noted: "what the world needs is people who have come alive."[160]

What follows are further, more concrete, suggestions for initiatives in collaborative dialogue and action that can combine these features by being: 1) integrative, 2) scalable 3) synergistic, and 4) a source of health, joy, and hope.

One of the most scalable and synergistic things that most readers could take as a next step involves redirecting our personal income. In redirecting our income to political change, responsible investment, and solidarity with others in need, our action can become scalable and synergistic in multiple ways. Chapter Five described methods for "meeting the future halfway" by successively reducing the percentage we spend on personal material consumption. These included "giving the gift of gifts", holding "marchathons" with political allies, forming clubs for mutual support in choosing socially responsible investments, and cutting our personal material consumption by 10 percent each year over a period of five years.

It is important to stress that many people are in genuine need and should be receiving solidarity to support more personal consumption rather than less. But for a majority in the developed world, this is not the case. For those who are living on an unsustainable excess, ways of "meeting the future halfway" can not only serve to cut our own ecological footprint but also invite others to join with us in making a basic transition in our identity. Such actions invite us all to shift away from identifying as rational economic consumers and towards identifying, instead, as agents of meaningful historical change, as **history makers**.

Reaching out to one other to do this already starts to multiply our effect and scale up. It can also build "market demand" for organizations that get funded in this way. This will motivate those organizations to systematically recruit and support networks of people who give such gifts to transform their world. Capitalist corporations scale up through profit mechanisms that enable them to accumulate capital; history makers can scale up by drawing others to their ranks in ways that are replicable and support further collaboration.

As we noted in Chapter Five, despite being well off, for many people, the dramatic cutting of personal material consumption can seem difficult and even impossible. Yet divorce, job displacement, retirement, and other life events often force us to discover that it can be done and that the kind of impossibility involved is, in part, the kind that people face when they try to lose weight and can't or try to quit an addiction and find that it is impossible. The challenges of obesity, addiction and similar problems, may be quite difficult and even sometimes genuinely intractable for a variety for reasons. However, in many cases, there is increasingly more good science as well as sound and effective practice in counselling, team effort, community support, online apps, and other methods that can help people to achieve what otherwise seems impossible.

We need to find other folks interested in reducing our ecological footprints and shifting our material consumption. We need to develop coordinated programs to fund research, development and implementation of programs that inspire, nurture, and sustain efforts of people to cut our collective consumption 50 percent or more and make the transition to being History Makers. Think of combining the most successful features of Noom, Alcoholics Anonymous and the Ecological Footprint Project with other kinds of personal change programs. Picture individualizing them for different community cultures and patterns of consumption.[161]

Systemic changes need to come not only from the ground up but also the top down. Everyone with a leadership role in an organization needs to consider how best to initiate scalable and synergistic social change as political/economic entrepreneurs. As we noted in Chapter Five, doing so will involve redefining prevailing assumptions. Potential clients will include not just paying customers, but every stakeholder. Potential products will include not just the stuff shipped out the front door but any change in the world a potential client might desire. Costs and benefits will include not just the money paid out or taken in, but any changes in the world that affect the net, long term value of the enterprise. Essentially the same shifts can be taken by leaders of NGOs. As leaders shift to seeing the world in these terms and adopting this new, more capacious identity, they will find that their political/economic entrepreneurship will help create a world which is supportive of their organizations. Raising the ethics of the playing field in markets will have synergistic effects not only on the markets but on the social and political institutions that frame them. And those synergistic effects will bootstrap the scaling up of shifts towards a civilization in which collaborative dialogue is used to guide our political economy in wiser ways.

Participants in governments should adopt a similar priority and undertake analogous initiatives for systematic change in the goals set and the ways they are pursued. Instead of seeking ever greater monetary GDP at municipal, state and federal levels, citizens and political leaders should shift to looking at multiple criteria for assessing the progress and well-being of communities. They should aim at promoting health, education, ecological resilience, security, and other values in a balanced way that deals with tradeoffs through collaborative dialogue. When conflicts prove difficult to resolve we should practice and promote nonviolent forms of satyagraha to discern, demonstrate and defend emergent objective moral truths about the best ways to resolve conflicts.

These shifts away from the traditional practices of purely Economic Rationality and *realpolitik* are essential to reducing ecological footprints, funding needed change, scaling up infrastructure, and sustaining it at the levels urgently required. There are a host of people already seeking to make such changes in their personal and corporate behavior and promote them in others. As we become clearer about the arenas where we, as individuals, feel most led to work, we can find folks already taking steps in these directions in visionary ways. A collaborative listing of organizations is available at this book's website.[162]

If a foundation, government agency, corporation or individual has a chunk of discretionary funding available, what specific types of pilot programs might they best prioritize?

One logical place to explore might be places at the intersection between rapidly advancing investment in methods of artificial intelligence and significant engagement by social activists. The school to prison pipeline provides an example. On the one hand, there is money being poured into the development of devices that can monitor ways children physically enter and attend schools, perform in classes, score on tests, encounter disciplinary controls, engage with social services, and progress through the system. Analogous heavy investments are being made in police and criminal justice systems to monitor highway traffic, surveil public spaces, provide dispatch services, give data to officers in the field, track suspects who enter the system, advise judges setting bail, and run prisons. Meanwhile, there are a host of concerned parents, community activists, bureaucratic reformers, policy makers, and citizens who are organizing to try to correct, improve and transform the ways these systems function.

The concerns that social change and tech folks face here are all clearly interconnected and systemic. Further, it is very clear that many of the problems that plague these systems arise because of poorly informed, one-sided, unilateral processes of judgment and inference which could be dramatically improved through processes of collaborative dialogue. There are any number of angles or perspectives from which a useful pilot project could be initiated in these systems. Such projects could prove fruitful not only in promoting important local change but in developing exemplary models to emulate in a wide range of other settings. Such a pilot project might also explicitly explore integrating forms of human and artificial intelligence with natural intelligence in ways, for instance, that emotional support animals and community gardens can improve schools and prisons.

Farms, forests, and fisheries provide fruitful sites for pilot projects that explore the integration of natural intelligence with human and artificial forms of it. Food systems around the world are the focus of intensive technological development and activism on social justice and ecological concerns. As with the school to prison pipeline, there are any number of perspectives on our "spade to spoon" pipelines from which pilot projects could be launched to provide exemplary proofs of concept. They could explore ways the monoculture systems of the "smarter planet" could be steered away from ecological collapse towards more just and resilient systems. How can collaborative dialogue include the voices and perspectives of all the intelligent people and creatures interacting in the system? Pilot projects on food are a priority because our lives so clearly depend on it.

Pilot projects could also be especially useful where there are insightful traditions of collaborative dialogue but even though advanced technology is lagging. These could include Indigenous communities trying to hold on to their land, language, and culture. Carried out with care and respect, such projects might benefit those who have been marginalized, and provide opportunities to learn from their practices of collaborative dialogue in councils, restorative justice, stewardship of the landscape, and interactions with people and creatures they encounter. In efforts to conserve and enhance language, culture, and agriculture, Indigenous communities may push technology development in important new directions.

The methods of collaboration and learning found in Indigenous communities might, for instance, provide crucial insight into the ways embodied humans can learn through dialogue with a few examples embedded in context. Imagine what could be learned by undertaking a pilot project with Indigenous young people and their elders on developing new forms of social media that focus on just, meaningful, peace-promoting ways of engaging people with each other.

In the context of the social/technological divide, other fruitful pilot projects could be online centers for sharing social practices and software methods for collaboration. Sites like GitHub already provide places where programmers collaborate in developing and sharing code. From the tech side, folks could work to make such sites more user friendly and accessible so non-tech people can more easily raise issues about software and evaluate results of changes. The development of models for access and libraries of code that incorporate strategies of collaborative dialogue could provide resources that are scalable in use because of their immediate online access. Such collaboration could yield significant synergies. When properly adapted to differences in circumstances, the strategies of collaborative dialogue that are successful in one setting often prove useful in others.

Chapter Seven noted the need for AI research here. A central priority should be the development of hybrid models that encode core strategies aimed at ethical consensus rooted in emergent, objective moral values. Just as we need inference engines to guide the mathematical reasoning of systems using neural nets, we also need collaborative dialogue strategies to guide the ethical reasoning of such systems.

Robotics provides another setting for pilot projects advancing systems of collaborative dialogue and a wiser Earth. One of the most dangerous developments in the drive towards a "Smarter Planet" is the massive investment in ever more sophisticated robotic weapon systems. They are ever more sophisticated, destructive, cheap, and widely available. And they are being ever more widely deployed by both police and military in ways that push our political systems toward reliance on violence and the logic of *realpolitik*. To counter this, we need to focus resources on pilot projects that develop robots serving nonviolent ends in nonviolent ways. As noted in Chapter Five, one promising test-case would be robots used by police to negotiate with armed and dangerous people threatening others as well as themselves. Consider the current practice of sometimes sending in a robotic bomb to blow up a veteran with PTSD who is trying to commit "suicide by cop". What if, instead, we explore sending in nonviolent robotic devices designed to de-escalate situations and improve conditions for people? Robots are already being developed for nonviolent use in settings like disaster rescue. Those innovations provide useful starting points for developing nonviolent robots for military settings.

In most contexts of modern warfare, the biggest challenge is to win over hearts and minds. Lethal autonomous weapon systems that bomb and blast tend to do the opposite. They polarize and alienate the friends and family of the people they destroy and often win the battle at the cost of losing the war. These drones distance their soldiers from harm's way but at the cost of harming their fundamental mission. Military establishments that aim to win wars to secure the peace are in stark need of pilot projects developing robotics that allow them to engage safely but collaboratively with civilian populations. Those people are often open to realigning their allegiances and are also in need of food, water, medicine, information, and opportunities to explain their problems and seek cooperation in coping with them.

There is a major danger in developing such non-violent robotic systems. They could easily exacerbate power imbalances and provide velvet gloves for iron fists of oppression. It would be a central challenge to ensure that devices introduced are genuinely nonviolent in the full sense. They must persuade people to act by appealing to their own interests and their own insights into emergent objective moral truths. They must collaborate in dialogue that yields genuine, voluntary agreement rather than numbed or terrified capitulation. In part, the challenge is to develop systems that empower people who are marginalized, giving, rather than taking away, resources. One challenge is to develop codes of ethics and ways of institutionalizing them that properly motivate and guide the research of the people developing these systems.

Developing and implementing AI codes of ethics has, fortunately, become a major priority for researchers across the world. Codes and creative ideas for implementing them have proliferated. An especially important venue for coordinating these efforts has been provided by UNESCO and resulted in 2021 in an agreement on the part of member states of the UN on the *Recommendation on the Ethics of Artificial Intelligence.*[163] It includes important elements for developing practices of AI as collaborative wisdom that could move us towards a wiser Earth. A major priority should be the explicit, systematic development of AI along these lines and the energetic pursuit of those kinds of dialogue and action at international and other levels. The UNESCO site on AI provides one useful venue for seeking out others and initiating collaborations. There are a host of others using websites to connect and collaborate on transformations of our economy, politics, technology, ethics, spirituality, and a wide range of social, cultural, and ecological concerns related to them. A number of these are listed on this book's website

The question of what to do next is one we must each face as individuals and as members of communities. What are the practical implications of the web of issues raised in this book? In part, the question about what to do next is also a question of sanity. It is a question about how we can each nurture and sustain a coherent mind and life in connecting our thoughts and actions. If we have reached clearness about things that need to be done, then we should let ourselves go forward with what needs doing. A sign that we have reached genuine clearness is that we are then led to act.

If, on the other hand, we continue to be unclear about these profound concerns, we still need to tentatively try out ideas. We need to express our feelings and experiment with possibilities that might open paths to greater hopes. Such explorations are necessary, not only for our personal mental health, but for the morale and spiritual health of the communities we live in and depend on. We need to act to affirm our sense of commitment and solidarity with the other folks who are taking the risk of thinking through these things with us.

Even if we are in a serious muddle, we must share the experiment of at least trying something. If we fail, we learn. Amidst the muddles we are in, we do well to recall the wisdom captured in the title of a book by two pathfinders in research on collaborative dialogue, Myles Horton and Paulo Freire: *We Make the Road by Walking*.[164] The path to wisdom is a trail of adventures on which even when we don't have a good day, we at least have a good story. It is just such stories that can give meaning to our lives and let us thrive as participants in history in the making. So where are you? What's happening? Who are you talking with lately? What will you do next?

Endnotes

Preface
1) Cox, 1986.

Chapter One: Introduction
2) Plato, Republic, p. 473d, accessed through: <http://www.perseus. tufts.edu/hopper/text?doc=Perseus%3Atext%3A1999.01.0167%3A-book%3D5%3Asection%3D473d , translation from the Greek: . . καὶ τοῦτο εἰς ταὐτὸν συμπέσῃ, δύναμίς τε πολιτικὴ καὶ φιλοσοφία, . . . , οὐκ ἔστι κακῶν παῦλα.>

3) For adopting a broader conception of human intelligence than the traditional idea associated with Stanford-Binet tests, see Gardner, 2011. For an exploration of various conceptions of intelligence applied to machine systems, see Legg and Hutter, 2007. The definition adopted here provides a minimal starting point that is intentionally broad enough to include successful forms of activity in mechanical thermostats, worms, and even plants that adapt by evolving rather than behavioral modification. This allows for a more comprehensive, human ecological approach to integrating fruitful elements of systems that include humans and other natural creatures as well as machines.

4) On the distinction between complicated vs. wicked problems see, for instance, Kolko, 2012. For some other conceptualizations of wisdom, see, for instance, Ferrari and Weststrate, 2016. The definition adopted here is intended to be broad and inclusive to allow incorporation of notions of wisdom from diverse cultural and spiritual communities. This is done to frame the inquiry in ways that allow for dialogue between those traditions to foster collaborative discovery of ever better ways to understand and pursue wisdom.

5) Kimmerer, 2015, p. x.

6) brown, 2017, p. 4.

7) Meadows, 2008, p. 4.

8) Plumwood, 2002, p. 5.

9) Kauffmann, 2010, p. ix.

10) The conception of dialogical reasoning developed here is informed by study of related notions of dialogue and dialectic in, for instance, Plato and Reeve, 1992; Hegel, 2019; Marx, 2007; Buber, 1971; Wittgenstein, 1973; MacIntyre, 2007; Hansen, 2000; and Everett, 2009. However, the conception does not adopt anyone of them wholesale. Instead, following Wittgenstein, it treats dialogue as a family resemblance notion describing a wide range of social "practices" in MacIntyre's sense of that term. Structures of dialogue vary profoundly as illustrated, for instance, by Chad Hansen's A Daoist Theory of Chinese Thought and Everett's study of the Pirahã in the Amazon. The intent of this book is to develop a phil-

osophically rich, sophisticated conception of dialogue through extended discussion in multiple contexts that propose non-creedal accounts of its core methods and epistemic, ontological, and ethical characteristics. In most general terms, the philosophical method employed here is a version of critical participatory research as described in Cox, 1986. It has sought to enrich that method with Quaker practices of spirit-led research as described in Cox et al., 2014.

11) On history of ethics and AI see, for instance, Wallach and Allen, 2008; Arkin, 2009; Armstrong, 2014; Barrat, 2015; Bostrom, 2016; Gunkel, 2017; Anderson and Anderson, 2018; Russell, 2020; Russell and Norvig, 2021; Tegmark, 2018; and Yudkowsky, 2022.

12) Goldstein, 2015, pp. 100-120.

13) See Stuart Russell's comments on this which are discussed in Chapter Seven, below, and come from Russell, 2020, p. 213. See also Tegmark's Life 3.0 assumes rational agents are substrate independent forms of algorithmic reasoning.

14) To listen to this song, "I'm gonna slow right down", you can use the QR code given in the text or go to the url here: <https://smarterplanetorwiserearth.com/2023/04/01/im-gonna-slow-right-down>. This and all the songs included in this book are available for free download at: <https://smarterplanetorwiserearth.com/2023/04/01/songs-for-a-wiser-earth/>.

Chapter Two: Golden Rule/Rainbow Rule

15) On right relationship, see Garver, et al 2012.

16) The U. S. Training and Industrial School was an influential model for American Indian boarding schools. Its founder, Captain Richard H. Pratt used this phrase to encapsulate its guiding philosophy -- see Pratt, 1892.

17) For examples and proposals to base a Global Ethic on the Golden Rule, see Swidler, pp. 44 ff.

18) This core idea has been explored in the context of medical ethics under the label of a "Platinum Rule", Wallis 2023 and Chochinov 2022. The rainbow label may serve better to capture the intent of intrinsically valuing different points of view in decolonizing ways rather than the more limited frame of serving customer interests more effectively.

19) Kaur, 2021, pp. 10-11.

20) Hager and Mawopiyane, 2022, pp. xi-xii.

21) Upstander Project, 2022.

22) On Yucatecan practices of milpa agroecology, see Terán and Rasmussen, 1994, and for its conflicted setting in modern development, see Cruz, 1996.

23) Cruz, 1996.

24) For critical analysis of the World Bank and related institutions from a former insider, see Stiglitz, 2007. Also, World Social Forum, 2022.

25) Kelly, 2011.

26) To listen to this song, "Todos somos otros," <https://smarterplanetor-wiserearth.com/2023/04/01/todos-somos-otros>.

Chapter Three: Challenges of the Rainbow Rule

27) For Quaker history and practices see Brinton and Bacon, 1965. For an ethnographic study of contemporary Quaker methods, see Sheeran, 1983.

28) Fisher, et al 2011; Lederach, 1994; Bondurant, 1988; and Ramsbotham, et al, 2016.

29) Martin, 2022.

30) To listen to this song, "To Hear With the Heart", <https://smarterplanetor-wiserearth.com/2023/04/01/to-hear-with-the-heart/>.

Chapter Four: Ethics as Collaborative Dialogue

31) Sandel, 2009.

32) Bentham, 2017.

33) For his introduction of core ideas, see Kant, 1993. For an attempt at a coherent explanation consistent with his transcendental philosophy, see Cox, 1984.

34) Kohlberg, 1981.

35) Gilligan, 2016; Noddings, 2013; Ruddick, 1995.

36) Fisher, et. al., 2011.

37) Ramsbotham, et. al., 2016; Nan, et al., 2011.

38) Fisher, et. al., 2011.

39) Gordon, 1969; Straus and Layton, 2002; Innes and Booher, 2018.

40) Lederach and Burgess, 1996; Chew, 2001; Nan, et. al., 2011.

41) On these methods of social research and action as expression, project, and practice, see Part III of Cox, 1986. See also the especially illuminating account of participatory, community-based methods in the Freire tradition in Richards, 2017.

42) Rawls, 1999 and Rawls, 2001.

43) MacIntyre, 2007, p. 153.

44) Fisher, 1964.

45) On the continuity of emotion with reason, see Jaggar, 1989; Collingwood, 2023; Cox, 1986; and Gendlin, 1982.

46) On emergent objective moral truth in Quaker and Gandhian traditions, see Rediehs, 2015.

47) On the origins of this practice, see Gandhi, 2018. For his articulation of core ideas, Gandhi, 2009; for his lifelong experiments, see Gandhi,

1983. For a systematic account of these, see Bondurant, 1988. On Gandhi's relevance to our current scene, see Allen, 2019. For an independent, objective history of Gandhi's life and work, see Guha, 2019.

48) Go to this url to listen to this song, "Walk With Me": <https://smarterplanetorwiserearth.com/2023/04/01/walk-with-me>

Chapter Five: Economics as History Making

49) On climate change, see Intergovernmental Panel on Climate Change, 2023. On pollution see Hill, 2020. On species loss see Kolbert, 2015.

50) See Smith, 2013, for the original formulation and Heilbroner, 1999, for the context of the Smith's ideas and their influence.

51) For a classic and influential formulation of this view, see Friedman, 1966, chapter one.

52) Hardin, 1968.

53) Ostrom, 2015.

54) Ciscel, et. al., 2011.

55) Cox, 2019.

56) Esteva, 1987, 2014; Freire and Macedo 2018.

57) On challenges measuring health and analogies with ecological well-being, see Goldberg, et. al., 2015. For a critique of cost/benefit analysis and sophisticated alternatives for measuring the success of programs in the developing world, see Richards, 2017.

58) UNDP, 2022; OHI, 2022; and UNHR, 2022.

59) See Appendix One on these points at: <https://smarterplanetorwiserearth.com/2023/04/01/book-appendices/>.

60) US Census Bureau, 2023

61) Cox, 2013. On reducing consumption in culturally specific ways, see Mackinnon, 2021. For creative ways to invest and retire at 42, see "Mr. Money Moustache", 2023.

62) To listen to "350 to Save the Sky" go to: <https://smarterplanetorwiserearth.com/2023/04/01/350-to-save-the-sky>.

63) Daly and Cobb, 1994.

64) For a nuanced, extended analysis of the need for degrowth, Kallis, 2018.

65) Wackernagel, et al, 2017.

66) Dreby, 2012; Dreby and Lumb, 2012; Lakey, 2017; and Center for Social Innovation, 2023

67) Khanna, 2022, pp. 2-4.

Chapter Six: Politics as Nonviolent Conflict Transformation

68) This analysis of peace is developed in detail in Cox 1986.

69) Thucydides, section 5:89.

70) D'Souza 2002, p. 164. Kissinger's dictum as quoted in D'Souza 2015 was "America has no permanent friends or enemies, only interests." For an elaboration on nation state as rational actor model see Allison 1999.

71) Social Network Rio+20, 2023.

72) Fetterly, 2007.

73) Ruddick 1995. See also Kaur, 2021, for birthing models of peacemaking.

74) Hanh, 2017.

75) Kimmerer, 2015.

76) For a description of this workshop methodology and the theory behind it, see Boulding, 1990.

77) For some examples of Boulding's work and key sources for ideas, see Boulding, 1988 and 1990; Freire and Macebo, 2018; Prutzman, 1977; the New York Quaker Project on Community Conflict, 1972; hooks, 2015; and Polak, 1973.

78) On the Marriage Equality movement, see Ball 2015. For liberation movements including South Africa, Polish Solidarity and others, see Sharp 2005.

79) Besides Bondurant's text and Gandhi's own Autobiography, Hind Swaraj and Satyagraha in South Africa, see Guha 2019. .

80) Guha does a very careful and professional job of assessing the criticisms that Arundhati Roy and others have made of internal contradictions and moral flaws in Gandhi's thought and practice. He does an especially good job of putting them in historical context in ways that allow for sympathetic understanding of Gandhi when that is appropriate and yet also not pulling any punches in dealing frankly and explicitly with personal and moral shortcomings, such as, for instance, in ways he sometimes dealt with his wife, children and others he was close to. See Guha 2019 and Roy 2017. Guha, 2019; Roy, 2017.

81) Gandhi, 2009, chapter 6.

82) For histories of such movements and analytical frameworks for understanding their dynamics, see Tilly, 2019; Sharp, 2005; Moyer, 2001; and Rediehs, 2022.

83) For an excellent documentary video describing the campaign in Nashville, see A Force More Powerful, 1999. For the larger context of this in the Civil Rights movement, see Carson, et al, 1991.

84) Bondurant, 1988; Guha, 2019; Gandhi, 2009, and 1983.

85) Chenoweth and Stephen, 2012.

86) The accompanying slide here is from: <https://www.nakedcapitalism.com/2012/02/erica-chenoweth-confronting-the- myth-of-the-rational-insurgent-2.html>.

87) Sharp, 1983.

88) Sharp, 2020.

89) For an historical overview of the emergence of key international institutions and cultural frameworks for doing this, see Boulding, 1990. For more current examples, see Hawken, 2008; Klein, 2015; Tilly, 2019; the People's Summit 2022, and the Wikipedia article on the World Social Forum.

90) To hear "There's a Change that's a'Comin'", go to: <https://smarterplanetorwiserearth.com/2023/04/01/theres-a-change-thats-a-comin>.

Chapter Seven: Artificial Intelligence as Collaborative Wisdom

91) Toffler, 1984.

92) For a more nuanced account, see Borgmann, 1987; Heidegger, 2013; and the especially helpful exploration of these issues by Dreyfus, 1992.

93) For accounts of the history of AI, see Kurzweil, 2006; and Tegmark, 2018.

94) IBM, 2015.

95) Turing, 1950.

96) Turing, 1950.

97) Russell and Norvik, 2021.

98) Turing, 1950.

99) Turing 1950.

100) Turing, 1950.

101) Turing 1950. For a discussion of Russell's paradox, see DeLong, 2004.

102) For a further exploration of the characteristics of a modern consumer family approach to heating systems and a wiser earth alternative set of practices as found in the Downeast region of Maine, see Cox, 2018.

103) On the "uncanny valley", see Mori 2012.

104) Turing, 1950.

105) GPT-3, 2020.

106) Kasparov, 2017.

107) On the history of studies of ethics and AI see, Wallach and Allen, 2008; Armstrong, 2014; Barratt, 2015; Bostrom, 2016; Gunkel, 2017; Anderson and Anderson, 2018; Russell, 2020; and Tegmark, 2018; and Yudkowsky, 2022.

108) Russell and Norvig, 2021, p. xii.

109) On autonomous robotic and cyber weapons see Singer, 2009; and Scharre, 2019.

110) There has been considerable discussion of the challenges of getting AI to be friendly or align with human values. See for instance: Bostrom,

2016; Russell, 2020; and Yudkowsky, 2022. There has been much less attention to these two complications, in part because most AI researchers adopt Utilitarian frameworks that make it difficult to avoid moral relativism and the related realpolitik frame of thought. If values reduce to utility preferences, then it becomes difficult to identify objectively good moral agents, let alone figure out how to get ASI to align with them.

111) For extensive ideas about design justice, see Costanza-Chock, 2020.

112) See the Appendix on "Talking Homes" at: <https://smarterplanetorwiserearth.com/2023/04/01/book-appendices/. See also Toffler, 1984.

113) Benjamin, 2019. For further examples of ways coding may run awry, see, also, O'Neil, 2017, and D'Ignazio and Klein, 2020.

114) Lederach and Burgress, 2017; Krog and Hunter-Gault, 2000; Hager and Mawopiyane 2022; and Ramsbotham et. al., 2016.

115) A fascinating complement to work like Kimmerer's which explores methods to develop paths to dialogue with nature from a Settler point of view is provided by Simard, 2022.

116) See the influential Stone, 2010. On developing ecological law and extending it in creative and resilient ways, see Garver, 2022.

117) Chalmers, 1997.

118) On the need to adopt an intentional stance and employ concepts of purpose and teleological or teleonomic ideas in interpreting the evolution and behavior of natural organisms, see Dennett, 1996 and Mayr, 2004.

119) For an invitation to reflect further on how our type of flesh may or may not be relevant to the question of consciousness, see the delightful short film, "They Are Made of Meat", O'Regan, 2013.

120) On alternative structures for corporations see: Dreby and Lumb, 2012; Dreby, Helmuth and Mansfield, 2012; Lakey, 2017; and Bornstein, 2007.

121) Kimmerer, 2015.

122) Keller, 1983.

123) To listen to "Breath on the Water", go to: <https://smarterplanetorwiserearth.com/2023/04/01/breath-on-the-water/>.

124) Russell, 2020, p. 247.

125) Russell, 2020, p.213.

126) Gandhi, 2009, Chapter 15, "Brute Force".

127) Strategies for developing hybrid models of relevant sorts have been investigated for some time by Ben Goertzel and others. See Goertzel and Pennachin, 2007; and Goertzel and Pitt, 2012.

128) For access to the program "Ethel the Ethical Robot" and a discussion of its uses in introducing ideas of dialogical approaches to programing in elementary ways, see: <https://breathonthewater.com/2022/05/16/resources-for-teaching- dialogical-approaches-to-ai-andcomputer-programming>.

129) <https://www.mycallisto.org> downloaded 6/1/2022

130) <https://consulproject.org/en/> downloaded 6/1/2022.

131) <https://GitHub.com/consul/consul> downloaded 6/1/2022.

132) For a useful starting point to explore family therapy approaches, see: <https://en.wikipedia.org/wiki/Family_therapy>.

133) Tegmark, 2018, pp. 65-67.

134) In the context of AI, one classic exploration of these ideas was provided by Hubert Dreyfus. See Dreyfus, 1992.

135) For a much fuller account of ways meaning may emerge through artistic and other forms of bodily expression, projects, practices, and traditions as well as implications this has for understanding rationality and the theory of action, see Cox, 1986, Part III.

136) For a fascinating example of the emergence of meaning combining Analytic and Continental traditions in philosophy, see Hacking, 2006.

137) For the ultimate and most minimal iteration of the Chomsky hypothesis which argues simply that recursion "is the only uniquely human component of language", see Hauser, Chomsky, and Fitch, 2002. On the Pirahã language and its significance in understanding the fundamentally contextual and emergent nature of language, see Everett, 2009.

138) Collingwood, 2023, p. 257.

139) Wareham, "Stopping Killer Robots" and Cox, 2016.

140) Russell 2021, pp. 172-173

141) For Quaker Institute for the Future experiments with "Meetings for Worship for the Conduct of Research" and spirit-led research methods, see Cox 2014.

142) On animal perceptual intelligence, see <https://www.theguardian.com/technology/2018/nov/04/five-diseases-that-dogs-can-detect. To draw on Traditional Ecological Knowledge and connect it to Western scientific traditions, see: Anderson 1996; Kimmerer 2015; and Wikipedia's useful "Traditional Ecological Knowledge".

Chapter Eight: Dialogue Across Creeds and Cultures

143) From II Corinthians, 3:6, Zondervan, NIV, Holy Bible, Compact, Paperback, Comfort Print.

144) On the role of testimonies in the Quaker tradition see Brinton 1965 and Sheeran 1983. For a sample document see the New England Yearly Meeting of Friends 1986. On the Quaker testimony regarding ecology, see, Ratcliffe 2019. On the Quaker Earthcare witness see <https://quakerearthcare.org/about-us>.

145) On this understanding of the Quaker peace testimony, see Cox 1986, ch. 17.

146) For examples of Quaker failings in these ways, see Brinton, 1965, ch. 9, and McDaniel and Julye, 2018.

147) For Aristotle's influence on models of reasoning in the Abrahamic traditions, see Adamson 2016a, 2016b, 2018. 2022.

148) Rumi's poem as quoted in Adamson 2018, p. 350.

149) For introductions to many of these traditions and relevant comparisons, see Smith 2009. For the Fourteen Precepts, see Hanh 2017.

150) For descriptions of negative theology in different Abrahamic traditions see Adamson 2016b and 2019 as well as Armstrong 1984. For examples from Hindu and Buddhist traditions like Nagarajuna, see Adamson, 2022.

151) To listen to this adaptation of "Wade in the Water", go to: <https://smarterplanetorwiserearth.com/2023/04/01/wade-in-the-water>.

152) Stuart A. Kaufmann, *Reinventing the Sacred: A New View of Science, Reason, and Religion*, p. x.

153) "I Have a Dream Speech" by Martin Luther King .Jr HD (Subtitled), <https://www.youtube.com/ watch?v=vP4iY1TtS3>.

154) For the notion of Design Space, see Dennett 1996. For ways to articulate the metaphysics of Design Space and the epistemology of spiritual leadings in research, see Cox 2014, ch. 4.

155) See Appendix Four online, "Oh my dear! -- how shall we peace this all together? . . . out of the Silence, fracturing into a larger whole . . ." at: <https://smarterplanetorwiserearth.com/2023/04/01/book-appendices>.

156) To listen to "In the Silence", go to: <https://smarterplanetorwiserearth.com/2023/04/01/in-thesilence>.

Chapter Nine: Bridging into the Future

157) Turing, 1950.

158) Gandhi, 2009, p. 81.

159) Macy and Johnstone, 2022.

160) A quotation attributed to Horward Thurman.

161) See <https://www.noom.com/about-us/; <https://www.aa.org/; and https://www.footprintnetwork.org/resources/footprint-calculator>.

162) <https://smarterplanetorwiserearth.com/>.

163) UNESCO, 2022.

164) Horton and Freire, 1990.

Bibliography

A Force More Powerful, Episode 2: "Nashville "We Were Warriors", 1999. <youtube.com/watch?v=gs14dOW2lFw>.

Adamson, Peter, 2014. *Classical Philosophy: A History of Philosophy without Any Gaps*, Volume 1. Oxford UK: Oxford University Press.

———, 2015. *Philosophy in the Hellenistic and Roman Worlds: A History of Philosophy without Any Gaps,* Volume 2. Oxford UK: Oxford University Press.

———, 2016 *Philosophy in the Islamic World: A History of Philosophy without Any Gaps*, Volume 3. 1st edition. Oxford UK: Oxford University Press.

———, 2019 *Medieval Philosophy: A History of Philosophy without Any Gaps,* Volume 4. Oxford ; New York NY: Oxford, UK: Oxford University Press.

Adamson, Peter, and Jonardon Ganeri, 2022. *Classical Indian Philosophy: A History of Philosophy without Any Gaps*, Volume 5. Oxford, UK: Oxford University Press.

Albert Einstein Institution. "Albert Einstein Institution: On Nonviolent Action." Accessed July 1, 2023. <aeinstein.org/on-nonviolent-action>.

Allen, Douglas, 2019. *Gandhi after 9/11: Creative Nonviolence and Sustainability.* New Delhi, India: Oxford University Press.

Allison, Graham, and Philip Zelikow, 1999. *Essence of Decision: Explaining the Cuban Missile Crisis.* New York NY: Pearson P T R.

Anderson, E. N., 1996. *Ecologies of the Heart: Emotion, Belief, and the Environment. 1st edition.* New York: Oxford University Press.

Anderson, Michael, and Susan Leigh Anderson, eds., 2018. *Machine Ethics.* 1st edition. Cambridge, UK: Cambridge University Press.

Andresen, Julie Tetel, and Phillip M. Carter, 2016. *Languages In The World: How History, Culture, and Politics Shape Language.* New Yoork, NY: John Wiley and Sons.

Arkin, Ronald, 2009. *Governing Lethal Behavior in Autonomous Robots.* Boco Raton FL: Chapman and Hall/CRC

Armstrong, Karen, 1994. *A History of God: The 4,000-Year Quest of Judaism, Christianity and Islam.* New York NY: Ballantine Books.

Armstrong, Stuart. 2014. *Smarter Than Us: The Rise of Machine Intelligence.* Machine Intelligence Research Institute.

Ball, Molly, 2015. "How Gay Marriage Won." *The Atlantic*, July 1, 2015. <theatlantic.com/politics/archive/2015/07/gay-marriage-supreme-court-politics-activism/397052>.

Barratt, James, 2015. *Our Final Invention.* New York NY: Griffin.

Benjamin, Ruha, 2019. *Race After Technology: Abolitionist Tools for the New Jim Code.* Medford MA: Polity.

Bentham, Jeremy. 2017. *An Introduction to the Principles of Morals and Legislation.* CreateSpace Independent Publishing Platform.

Bondurant, Joan Valerie, 1988. *Conquest of Violence: The Gandhian Philosophy of Conflict.* Princeton NJ: Princeton University Press.

Borgmann, Albert, 1987. *Technology and the Character of Contemporary Life: A Philosophical Inquiry.* Chicago: The University of Chicago Press.

Bornstein, David, 2007. *How to Change the World: Social Entrepreneurs and the Power of New Ideas,* Oxford ; New York: Oxford University Press.

Bostrom, Nick, 2016. *Superintelligence: Paths, Dangers, Strategies.* Oxford, United Kingdom ; New York NY: Oxford University Press.

Boulding, Elise, 1989. *One Small Plot of Heaven: Reflections on Family Life by a Quaker Sociologist.* Wallingford, PA: Pendle Hill Publications.

———, 1990. *Building a Global Civic Culture: Education for an Interdependent World.* Syracuse, NY: Syracuse University Press.

Boulding, Kenneth, 1964. "The Evolutionary Potential of Quakerism" *Pendle Hill Pamphlet* No. 136, Wallingford, PA: Pendle Hill Publications. <pendlehill.org/product/evolutionary-potential-quakerism> Accessed July 1, 2023

Brinton, Howard H., and Margaret Hope Bacon, 1965. *Friends for 350 Years: The History and Beliefs of the Society of Friends.* Wallingford, PA: Pendle Hill Publications.

brown, adrienne maree, 2017. *Emergent Strategy: Shaping Change, Changing Worlds.* Chico, CA: AK Press.

Brown, Peter G. and Geoffrey, 2009. *Right Relationship: Building a Whole Earth Economy.* Oakland CA: Berrett-Koehler.

Brown, Peter, and Peter Timmerman, 2015., eds. *Ecological Economics for the Anthropocene: An Emerging Paradigm.* New York NY: Columbia University Press.

Buber, Martin, 1971. *I And Thou.* Translated by Walter Kaufmann. New York NY: Touchstone.

Bureau, US Census, 2020. *Income and Poverty in the United States: 2020.* U.S. Census Bureau. <census.gov/library/publications/2021/demo/p60-273.html> Accessed July 1, 2023.

Carson, Clayborne, David J. Garrow, Gerald Gill, Vincent Harding, and Darlene Clark Hine, eds., 1991. *The Eyes on the Prize Civil Rights Reader: Documents, Speeches, and Firsthand Accounts from the Black Freedom Struggle.* 4th printing edition. New York NY: Penguin Books.

Carter Center. *The Carter Center: Waging Peace. Fighting Disease. Building Hope.* <cartercenter.org> Accessed July 1, 2023.

Center for Social Innovation. "Who We Are." *Centre for Social Innovation* <socialinnovation.org/about/who-we-are> accessed July 1, 2023.

Chalmers, David J., 1997. *The Conscious Mind: In Search of a Fundamental Theory.* New York NY: Oxford University Press.

Chenoweth, Erica, and Maria Stephan, 2012. *Why Civil Resistance Works: The Strategic Logic of Nonviolent Conflict.* New York NY Chichester, West Sussex: Columbia University Press.

Chew, Pat K., ed., 2001. *The Conflict and Culture Reader.* New York NY: NYU Press.

Christian, Brian, 2020. *The Alignment Problem: Machine Learning and Human Values.* New York NY: W. W. Norton & Company.

Chochinov, Harvey Max. "The Platinum Rule: A New Standard for Person-Centered Care." *Journal of Palliative Medicine* Vol 25, no. 6 (June 2022): 854–56. <doi.org/10.1089/jpm.2022.0075>. Accessed July 1, 2023.

Ciscel, David, Keith Helmuth, and Sandra Lewis, 2011. "How on Earth Do We Live Now? Natural Capital, Deep Ecology and the Commons." *QIF Focus Book* #2, Quaker Institute for the Future. Caye Caulker, Belize: Produccicones de la Hamaca, 2011.

Collingwood, R. G., 1923. *The Principles of Art.* Case Press, republished 2013 by Briston UK: Read and Co. Books.

Costanza-Chock, Sasha, 2020. *Design Justice: Community-Led Practices to Build the Worlds We Need.* Cambridge, MA: The MIT Press.

Cox, Gray, 1984. *The Will at the Crossroads: A Reconstruction of Kant's Moral Philosophy.* Lanham, MD: University Press of America.

———, 1985. "Bearing Witness: Quaker Process and a Culture of Peace." *Pendle Hill Pamphlet* No. 262. Wallingford PA: Pendle Hill Publications <pendlehill.org/product/bearing-witness-quaker-process-culture-peace> Accessed July 1, 2023.

———, 1986. "Modern Consumer Families and Self-Reliant Maine Yankees: Two Cultures of Residential Heating" *The Maine Journal of Conservation and Sustainability* - University of Maine. June 8, 2018. <umaine.edu/spire/2018/06/08/cox> Accessed July 1, 2023.

———, 1986. *The Ways of Peace: A Philosophy of Peace As Action.* New York NY: Paulist Press.

———, 2013. "A Proposal to Cut US Citizen's Consumption in Half." *Breathonthewater*, April 23, 2013. <breathonthewater.com/2013/04/23/a-proposal-to-cut-us-citizens-consumption-in-half> Accessed July 1.2023.

———, 2016. "Arming Nonviolent Drones." *Mount Desert Islander*, July 22, 2016.

Cox, Gray; Charles Blanchard, Geoff Garver, Keith Helmuth, Leonard Joy, Judy Lumb, and Sara Wolcott, 2014. "A Quaker Approach to Research: Collaborative Practice and Communal Discernment." *QIF Focus Book* #7, Quaker Institute for the Future. Caye Caulker, BELIZE: Producciones de la Hamaca.

Cox, J. Gray, 2019. "Pollinators for a Truly Smarter Planet: Using Gandhian Traditions of Dialogical Reasoning to Frame and Foster Rural Development." *Journal of Rural Development 38*, no. 3 (September 30, 2019): 426–51. <doi.org/10.25175/jrd/2019/v38/i3/147919>. Accessed July. 1, 2023

Cox, John Gray, 2015. "Reframing Ethical Theory, Pedagogy, and Legislation to Bias Open Source AGI Towards Friendliness and Wisdom." *Journal of Evolution and Technology* 25, no. 2 (November 2015): 39–54.

Cruz, Alicia Re, 1996. *The Two Milpas of Chan Kom: Scenarios of a Maya Village Life.* Albany NY: SUNY Press.

Daly, Herman E., and John B. Cobb Jr, 1994. *For The Common Good: Redirecting the Economy toward Community, the Environment, and a Sustainable Future.* Boston MA: Beacon Press.

DeLong, Howard, 2004. *A Profile of Mathematical Logic.* Garden City NY: Dover Publications.

Dennett, Daniel Clement, 1996. *Darwin's Dangerous Idea.* New York NY: Simon & Schuster.

D'Ignazio, Catherine, and Lauren F. Klein, 2020. *Data Feminism.* Cambridge MA: The MIT Press.

Dreby, Ed, Keith Helmuth, and Margaret Mansfield, 2012. "It's the Economy, Friends: Understanding the Growth Dilemma." *QIF Focus Book #5*, Quaker Institute for the Future. Caye Caulker, BELIZE: Producciones de la Hamaca.

Dreby, Ed, and Judy Lumb, eds., 2012. "Beyond the Growth Dilemma: Toward an Ecologically Integrated Economy." *QIF Focus Book #6*, Quaker Institute for the Future. Caye Caulker, BELIZE: Produccicones de la Hamaca.

Dreyfus, Hubert L., 1992. *What Computers Still Can't Do: A Critique of Artificial Reason.* Cambridge, MA: The MIT Press.

D'Souza, Dinesh, 2015. *What's So Great About America.* Washingtton, D.C.: Regnery Publishing.

Dudiak, Jeffrey, 2015. "Befriending Truth: Quaker Perspectives," Volume 2 of Friends Association for Higher Education's *Quakers & the Disciplines.* Gainesville GA: Full Media Services.

Einhorn, Catrin, 2022. "Researchers Report a Staggering Decline in Wildlife. Here's How to Understand It." *The New York Times*, October 12, 2022, <nytimes.com/2022/10/12/climate/living-planet-index-wildlife-declines.html>.

Esteva, Gustavo, 1987. "Regenerating People's Space." *Alternatives* 12, no. 1 (January 1, 1987): 125–52. <doi.org/10.1177/030437548701200106>. Accessed July 1, 2023.

Esteva, Gustavo, Madhu Suri Prakash, Pnina Werbner, Richard Werbner, and Vandana Shiva, 2014. *Grassroots Postmodernism: Remaking the Soil of Cultures.* London: Zed Books.

Everett, Daniel L., 2009. *Don't Sleep, there Are Snakes: Life and Language in the Amazonian Jungle.* New York NY: Vintage.

Ferrari, Michel, and Nic M. Weststrate, eds., 2016. *The Scientific Study of Personal Wisdom: From Contemplative Traditions to Neuroscience.* Reprint of the original 1st ed. 2013 edition. New York NY: Springer.

Fetterly, Judith, 2007. "On Sexism as a Spiritual Disaster." *Friends Journal*, February issue. <friendsjournal.org/2007013>.

Fisher, Roger, 1964. "Fractionating Conflict." *Daedalus* 93, no. 3: 920–41.

Fisher, Roger, William L. Ury, and Bruce Patton, 2011. *Getting to Yes: Negotiating Agreement Without Giving In.* New York NY: Penguin Publishing Group.

Freire, Paulo, and Donaldo Macedo, 2018. *Pedagogy of the Oppressed*: 50th Anniversary Edition. New York NY: Bloomsbury Academic.

Friedman, Milton, 1966. *Essays in Positive Economics.* Chicago: University of Chicago Press.

Gandhi, Mohandas Karamchand, 1983. *Autobiography: The Story of My Experiments with Truth.* Garden City NY: Dover Publications.

Gandhi, Mohandas, 2009. *Gandhi: "Hind Swaraj" and Other Writings Centenary Edition.* Edited by Anthony J. Parel. Centenary edition. Cambridge UK: Cambridge University Press.

Gandhi, M. K., 2018. *Satyagraha in South Africa.* <sas.upenn.edu>.

Gardner, Howard E., 2011. *Frames of Mind: The Theory of Multiple Intelligences.* New York NY: Basic Books.

Garver, Geoffrey, 2022. *Ecological Law and the Planetary Crisis: A Legal Guide for Harmony on Earth.* Oxfordshire UK: Routledge Explorations in Environmental Studies.

Gendlin, Eugene T., 1982. *Focusing.* 2nd edition. New York NY: Bantam.

Gilligan, Carol, 2016. *In a Different Voice: Psychological Theory and Women's Development.* Cambridge. MA: Harvard University Press.

Goertzel, Ben, and Cassio Pennachin, 2007. "The Novamente Artificial Intelligence Engine." in *Cognitive Technologies*, edited by Ben Goertzel and Cassio Pennachin, pp 63–129. Berlin, Germany: Springer Berlin Heidelberg. <doi.org/10.1007/978-3-540-68677-4_3>. Accessed July 1, 2023.

Goertzel, B. and J. Pitt, 2012. "Nine Ways to Bias Open-Source AGI Towards Friendliness." *Journal of Evolution and Technology* 22 (1): 116-131.

Goldberg, Mark S., Geoffrey Garver, and Nancy E. Mayo, 2015. "Revisiting the Metaphor of Human Health for Assessing Ecological Systems and Its Application to Ecological Economics." In *Ecological*

Economics for the Anthropocene: An Emerging Paradigm, Ed. by Peter G. Brown and Peter Timmerman, pp. 190–207. New York NY: Columbia University Press.

Goldstein, Rebecca, 2015. *Plato at the Googleplex: Why Philosophy Won't Go Away.* New York NY: Vintage.

Gordon, William J. J., 1969. *Synectics: The Development of Creative Capacity.* New York NY: Collier-Macmillan.

GPT-3, 2020. "A Robot Wrote This Entire Article. Are You Scared yet, Human?" *The Guardian*, September 8, 2020, <theguardian.com/commentisfree/2020/sep/08/robot-wrote-this-article-gpt-3>.

Guha, Ramachandra, 2019. *Gandhi 1914-1948: The Years That Changed the World.* London UK: Penguin.

Gunkel, David J., 2017. *The Machine Question: Critical Perspectives on AI, Robots, and Ethics.* Cambridge, MA: The MIT Press.

Guthrie, William C., 1971. *Greeks and Their Gods.* Boston MA: Beacon Press.

Hacking, Ian, 2006. *The Emergence of Probability: A Philosophical Study of Early Ideas about Probability, Induction and Statistical Inference.* New York NY: Cambridge University Press.

Hager, Shirley N., and Mawopiyane, 2022. *The Gatherings: Reimagining Indigenous-Settler Relations.* Toronto, Canada: Aevo UTP.

Hanh, Thich Nhat, and Jack Kornfield, 2005. *Being Peace.* 2nd edition. Berkeley, CA: Parallax Press.

Hanh, Thich Nhat, 2017. "The Fourteen Precepts of Engaged Buddhism", *Lions Roar: Buddhist Wisdom for Our Time.* April 12, 2017. <lionsroar.com/the-fourteen-precepts-of-engaged-buddhism> Accessed July 1, 2023.

Hansen, Chad, 2000. *A Daoist Theory of Chinese Thought: A Philosophical Interpretation.* New York NY: Oxford University Press.

Hardin, Garrett, 1968. "The Tragedy of the Commons." *Science*, New Series 162, no. 3859: 1243–48.

Hauser, Marc D., Noam Chomsky, and W. Tecumseh Fitch, 2002. "The Faculty of Language: What Is It, Who Has It, and How Did It Evolve?" *Science* 298, no. 5598 (November 22, 2002): 1569–79. <doi.org/10.1126/Science.298.5598.1569>. Accessed July 1, 2023.

Hawken, Paul, 2008. *Blessed Unrest: How the Largest Social Movement in History Is Restoring Grace, Justice, and Beauty to the World.* New York NY: Penguin Books.

Hegel, Georg, 2019. *The Phenomenology of Spirit.* Cambridge UK: Cambridge University Press.

Heidegger, Martin, 2008. *Being and Time.* New York NY: Harper Perennial Modern Classics.

Heidegger, Martin, 2013. *The Question Concerning Technology, and Other Essays.* New York NY: Harper Perennial Modern Classics.

Heilbroner, Robert L., 1999 *The Worldly Philosophers: The Lives, Times And Ideas Of The Great Economic Thinkers,* Seventh Revised edition. New York NY: Touchstone.

Hill, Marquita K., 2020 *Understanding Environmental Pollution.* 4th edition. Cambridge, UK: Cambridge University Press.

Hofkirchner, Wolfgang, 2020. "Intelligence, Artificial Intelligence and Wisdom in the Global Sustainable Information Society." *Proceedings of Institute for a Global Sustainable Information Society (GSIS),* 1220 Vienna, Austria <mdpi.com/2504-3900/47/1/39>. Accessed July 1, 2023.

hooks, bell, 2014. *Talking Back: Thinking Feminist, Thinking Black.* New York NY: Routledge.

Horton, Myles, and Paulo Freire, 1990. *We Make the Road by Walking: Conversations on Education and Social Change.* Philadelphia, PA: Temple University Press.

IBM, 2015. "IBM Builds a Smarter Planet," *IBM,* October 1, 2015. <ibm.com/smarterplanet/us/en/>. Accessed July 1, 2023.

Innes, Judith E., and David E. Booher, 2018. *Planning with Complexity: An Introduction to Collaborative Rationality for Public Policy.* New York NY: Routledge.

Intergovernmental Panel on Climate Change, 2023. "Climate Change 2023: Sixth Assessment Report" <ipcc.ch/ar6-syr>. Accessed July 1, 2023.

Intergovernmental Platform on Biodiversity and Ecosystem Services (IPBES), 2019. "Summary for Policymakers of the Global Assessment Report on Biodiversity and Ecosystem Services." Zenodo, November 25, 2019. <doi.org/10.5281/zenodo.3553579>.

Jaggar, Alison M., 1989. "Love and Knowledge: Emotion in Feminist Epistemology." *Inquiry* 32, no. 2 (January 1989): 151–76. <tandfonline.com/doi/abs/10.1080/00201748908602185>. Accessed July 1, 2023.

Jeste, Dilip V., Sarah A. Graham, Tanya T. Nguyen, Colin A. Depp, Ellen E. Lee, and Ho-Cheol Kim, 2020. "Beyond Artificial Intelligence: Exploring Artificial Wisdom." *International Psychogeriatrics* 32, no. 8 (August 2020): 993–1001. <doi.org/10.1017/S1041610220000927>.

Kageki, Norri, and Mori Masahiro, 2012. "An Uncanny Mind: Masahiro Mori on the Uncanny Valley and Beyond." *IEEE Spectrum,* June 12, 2012. <spectrum.ieee.org/an-uncanny-mind-masahiro-mori-on-the-uncanny-valley>.

Kallis, Giorgos, 2018. *Degrowth.* Newcastle upon Tyne UK: Agenda Publishing.

Kant, Immanuel, 1993. *Grounding for the Metaphysics of Morals: With On a Supposed Right to Lie Because of Philanthropic Concerns.* Translated by James W. Ellington. Third Edition. Indianapolis IN: Hackett Publishing Company.

Kasparov, Garry, 2017. *Deep Thinking: Where Machine Intelligence Ends and Human Creativity Begins.* New York NY: PublicAffairs.

Kauffman, Stuart A., 2010. *Reinventing the Sacred: A New View of Science, Reason, and Religion.* New York NY: Basic Books.

Kaur, Valarie, 2021. *See No Stranger: A Memoir and Manifesto of Revolutionary Love.* New York NY: One World.

Keller, Evelyn Fox, 1983. *A Feeling for the Organism: The Life and Work of Barbara McClintock.* San Francisco: W.H. Freeman.

Kelly, Kevin, 2011. *What Technology Wants.* London: Penguin Books.

Khanna, Ro, and Amartya Sen, 2022. *Dignity in a Digital Age: Making Tech Work for All of Us.* New York NY: Simon & Schuster, 2022.

Kim, Tae Wan, and Santiago Mejia, 2019. "From Artificial Intelligence to Artificial Wisdom: What Socrates Teaches Us." *Computer* 52, no. 10 (October 2019): 70–74. <doi.org/10.1109/MC.2019.2929723>. Accessed July 1, 2023.

Kimmerer, Robin Wall, 2015. *Braiding Sweetgrass: Indigenous Wisdom, Scientific Knowledge and the Teachings of Plants.* First Paperback edition. Minneapolis, MN: Milkweed Editions.

King, Jr. Martin Luther,1963. *Recording of "I Have a Dream Speech"* by Martin Luther King, Jr HD (Subtitled), <youtube.com/watch?v=vP4iY1TtS3s>. Accessed July 1, 2023

Kitzmann, Harald, Viktoria Yatsenko, and Markus Launer, 2021. "Artificial Intelligence and Wisdom". *Management.* Vol. 5 (27) 22-27, 2021. <doi.org/10.13140/RG.2.2.33802.59844>.

Klein, Naomi, 2015. *This Changes Everything: Capitalism vs. The Climate.* Reprint edition. New York NY: Simon & Schuster.

Kohlberg, Lawrence, 1981. *The Philosophy of Moral Development: Moral Stages and the Idea of Justice.* 1st edition. San Francisco CA: Harper & Row.

Kolbert, Elizabeth, 2015. *The Sixth Extinction: An Unnatural History.* Reprint edition. New York NY: Picador.

Kolko, Jon, 2012. *Wicked Problems: Problems Worth Solving: A Handbook & A Call to Action.* Austin TX: AC4D.

Krog, Antjie, and Charlayne Hunter-Gault, 2000. Country of My Skull: Guilt, Sorrow, and the Limits of Forgiveness in the New South Africa. Reprint edition. New York NY: Crown.

Kurzweil, Ray, 2006. *The Singularity Is Near: When Humans Transcend Biology.* New York NY: Penguin Books.

Lakey, George, 2017. *Viking Economics: How the Scandinavians Got It Right-and How We Can, Too.* Reprint edition. Hoboken NJ: Melville House.

Lederach, John, 1994. *Preparing For Peace: Conflict Transformation Across Cultures. Syracuse,* N.Y: Syracuse University Press. Also available as *The Little Book of Conflict Transformation* <beyondintractability.org/essay.transformation>.

Legg, Shane, and Marcus Hutter, 2007. "Universal Intelligence: A Definition of Machine Intelligence." *Minds and Machines* 17 (no. 4): 391–444. <link.springer.com/journal/11023/volumes-and-issues/17-4>. Accessed July 1, 2023.

Lederach, John Paul, and Heidi Burgress, 2017. "Conflict Transformation." *Beyond Intractability*, July 6, 2016. <beyondintractability.org/essay/transformation> Accessed July 1, 2023.

Lee, Kai-Fu, 2021. *AI Superpowers: China, Silicon Valley, and the New World Order.* Reprint edition. Boston, Mass. New York NY: Mariner Books.

Leopold, Aldo, and Barbara Kingsolver, 2020. *A Sand County Almanac: And Sketches Here and There.* Illustrated edition. Oxford University Press.

Lopez, C. Todd, 2022. "DOD Adopts 5 Principles of Artificial Intelligence Ethics." *U.S. Department of Defense.* <defense.gov/News/News-Stories/Article/Article/2094085/dod-adopts-5-principles-of-artificial-intelligence-ethics>.

MacIntyre, Alasdair, 2007. *After Virtue: A Study in Moral Theory, Third Edition.* 3rd edition. Notre Dame, Ind: University of Notre Dame Press.

MacKinnon, J. B., 2021. *The Day the World Stops Shopping: How Ending Consumerism Saves the Environment and Ourselves.* New York NY: Ecco.

Macy, Joanna, and Chris Johnstone, 2022. *Active Hope: How to Face the Mess We're in with Unexpected Resilience and Creative Power.* Revised edition. New World Library.

Martin, Courtney, 2022. "Shut up and Repair." *The Examined Family*, March 23, 2022. <courtney.substack.com/p/shut-up-and-repair>.

Marx, Karl, 2007. *Economic and Philosophic Manuscripts of 1844.* Illustrated edition. Mineola NY: Dover Publications.

Mayr, Ernst, 2004. *What Makes Biology Unique?: Considerations on the Autonomy of a Scientific Discipline.* New York NY: Cambridge University Press.

McDaniel, Donna, and Vanessa D. Julye, 2009. *Fit for Freedom, Not for Friendship: Quakers, African Americans, and the Myth of Racial*

Justice. Philadelphia, Pa: QuakerPress of FGC.

Meadows, Donella H., 2008. *Thinking in Systems.* Edited by Diana Wright. White River Junction, VT: Chelsea Green Publishing.

Moyer, Bill, JoAnn McAllister, Mary Lou Finley, and Steven Soifer, 2001. *Doing Democracy: The MAP Model for Organizing Social Movements.* Gabriola Island, B.C.: New Society Publishers.

Mr. Money Moustache, 2023. <mrmoneymustache.com>.

Nan, Susan Allen, Zachariah Cherian Mampilly, and Andrea Bartoli, eds., 2011. *Peacemaking.* Santa Barbara, CA: Praeger.

New England Yearly Meeting of Friends, 1986. *Faith and Practice of New England Yearly Meeting of Friends.* New England Yearly Meeting of Friends.

New York Quaker Project on Community Conflict, 1972. "Creative Response to Conflict – Conflict Resolution Education Connection". <creducation.net/intl-orgs/creative-response-to-conflict>. Accessed July 1, 2023.

Noddings, Nel, 2013. *Caring: A Relational Approach to Ethics and Moral Education.* Second Edition, Updated. Berkeley, CA.: University of California Press, 2013.

Nonviolent Peaceforce, 2023. "Unarmed Civilian Protection Across Generations". <nonviolentpeaceforce.org>. Accessed July 1, 2023.

OHI, 2022. "Ocean Health Index." <oceanhealthindex.org>. Accessed July 1, 2023.

O'Neil, Cathy, 2017. *Weapons of Math Destruction: How Big Data Increases Inequality and Threatens Democracy.* Reprint edition. New York NY: Crown.

O'Regan, Stephen, 2013. *They're Made Out of Meat.* youtube.com/watch?v=7tScAyNaRdQ.

Ostrom, Elinor, 2015. *Governing the Commons.* Reissue edition. Cambridge, United Kingdom: Cambridge University Press.

Peoples Summit, 2022. Rio+20 Portal: Building the Peoples Summit Rio+20. <rio20.net/en/iniciativas>.

Plato, and C. D. C. Reeve, 1992. Republic. Translated by G. M. A. Grube. 2nd edition. Indianapolis: Hackett Publishing Company, Inc., 1992.

Prine, John, 2007. "Paradise" <youtube.com/watch?v=DEy6EuZp9IY>.

Plumwood, Val, 2002. *Environmental Culture: The Ecological Crisis of Reason.* 1st edition. London ; New York NY: Routledge.

Polak, Fred, 1973. *The Image of the Future.* Amsterdam, Netherlands: Elsevier Scientific Publishing Company.

Popkin, Gabriel, 2022. "Are Trees Talking Underground? For Scientists, It's in Dispute." *The New York Times*, November 7, 2022. <nytimes.com/2022/11/07/science/wood-wide-web-trees-fungi-talking.html>.

Pratt, Richard H., 1892. "Kill the Indian, and Save the Man"
Capt. Richard H. Pratt on the Education of Native Americans.
<historymatters.gmu.edu/d/4929> Accessed July 1, 2023.

Prutzman, Priscilla, 1997. *The Friendly Classroom for a Small Planet: A Handbook on Creative Approaches to Living and Problem Solving for Children.* Gabriela Island BC: New Society Publishers.

Ramsbotham, Oliver, Tom Woodhouse, and Hugh Miall, 2016. *Contemporary Conflict Resolution.* 4th edition. Cambridge MA: Polity.

Ratcliffe, Jennie M., 2019. *Nothing Lowly in the Universe: An Integral Approach to the Ecological Crisis.* 2nd ed. edition. Hillsborough, NC: Crundale Press..

Rawls, John, 1999. *A Theory of Justice.* 2nd edition. Cambridge, MA: Belknap Press: An Imprint of Harvard University Press.

Rawls, John, 2001. *Justice as Fairness: A Restatement.* Edited by Erin I. Kelly. 2nd edition. Cambridge, Mass: Belknap Press: An Imprint of Harvard University Press.

Rediehs, Laura, 2015. "Truth and Nonviolence: Living Experimentally in Relation to Truth." In *Befriending Truth: Quaker Perspectives,* 164–81. Friends Association of Higher Education.

Richards, Howard, 2017. *The Evaluation of Cultural Action: An Evaluative Study of the Parents and Children Program.* London UK: Palgrave MacMillan.

Roy, Arundhati, 2017. *The Doctor and the Saint: Caste, Race, and Annihilation of Caste, the Debate Between B.R. Ambedkar and M.K. Gandhi.* Annotated edition. Chicago IL: Haymarket Books.

Ruddick, Sara, 1995. *Maternal Thinking: Toward a Politics of Peace.* Boston MA: Beacon Press.

Rumi, Jalal al-Din, 2004. *The Essential Rumi,* New Expanded Edition. Translated by Coleman Barks and John Moyne. San Francisco CA: Harper One.

Russell, Stuart, 2020. *Human Compatible: Artificial Intelligence and the Problem of Control.* Reprint edition. New York NY: Penguin Books.

Russell, Stuart and Peter Norvig, 2021. *Artificial Intelligence: A Modern Approach,* Global Edition. 4th edition. London UK: Pearson Series in Aritificial Intelligence.

Sandel, Michael, 2009. *Justice: What's The Right Thing To Do?* Episode 1: "The Moral Side Of Murder," Harvard University. <youtube.com/watch?v=kBdfcR-8hEY>.

Scharre, Paul, 2019. *Army of None: Autonomous Weapons and the Future of War.* New York NY: W. W. Norton & Company.

Sharp, Gene, 1983. *Making Europe Unconquerable: A Civilian-Based Deterrence and Defense System.* Cambridge, Mass: Harper Collins College Div.

Sharp, Gene, 2020. *The Politics of Nonviolent Action.* Albert Einstein Institution.

Sharp, Gene, Joshua Paulson, Christopher A. Miller, and Hardy Merriman, 2005. *Waging Nonviolent Struggle: 20th Century Practice And 21st Century Potential.* Boston: Extending Horizons Books.

Sheeran, Michael J., 1983. *Beyond Majority Rule: Voteless Decisions in the Religious Society of Friends.* New edition. Philadelphia PA: Philadelphia Yearly Meeting of Religious Society of Friends.

Simard, Suzanne, 2022. *Finding the Mother Tree: Discovering the Wisdom of the Forest.* New York NY: Vintage.

Singer, P. W., 2009. *Wired for War: The Robotics Revolution and Conflict in the 21st Century.* New York NY: Penguin Books.

Smith, Adam, 2013. *The Wealth of Nations.* CreateSpace Independent Publishing Platform.

Smith, Huston, 2009. *The World's Religions.* 2nd ed. edition. New York NY: HarperOne.

Social Network Rio+20, 2023. "Rio+20 Portal | Building the Peoples Summit Rio+20." <rio20.net/en/iniciativas>.

Stiglitz, Joseph E., 2007. *Making Globalization Work.* Reprint edition. New York NY: W. W. Norton & Company.

Stone, Christopher D., 2010. *Should Trees Have Standing? Law, Morality, and the Environment.* 3rd edition. New York NY: Oxford University Press.

Straus, David, and Thomas C. Layton, 2002. *How to Make Collaboration Work: Powerful Ways to Build Consensus, Solve Problems, and Make Decisions.* San Francisco CA: Berrett-Koehler Publishers.

Tegmark, Max, 2018. *Life 3.0: Being Human in the Age of Artificial Intelligence.* London UK: Penguin UK.

Terán, Silvia, and Christian H. Rasmussen, 1994. *La milpa de los mayas: la agricultura de los mayas prehispánicos y actuales en el noreste de Yucatán.* Yucatán: <cephcis.unam.mx/wp-content/uploads/2020/04/milpa-de-los-mayas.pdf>.

Thucydides. "History of the Peloponnesian War," *Wikisource.*

Thurman, Howard. "Ask Yourself What Makes You Come Alive, and Go Do That, Because What the World Needs Is People Who Have Come Alive" *Quote Investigator.* <quoteinvestigator.com/2021/07/09/come-alive>.

Tilly, Charles, Ernesto Castañeda, and Lesley J. Wood, 2019. *Social Movements, 1768 - 2018.* 4th edition. New York NY: Routledge.

Toffler, Alvin, 1984. *Future Shock.* New York NY: Bantam.

Turing, A. M., 1950. "Computing Machinery and Intelligence." *Mind LIX*, no. 236 (October 1, 1950): 433–60. <doi.org/10.1093/mind/LIX.236.433>.

UNDP, 2022. "Human Development Report 2021/22" *UNDP HDR.* <report.hdr.undp.org>.

UNESCO, 2022. "Recommendation on the Ethics of Artificial Intelligence" UNESCO Digital Library." <unesdoc.unesco.org/ark:/48223/pf0000381137>.

UNHR, 2022. "Universal Human Rights Index —Human Rights Recommendations." <uhri.ohchr.org/en>.

Upstander Project, 2022. "The Maine Wabanaki-State Child Welfare Truth and Reconciliation Commission." *Upstander Project.* <upstanderproject.org/learn/guides-and-resources/first-light/truth-and-reconciliation-commision>.

US Census Bureau, 2020. "Income and Poverty in the United States: 2020." *Census.gov.* <census.gov/library/publications/2021/demo/p60-273.html>.

Wackernagel, Mathis, Laurel Hanscom, and David Lin, 2017. "Making the Sustainable Development Goals Consistent with Sustainability." *Frontiers in Energy Research* 5. <frontiersin.org/article/10.3389/fenrg.2017.00018>.

Wallach, Wendell, and Colin Allen, 2008. *Moral Machines: Teaching Robots Right from Wrong.* Oxford University Press.

Wallis, Claudia, 2023. "Better Patient Care Calls for a Platinum Rule to Replace the Golden One." *Scientific American*, February, 2023.

Wareham, Mary, 2020. "Stopping Killer Robots." *Human Rights Watch*, August 10, 2020. <hrw.org/report/2020/08/10/stopping-killer-robots/country-positions-banning-fully-autonomous-weapons>.

Wikipedia. "Smarter Planet." In *Wikipedia*, May 2, 2022. https://en.wikipedia.org/w/index.php?title=Smarter_Planet&oldid=1085881713.

———. "Traditional Ecological Knowledge." In *Wikipedia*, November 4, 2022. <en.wikipedia.org/w/index.php?title=Traditional_ecological_knowledge&oldid=1120031420>.

———. "World Social Forum." In *Wikipedia*, January 13, 2022. https://en.wikipedia.org/w/index.php?title=World_Social_Forum&oldid=1065509649.

Williams, Deborah H., and Gerhard P. Shipley, 2020. "Enhancing Artificial Intelligence with Indigenous Wisdom." *Open Journal of Philosophy* 11, no. 1 (December 18, 2020): 43–58. https://doi.org/10.4236/ojpp.2021.111005.

Wink, Walter, 1999. *The Powers That Be: Theology for a New Millennium.* New York NY: Harmony.

Wittgenstein, Ludwig, 1973. *Philosophical Investigations.* Translated by G. E. M. Anscombe. 3rd edition. Englewood Cliffs NJ: Pearson.

World Social Forum, 2021. "World Social Forum Online 20 Years."
<https://www.ituc-csi.org/wsf2021>.

Wu, Kun, 2020. "Introduction to the Fourth International Conference
on Philosophy of Information, Berkeley, California, USA, 2–6 June
2019". *MDPI Proceedongs* 47, no. 1 (2020): 39. <mdpi.com/2504-
3900/47/1/32>.

Yudkowsky, Eliezer. 2022. "The Library—LessWrong." <lesswrong.
com/library>.

Zondervan. 2022. *NIV, Holy Bible*, Compact, Paperback, Burgundy,
Comfort Print. Compact edition. Grand Rapids: Zondervan.

Appendices

Appendices are online here:
https://smarterplanetorwiserearth.com/2023/04/01/book-appendices/

Index

Gray Cox is a professor of philosophy, peace studies and language learning at College of the Atlantic where he as has also led the development of study abroad programs in Mexico and France. His studies included a B.A. at Wesleyan University, 1974, and a Ph.D. in Philosophy, at Vanderbilt University, 1981. He has written a wide variety of papers in philosophy, social theory, and artificial intelligence as well as four books (*p. iv*). He was Principal Investigator on the project, "Modern Consumer Families and Self-Reliant, Maine Yankees: Two Cultures of Residential Heating." He is a long-term member of Acadia Friends Meeting and a founding member and current Clerk of the Quaker Institute for the Future <quakerinstitute.org>. He trained with Elise Boulding and Warren Ziegler in methods for leading Imaging a World Without Weapons Workshops and has led a number over the years. He plays guitar and bones, and writes songs for shared joy and social change. He has recorded several albums of original music in English, Spanish and French <graycox.bandcamp.com>. He blogs occasionally at <breathonthewater.com>. He lives with his wife in Bar Harbor, Maine, where they enjoy gardening, hiking, and the search for the way life ought to be.

Acknowledgements

This book has been the fruit of much study and many conversations in which I have been helped enormously by many different people and groups. Foremost, I would like to thank Judy Lumb who worked for several years with me on this material as part of a QIF Circle of Discernment and then as the Managing Editor provided editing and layout for the final version. Her insight, professional skill, patience, persistence, and depth of experience both in publishing and in Quaker practice, were absolutely invaluable. I would also like to thank Michael Sommerville and Producciones de la Hamaca for all their congenial, professional work on layout and the process of bringing the publication of this book to completion.

In developing basic ideas for the cover it was a pleasure to work, initially, with Jess Boch and Dru Colbert and then have them filled out and refined by Ben Troutman. I am also very grateful to other Friends who participated at points in the Circle of Discernment and provided invaluable reflections and advice including Larry Jordan, Charlie Blanchard, and Geoff Garver. Keith Helmuth played a key role in providing advice on framing and developing the project and packaging the final form of it.

This book has been the fruit of much study and many conversations in which I have been helped enormously by many different people and groups. Foremost, I would like to thank Judy Lumb who worked for several years with me on this material as part of a QIF Circle of Discernment and then as the Managing Editor provided editing and layout for the final version. Her insight, professional skill, patience, persistence, and depth of experience both in publishing and in Quaker practice, were absolutely invaluable. Other Friends who participated at points in that Circle of Discernment and provided invaluable reflections and advice included Larry Jordan, Charlie Blanchard, and Geoff Garver. Keith Helmuth played a key role in providing advice on framing and developing the project and packaging the final form of it.

Work on that Circle of Discernment project grew out of a variety of other, earlier collaborations which included courses on AI and ethics that I team taught with Ed Snyder and Ron Beard in the

Acadia Senior College and classes I offered at College of the Atlantic. Ron provided an exemplary model for facilitating collaborative dialogue. Ed provided intellectual and moral mentoring that helped me invaluably in wrestling with questions about the structure of the moral arc of history. I benefited invariably both with the challenges, wisdom, and energy shared by students in all these classes. I have, likewise, benefited enormously from the participants who engaged with me on this material in workshops offered in Summer Research Seminars of the Quaker Institute for the Future and presentations at conferences of the Society for Human Ecology, Friends Association on Higher Education, and the Annual Conference of the International Society for MacIntyrean Enquiry. In the 2022 NIC.br Annual Workshop of Survey Methodology of the National School of Statistical Science in São Paulo, Brazil, I was especially grateful for the chance to discuss conceptions of dialogical approaches to AI with Alexandre Barbosa and the wonderful community of collaborative colleagues he drew together including, especially, Ellen Helsper, David Marker, Vijay Nair, Marielza Oliveira , Joao Pita Costa, Marlei Pozzebon, and João Paulo Veiga.

As part of work on this material, I sat in on a series of courses dealing with AI related material and am very grateful to the colleagues who let me do so and who were so tolerant and supportive of me as a student: Dave Feldman, Dan Gatti, and Kyle Shank. Over the last quarter century, I also have had the opportunity to teach – and study – in Mexico in ways that enriched my understanding of cross-cultural exchange in different ecological landscapes and I am very grateful to the people who collaborated, co-mentored, and nurtured me in those adventures including Doug Barkey, Tere Castillo, Federico Dickinson, José Ines Loria, Francisco Rosado May, Suzanne Morse and, most especially, Karla Peña Zapata. The understanding of collaborative dialogue developed in this book grows out of my earlier work in peace studies and I am especially grateful for help in that which I received from Elise Boulding, Caroline Higgins, and Howard Richards. Work on insights and ideas about Do It Ourselves technologies and culture discussed in Chapter Six was supported by a 2009-2011 National Science Foundation Grant # 0904155 obtained through a Maine EPSCOR grant on "Developing Our Energy Future" received by the College of the Atlantic, administered by the University of Maine under the "Maine's Sustainability Science Initiative. I benefited from the chance to work and write on those issues with Moises Flores Baca, Nicholas C. Harris, Renae Lesser, Phineas Ramsey, Miguel Valencia, Stephen Wagner, and Jacob Wartell.

Rich Hilliard was very helpful in revising material for Chapter Six and I am especially grateful for the time he took to do so.

I am grateful to the many other people who at various points discussed ideas or read earlier drafts of material incorporated in this book and provided very helpful comments including: Doug Allen, Beth Bertrand, Michael Birkel, Susan Cozzens, Tom Crickelair, David Einhorn, John Howell, Shirley Hager, Brian Jennings, Jimmy Pryor, Laura Rediehs, Donald Smith, Ram Subrahmanian, Katie Wasserman, Steve Wessler, Todd West, Chuck Whitney, Jim Willis, and Sara Jolena Wolcott.

My collaboration with Phileas Dazeley-Gaist as a research assistant working on this book has been especially valuable, stimulating and delightful.

My wife, Carolyn, has been supportive all along in all the right ways, for which I am ever so deeply thankful

Not all of the excellent suggestions these folks offered made it into the final version of the book. In part, I am afraid, this is because not all of them made it into the intermediary vehicle my head provided. But I am profoundly grateful for all their efforts to help me think more clearly, deeply, accurately, and wisely about the challenges of living well in this new age that is rushing upon us.

Gray Cox.

living in the territory of the Wabanaki,

in Bar Harbor, Maine,

July 6, 2023